Women Playwrights

THE BEST PLAYS OF 1995

Smith and Kraus *Books For Actors*

CONTEMPORARY PLAYWRIGHTS SERIES

Christopher Durang Vol. I: 27 Short Plays
Christopher Durang Vol. II: Complete Full-Length Plays, 1975-1995
Horton Foote Vol. I: 4 New Plays
Horton Foote Vol. II: Collected Plays
John Guare: The War against the Kitchen Sink
A.R. Gurney Vol. I: 9 Early Plays
A.R. Gurney Vol. II: Collected Plays, 1977-1985
Israel Horovitz Vol. I: 16 Short Plays
Romulus Linney: 17 Short Plays
Jane Martin: Collected Plays, 1980-1995
Terrence McNally Vol. I: 15 Short Plays
Terrence McNally Vol.II: Collected Plays
William Mastrosimone: Collected Plays
Marsha Norman: Collected Plays
Eric Overmyer: Collected Plays
Lanford Wilson: 21 Short Plays
Lanford Wilson: Collected Plays, 1965-1970
20 One-Acts from 20 Years at the Humana Festival, 1975-1995
Humana Festival '93: The Complete Plays
Humana Festival '94: The Complete Plays
Humana Festival '95: The Complete Plays
Humana Festival '96: The Complete Plays
Women Playwrights: The Best Plays of 1992
Women Playwrights: The Best Plays of 1993
Women Playwrights: The Best Plays of 1994
Women Playwrights: The Best Plays of 1995
EST Marathon '94: One-Act Plays
EST Marathon '95: One-Act Plays
EST Marathon '96: One-Act Plays
Act One Festival '94: One-Act Plays
Act One Festival '95: One-Act Plays

If you require pre-publication information about upcoming Smith and Kraus books, you may receive our semi-annual catalogue, free of charge, by sending your name and address to *Smith and Kraus Catalogue, P.O. Box 127, One Main Street, Lyme, NH 03768. Or call us at (800) 895-4331, fax (603) 795-4427.***Smith and Kraus** *Books For Actors*

Women Playwrights

THE BEST PLAYS OF 1995

Introduction by Ellen Burstyn
Edited by Marisa Smith

Contemporary Playwrights Series

SK

A Smith and Kraus Book

Book
Kraus, Inc.
Lyme, NH 03768

Copyright © 1996 by Smith and Kraus
All rights reserved
Manufactured in the United States of America
Cover and Text Design by Julia Hill
Photo of Cecilia Fannon by John L. Blom ©1996
Photo of Jocelyn A. Beard by Bibiana H. Matheis ©1996

First Edition: September 1996
10 9 8 7 6 5 4 3 2 1

Library of Congress Cataloguing-in-Publication Data
Women Playwrights: The Best Plays of 1995
Women Playwrights Series
ISSN 1067-327X

94-10071
CIP

Contents

Introduction
by Ellen Burstyn

As I read these plays, each one so different in theme, plot, and style, I found myself asking, "could they have been written by a man?" Each time the answer was "no." Of course, I already knew that I was reading a collection of plays written by women, so I was certainly not a double blind test; nevertheless, there was some quality, some propensity, some persuasion that was distinctly feminine. It was a feminine consciousness I felt; though when I tried to describe what that meant, I was stumped. Every explanation sounded biased or superficial, even stereotypical.

When I turned to my library for help, to Carl Jung, whom I've always found a valuable guide, this is what I found:

> "A woman's consciousness is characterized more by the connected quality of Eros than by the discrimination or cognition of Logos."

It would have been alright if I stopped there, but I read on:

> "In men, Eros, the function of relationship, is usually less developed than Logos. In women, on the other hand, Eros is an expression of their true nature, while their Logos is often only a regrettable accident.

That made the hairs on the back of my neck rise up and align themselves in military formation. I looked at the plays again.

Emma's Child by Kristine Thatcher is a deeply moving drama about Jean and Henry, a couple in their 40s, who have arranged to adopt the baby of a teenager named Emma. Unfortunately, when Emma's child, Robin, is born, he has severe hydrocephalus. Jean and Henry are informed that Robin will not survive for long. Adoption proceedings are dropped. Emma leaves town and Jean finds herself drawn to the bedside and, against her husband's wishes, she begins to nurture the infant.

We never see Robin. He is in his crib or swathed in blankets when Jean eventually holds him. But what we do see by the end of his short, sad life is how, through the simple acts of tending and caring, Jean has been transformed into the mother of Emma's child.

Dance with Me by Jean Reynolds is like a piece of music: a trio where overlapped lines, lives, and loves combine and recombine in a series of amorous and emotional couplings. Ray meets Grace, they fall in love, Ray hires Grace to work in his office. Grace wants Ray to tell his wife, Ruth, about their love affair. Ray promises he will, but doesn't. Ruth hears about Grace and invites her home to tea. During the conversation, Grace tells Ruth about her boyfriend, and as they talk it dawns on Ruth who that boyfriend is. As Grace and Ruth weave a spell of sexually charged intimacy, Ray gets pulled into it, and all three voices blend, harmonize and interweave.

Vladivostok Blues by Jocelyn A. Beard is a well-plotted, satirical comedy about Sophia, a world famous Mexican soap opera star, who is kidnapped in Vladivostok by Piotr, who has her confused with her television personality and is trying to save her from the soap opera villain.

When Piotr's sister, Tasha, arrives, she and Sophia develop a rapport and soon concoct a scheme to convert the kidnapping into an international news event that leads us to the surprise ending. The bonding of the two women looks like Eros à la *Thelma and Louise* but turns out to be part of a richer love relationship.

Green Icebergs by Cecilia Fannon, which takes place in Tuscany, is a story about love in its modern and historical guise; the structure relies on a traditional model that examines two marriages. The partners seem to be mismatched with one interesting and creative person married to a dull spouse. During the course of the play, the couples disentangle with each other and are rematched with surprising implications.

Sacrilege by Diane Shaffer, in which I appeared on Broadway, is the story of Sister Grace, a nontraditional nun who runs the Houston Street Crisis Center and is in the forefront of the challenge to the Church's exclusion of women from the priesthood. The play is about her connection to Ramone, a Latino street tough whom she shepherds into the priesthood, as well as her longtime friendship with Cardinal King whose job it is to keep women like her out of the priesthood.

The phrase in Jung's statement that seemed helpful in defining feminine consciousness was "The connected quality of Eros." That is what the plays had in common. In all their different ways and styles, they were about people connecting or trying to connect or failing to connect...with a hydrocephalic child, with a husband, lover, friend, with a calling, with God. That is Eros. But was their Logos only "a regrettable accident"? I think not.

Logos asks, "How are things different? What are the individual parts that make up the universe?" Eros asks "How are those parts connected to form the whole?" Obviously men playwrights can write from the feminine aspect of their psyche just as women use their Logos in their dissection and differentiation of their characters and ideas. Both are needed for a comprehensive perception of our world. The Logos is in the construction, the Eros is in the themes.

Dance with Me

a play in two acts

Jean Reynolds

Dedicated to the memory of Patricia Mantica McAleese

BIOGRAPHY

Ms. Reynolds' first full-length play, *The Last Intimacy,* received a Roger L. Stevens Award from the Kennedy Center Fund for New American Plays. Her second full-length play, *Dance With Me,* received the 1995 Salter Award from the Beverly Hills Theatre Guild—Julie Harris Playwriting Competition and the 1995 Best Play Award from Playwrights First (NYC). *Dance With Me* has been optioned for production in Los Angeles and has gone through developmental work at Circle Repertory Company (NYC), Lost Nation Theatre (Montpelier, VT), and Stages (Los Angeles, CA). Ms. Reynolds' work has been performed in New York City and regionally. She is at work on a third full-length play.

AUTHOR'S NOTE

"Three is not a crowd when a husband, his wife and his mistress create a triangle of marital love, illicit passion and the evolving friendship of the two women. The play explores the mystery of intimate love—its bonds, its boundaries, and its power." —Marcella Meharg, dramaturg, Stages Theatre

ORIGINAL PRODUCTION

Dance With Me was originally presented at Stages Theatre, Los Angeles, CA, December 11, 1995. It was directed by Dick Dotterer with the following cast:

Grace	Jean Gilpin
Ray	Jim Norton
Ruth	Clare Wren

CAST

Grace: a woman in her late thirties or early forties (or older).
Ray: a man in his late thirties or early forties (or older).
Ruth: Ray's wife, same age.

SETTING

The bar car of a train, upstate New York.
The home of Ray and Ruth in a small town, upstate New York.

TIME

The 1950s

DANCE WITH ME

Scene: The bar car of a train, upstate New York, 1950s, night.
At Rise: Ray and Grace sit at a table by a window.

GRACE: *(Gazing out window.)* The light.

RAY: What?

GRACE: Out there.

RAY: Oh.

GRACE: The light.

RAY: Yes.

GRACE: Something about the light.

RAY: A rare configuration of the heavens.

GRACE: Oh.

RAY: *(Pause.)* Are you hungry? Shall I order something?

GRACE: No. No, thank you.

RAY: If you change your mind—

GRACE: I'll let you know.

RAY: Do let me know.

GRACE: The light intrigues me.

RAY: Why?

GRACE: The usual things appear...appear...unusual. I don't know how to say
what I am saying. The usual things are...changed.

RAY: Oh?

GRACE: Changed by the light.

RAY: How?

GRACE: You can see it, if you want.

RAY: Interesting.

GRACE: What?

RAY: The landscape.

GRACE: Yes.

RAY: Provocative.

GRACE: Yes.

RAY: Your wrists are so small.

GRACE: What?

RAY: Your wrists.

GRACE: I have a delicate bone structure.

RAY: You do.

GRACE: You prefer a woman with a delicate bone structure.

RAY: I do. *(Pause.)* What are you thinking?

GRACE: About you. Being alone with you.

RAY: There's no one here. Not even the waiter.

GRACE: Alone with you, in private.

RAY: What will you do in private that you won't do here?

GRACE: Put my hands on you.

RAY: Where will you put them? Your hands with the delicate bone structure?

GRACE: On you.

RAY: Do it. Do it now.

GRACE: Not in the bar car.

RAY: You've put your hands on me before in the bar car.

GRACE: Have I?

RAY: We'll go to the compartment. The porter will make up the bed.

GRACE: Let's stay here. For now. I want to think.

RAY: Thinking has nothing to do with it.

GRACE: I suppose not.

RAY: *(Pause.)* It's beginning to snow.

GRACE: The last before spring.

RAY: We're making small talk.

GRACE: So we are.

RAY: About the weather. *(Pause.)* I called last night.

GRACE: Oh?

RAY: Where were you?

GRACE: When?

RAY: Last night.

GRACE: Out. Walking.

RAY: Alone?

GRACE: I was alone.

RAY: When I call and you're not there—

GRACE: What?

RAY: If I thought you were…with someone.

GRACE: What would you do?

RAY: When I don't know where you are, when I can't find you…

GRACE: What? Tell me.

RAY: I become another man. A man I don't know.

GRACE: I was walking. Just walking.

RAY: You hate the cold.

GRACE: The moon woke me up.

RAY: If I could be with you—

GRACE: I went out to walk in the moonlight.

RAY: If I could be with you, I wouldn't have to wonder where you are, what you are doing.

GRACE: We could walk in the moonlight. *(Pause.)* Let's go away.

RAY: Away? We are away.

GRACE: Not just a night on the train or at a hotel, but away. Where we have time. Wouldn't it be good to have time?

RAY: Yes.

GRACE: Can we?

RAY: Perhaps.

GRACE: When?

RAY: Soon.

GRACE: I want a room high up. Overlooking a park. High up. Above the trees. Where we hear the wind. And the pigeons look in. No. I want a room by the sea. High up. I want to be high up. I want to hear the waves crashing below. I want to go to that place you took me to once. That small hotel on a point overlooking the sea. That place. I want to go there.

RAY: I'll see what I can do.

GRACE: Will you?

RAY: I'll try. I'll try.

GRACE: Will you?

RAY: Of course I will.

GRACE: Away. Where we are alone. Away. That's what I want.

RAY: I want that too. Of course I do.

GRACE: Why?

RAY: Don't ask silly questions.

GRACE: Tell me.

RAY: Your bone structure.

GRACE: Are you…Are you…?

RAY: What?

GRACE: Happy.

RAY: I'm happy with you.

GRACE: And when you're not with me?

RAY: I imagine you. I imagine your eyes, your hair, your hands, your…well,

everything, everything. Your touch, the sound of your voice, the way you
hold me.

GRACE: I imagine you.

RAY: When you're not with me?

GRACE: Yes.

RAY: What? What do you imagine?

GRACE: You.

RAY: What am I doing?

GRACE: You...you...

RAY: Tell me.

GRACE: No, no.

RAY: Tell me.

GRACE: Shall I?

RAY: Tell me.

GRACE: No.

RAY: All right, don't.

GRACE: All right, I will.

RAY: Go on.

GRACE: I imagine...well, what I imagine is something...something I do to you.

RAY: Do it.

GRACE: I cast a spell.

RAY: You have.

GRACE: To enchant you.

RAY: You have.

GRACE: So that no matter what I ask, anything, anything at all, no matter what,
no matter, anything, you will do it.

RAY: I am spellbound.

GRACE: So am I.

RAY: Are you?

GRACE: Is that what you want?

RAY: More than anything.

GRACE: More than—?

RAY: More than life.

GRACE: If that were true.

RAY: It is true.

GRACE: If it is—

RAY: You know it's true.

GRACE: What if I got off the train at the next station?

RAY: I wouldn't let you.

GRACE: You couldn't stop me.

RAY: I could.

GRACE: Not if I wanted to get off.

RAY: I'd stop you.

GRACE: How?

RAY: I'd stop you.

GRACE: I've thought about getting off. I've thought, I'll get off and I won't look back. I've thought, I'll go on without him.

RAY: You won't.

GRACE: Are you so certain of me?

RAY: No.

GRACE: *(Pause.)* What time is it?

RAY: Midnight.

GRACE: It was midnight when we met.

RAY: Was it?

GRACE: And midwinter.

RAY: It wasn't midwinter.

GRACE: It was.

RAY: When we met? It was April.

GRACE: April?

RAY: Early April.

GRACE: It was January. It was cold. The train was almost empty. Do you think about that moment? That moment we met?

RAY: And all the moments since.

GRACE: What about the bad moments?

RAY: There are none.

GRACE: Not one? Not one at all?

RAY: Not one.

GRACE: You were alone in the bar car. Then I walked in. I felt your eyes.

RAY: A bold look.

GRACE: You watched me.

RAY: You sat at a table close by.

GRACE: The bad moments are when I'm not with you.

RAY: You removed your coat, but kept it draped over your shoulders.

GRACE: It was cold.

RAY: You wore a red dress. The material appeared soft. I wanted to get up from my chair, go to you, kneel down, and put my face against your red dress.

GRACE: Why didn't you?

RAY: I did.

GRACE: Not at first.

RAY: No. Not at first.

GRACE: You wanted to.

RAY: I watched your reflection in the window. Our eyes met in the glass.

GRACE: Did you know then?

RAY: I knew. And you?

GRACE: I knew.

RAY: Your gaze…

GRACE: What?

RAY: Your gaze…affected me.

GRACE: You tried to look away.

RAY: I couldn't.

GRACE: Nor I.

RAY: You asked a question.

GRACE: *(She asks the question as she asked it the night they met.)* Do you always stare that way? Or is it me?
(They continue for a time, in the dialogue, to move back and forth between the present and the memory of the past.)

RAY: It's you. Please, may I join you?

GRACE: Buy me a drink.

RAY: All right.

GRACE: You moved to my table.

RAY: I don't usually do this.

GRACE: Really?

RAY: Are you hungry?

GRACE: No.

RAY: *(Pause.)* What's your name?

GRACE: Grace.

RAY: Grace. A lovely name.

GRACE: So I've been told.

RAY: Grace who?

GRACE: Just Grace.

RAY: No last name?

GRACE: You don't need to know my last name.

RAY: Shall I tell you my name?

GRACE: Later. If I ask.

RAY: *(Pause.)* Take off your coat.

GRACE: I'm cold.

RAY: You need brandy.

GRACE: I want gin.

RAY: Gin it is.

GRACE: Gin.

RAY: Whatever you want.

GRACE: Whatever?

RAY: Whatever's in my power.

GRACE: How much power do you have?

RAY: Depends on what you want.

GRACE: For now, gin will do.

RAY: Anything with it?

GRACE: A glass.

RAY: Ah.

GRACE: I can be amusing.

RAY: We'll amuse each other.

GRACE: You amuse me.

RAY: Why?

GRACE: Because you do.

RAY: Why?

GRACE: Men amuse me.

RAY: All men?

GRACE: Most men.

RAY: I'm not most men.

GRACE: *(Pause.)* The darkness slid by outside. Occasionally a small quick light was visible, a streetlight or a headlight at a crossing, the light from someone's home, but mostly the night looked back.

RAY: You pulled your coat tighter.

GRACE: I saw myself reflected in your eyes, caught there.

RAY: Talk to me. Tell me about yourself.

GRACE: You writing a book?

RAY: I think about you all the time.

GRACE: You just met me.

RAY: Since I met you, I think about you all the time.

GRACE: How about that gin?

RAY: Of course.

GRACE: You signaled the waiter. We sat in silence looking out into the night. In the distance, on a hill, a fire, some sort of fire. Flames...flames consuming...consuming the dark. The waiter brought my gin.

RAY: You picked up the glass.

GRACE: The best way to see the world—

RAY: And held it to the light.

GRACE: —is through a glass of gin.

RAY: I couldn't help…

GRACE: What?

RAY: Noticing you.

GRACE: Your eyes…

RAY: What about my eyes?

GRACE: They are impossible.

RAY: I've got a compartment. We'll be more comfortable there.

GRACE: You said you wanted to talk.

RAY: I do.

GRACE: What do you want to talk about?

RAY: Come with me.

GRACE: When I know you better.

RAY: If you come with me, you'll know me better.

GRACE: I could have moved on then, away from you, to another table, away. I
could have gotten off the train at the next station.

RAY: You could have.

GRACE: Where are we?

RAY: Near the border.

GRACE: What border?

RAY: The border between you and me.

GRACE: Ah. That border.

RAY: I want to see you again.

GRACE: To talk?

RAY: Talk?

GRACE: You'll miss your stop.

RAY: Grace, I want to see you again. How can I reach you?

GRACE: Perhaps we'll meet on the train.

RAY: When?

GRACE: The waiter leaned in and said, "Last call for Albany, Dr. Garrison."

RAY: You have a quality…a quality…I don't know how to describe it. A quality
few have, very few.

GRACE: Slow down, Dr. Garrison, slow down.

RAY: I get off in Albany. I work in the hospital there once a week and stay at the
Wellington Hotel. Other days I'm at my practice in Essex. Come to Albany
with me. I'll show you the city.

GRACE: I've seen it.

RAY: Not with me.

GRACE: Another time.

RAY: I pleaded with you.

GRACE: Another time.

RAY: When?

GRACE: I'll let you know.

RAY: Please come with me. I'll stay over an extra night. We'll have dinner at Keeler's and then hire a car and drive to Crooked Lake for the dancing.

GRACE: Are you a good dancer?

(Ruth appears in another area. What she says is in Ray's mind.)

RUTH: Are you a good dancer?

RAY: I am.

RUTH: I enjoy dancing.

GRACE: I enjoy dancing.

RAY: I am a very good dancer.

GRACE: Me too.

RUTH: It's what attracted me to you. Something about the dancing. Yes, something about that. On the verandah at Crooked Lake. My body against a man's body for the first time. I'd never danced with a man before. Only boys.

RAY: *(To Grace, as Ruth recedes from his mind.)* Do you have any luggage?

GRACE: You were insistent.

RAY: You resisted.

GRACE: Did I?

RAY: The train began to move.

GRACE: You missed your stop.

RAY: Yes. I missed my stop.

GRACE: They'll put you off at Hudson.

RAY: No.

GRACE: You can catch the northbound train back to Albany.

RAY: No.

GRACE: Don't you care that you missed your stop?

RAY: No.

GRACE: You're impulsive.

RAY: No.

GRACE: It appears that you are.

RAY: I've never done this before.

GRACE: Done what?

RAY: I've never—

GRACE: Been impulsive?

RAY: Missed my stop.

GRACE: Never?

RAY: You distracted me. It's your fault. No. The fault is mine. But fault is wrong. It's pleasure. My pleasure.

GRACE: You say you're a good dancer?

RAY: I am.

GRACE: You're the right height.

RAY: Am I?

GRACE: For a partner.

RAY: You must have had many partners.

GRACE: Are you a possessive man?

RAY: Yes.

GRACE: Shall I tell you the truth?

RAY: Of course.

GRACE: I am possessive too. Demanding. I get what I want.

RAY: I've never gotten what I want.

GRACE: You haven't wanted it enough.

RAY: Let's go to the compartment.

GRACE: The stop after Hudson is my stop.

RAY: Is that where you live?

GRACE: No.

RAY: Where do you live?

GRACE: If I tell you, will you stop asking questions?

RAY: Yes.

GRACE: A small town.

RAY: Which one?

GRACE: You said you would stop asking questions.

RAY: Do you take the train often? What's at the stop after Hudson?

GRACE: No more, please.

RAY: Is there someone…?

GRACE: Someone?

RAY: Someone waiting? A man? Oh. Ah, I see. Look, I'm sorry. I won't bother you. No, don't say anything. There's nothing to say. I don't know what made me…well, you know. You won't believe this—no reason you should—but I…I'm sorry. I'll get off at Hudson. I'm sorry.

GRACE: Don't.

RAY: Don't what?

GRACE: Don't be sorry.

RAY: Will you forgive me?

GRACE: Buy me another drink. And something to eat. I'm hungry.

RAY: I'm not the kind of man who pursues women on trains.

GRACE: What kind of man are you?

RAY: I'm not the kind of man who buys drinks for women.

GRACE: I asked. I asked you to buy me a drink.

RAY: No. I asked—

GRACE: That's not how it happened.

RAY: The man…the man who's waiting—

GRACE: I didn't say a man is waiting.

RAY: I'd be waiting.

GRACE: Would you?

RAY: Oh, yes.

GRACE: No man is waiting.

RAY: Why not?

GRACE: There is no man.

RAY: Oh.

GRACE: For the moment.

RAY: Ah.

GRACE: Ah?

RAY: Why did you ask me to buy you a drink?

GRACE: Your haircut.

RAY: My haircut?

GRACE: I think it was your haircut.

RAY: My haircut?

GRACE: Or the way you looked at me.

RAY: My haircut.

GRACE: Or the promise.

RAY: How did I look at you?

GRACE: The way you're looking at me.

RAY: What promise?

GRACE: The one in your eyes.

RAY: Do you believe in magic?

GRACE: Magic?

RAY: Yes.

GRACE: No.

RAY: Give me your hand.

GRACE: A fortune teller?

RAY: Please.

GRACE: You held my hand in yours a moment before turning it over.

RAY: A warm hand.

GRACE: I have good circulation.

RAY: A gentle hand.

GRACE: You traced the lines of my palm.

RAY: Where are you going?

GRACE: You tell me.

RAY: *(Touching her palm.)* This line…

GRACE: Yes?

RAY: This line tells a story.

GRACE: What story?

RAY: The story of a woman in a red dress and a man who missed his stop because of her.

GRACE: Are you an experienced palm reader?

RAY: A novice.

GRACE: So am I, a novice.

RAY: I want to see you again.

GRACE: What will your wife say?

RAY: My wife?

GRACE: What will she say? *(Pause.)* You're married, aren't you?

RAY: It's not the same thing. Not the same thing at all.

GRACE: What is it, then?

RAY: Not the same.

GRACE: Was it, in the beginning, the same?

RAY: No.

GRACE: Was it love?

RAY: Now who's asking the questions?

GRACE: Was it?

RAY: It was…different.

GRACE: How?

RAY: I don't want to talk about her.

GRACE: Why not?

RAY: I want to talk about you.

GRACE: I want to talk about her.

RAY: I want to know about you.

GRACE: I want to know about her.

RAY: What do you do?

GRACE: Do?

RAY: To pass the time.

GRACE: Not much.

RAY: What?

GRACE: *(Pause.)* I work in an office.

RAY: What office? Where?

GRACE: Tell me your first name, Dr. Garrison.

RAY: Ray.

GRACE: Ray.

RAY: Will you meet me again?

GRACE: Tell me her name.

RAY: Who?

GRACE: Your wife.

RAY: Ruth.

GRACE: Ruth.

RAY: Will you meet me again?

GRACE: Yes.

RAY: You will?

GRACE: It seems a natural thing to do. Natural.

RAY: To meet? A natural thing to do, natural to meet, yes.

GRACE: But unwise.

RAY: When the train arrived in Hudson, I didn't get off.

GRACE: We both knew you wouldn't.

RAY: How did we know?

GRACE: We felt it.

RAY: We went on.

    (Ruth appears in another area. She is in Ray's mind.)

RUTH: Is everything all right?

RAY: What makes you ask?

RUTH: Nothing.

RAY: Oh.

RUTH: Do I need a reason to ask my husband if everything's all right?

RAY: You sound as though you expect everything not be be all right. You never ask if everything's all right. I thought there was a reason you asked.

RUTH: Raymond?

RAY: Everything's all right.

RUTH: Is there something you want to tell me?

RAY: No.

GRACE: *(Interrupts Ruth in Ray's mind.)* People don't take the train the way they used to.

RAY: There was always a crowd in the bar car.

GRACE: Not always.

RAY: Even at midnight.

GRACE: The night we met the bar car was empty.

RAY: Empty?

GRACE: We were alone, and we danced.

RAY: We didn't dance.

GRACE: Yes, we danced.

RAY: Not on the train, not that night. Another night. At Crooked Lake.

GRACE: At Crooked Lake?

RAY: At the hotel there. We danced at Crooked Lake.

GRACE: I hadn't danced in a while. I hadn't had the right partner. You're a good dancer.

RAY: Later, we walked outside, down to the water.

GRACE: You wore a dark suit with tiny, almost invisible, stripes.

RAY: You rested your head on my chest, on my dark suit.

GRACE: The touch of your hand on my back.

RAY: The touch of your back on my hand.

GRACE: Ray?

RAY: You're too thin. You know what I'm going to do? I'm going to fatten you up, make you strong.

GRACE: Ray?

RAY: You looked up at me.

GRACE: We ought to have a child.

RAY: A child?

GRACE: To keep things going. To keep things moving along.

RAY: I looked into your eyes. I touched your hair. I said something.

GRACE: What?

RAY: You smiled.

GRACE: Oh! These shoes!

RAY: Take them off.

GRACE: Yes.

RAY: You bent down and undid the ankle straps on your high heels. You stepped out of them and we walked on the beach.

GRACE: The pebbles hurt my feet. I cut my foot.

RAY: It wasn't serious.

GRACE: I sat on a rock and you looked at my foot and kissed it where it was bleeding.

RAY: Did I?

GRACE: Take off your clothes.

RAY: What!?

GRACE: Let's go swimming.

RAY: Grace, it's too cold.

GRACE: No, it isn't

RAY: Someone will see us.

GRACE: Let them see us. Let them look.

RAY: You unbuttoned your blouse.

GRACE: Hurry up.

RAY: You undressed.

GRACE: You, too.

RAY: You stood on the beach, on the pebbles that hurt your feet, in the moonlight.

GRACE: We swam out to the raft.

RAY: Not that night.

GRACE: It was that night. It was.

RAY: You don't know it was that night.

GRACE: I know.

RAY: You think you know. You think you're certain, but it's only what you think. You want it to be the way you think it is, but it isn't.

GRACE: You want it to be the way you think it is.

RAY: We were on the grass by the lake.

GRACE: We were not.

RAY: Yes, we were, Grace.

GRACE: We were on the raft.

RAY: The grass.

GRACE: We swam out.

RAY: I put my coat on the grass.

GRACE: The water was warm.

RAY: We were lying on my coat.

GRACE: The raft was covered with canvas.

RAY: My pipe fell out of my pocket.

GRACE: I felt it against my back.

RAY: We were under a poplar tree.

GRACE: I looked up and saw the moon. *(Pause.)* That was the night I said we ought to have a child. I said we ought to have a child because I wanted a child. I wanted something of you, something…I wanted…something.

RAY: *(Pause.)* Maybe it was that night.

GRACE: I'm sure it was that night.

RAY: Yes.

GRACE: Your breath in my hair. Your whisper in my ear.

RAY: A summer night.

GRACE: Water slapping against the raft.

RAY: The train whistle in the distance.

GRACE: Dance music floating down from the hotel.

RAY: Stars in your hair.

GRACE: I believe, I do believe, yes, I do believe in magic.

RAY: You began it.

GRACE: You began it. You began it with your eyes. Looking at me, the way you looked at me. Looking at me. You began it. Looking at me, then speaking.

RAY: You spoke first. You said, "Do you always stare that way?"

GRACE: You spoke with your eyes.

RAY: You began it by inviting me to buy you a drink.

GRACE: It had already begun.

RAY: The thing is, to keep going.

GRACE: Where?

RAY: To keep going, that's the thing.

GRACE: Has the waiter abandoned us?

RAY: Do you want the waiter?

GRACE: No.

RAY: What's wrong?

GRACE: Nothing.

RAY: What is it?

GRACE: Ray, you know what it is.

RAY: Yes.

GRACE: Find a way for us to be together.

RAY: If I could let you go, I would. But I can't.

GRACE: Tell her about us.

RAY: I'll find a way.

GRACE: Ray?

RAY: Here's my plan. No, don't talk. Listen. I want you to work for me. Hear me out. Don't say no. Consider what it means. We'll see each other every day. You'll work in my office and we'll be together.

GRACE: All the time?

RAY: Not all the time.

(Dance music. Ray extends his hand, asking Grace to dance. Lights close in as they dance, indicating a passage of time.)

GRACE: Ray?

RAY: Hmmm?

GRACE: Tell her.

RAY: I will.

GRACE: When?

RAY: Grace. I will. Soon.

GRACE: You want us both.

RAY: You. I want you.

GRACE: And Ruth?

RAY: I don't want to think of Ruth. I'm with you, not Ruth.

GRACE: Now you're with me.

RAY: Now I'm with you.

GRACE: When you're not…when you're not with me, when you're with her—

RAY: Don't, Grace.

GRACE: When you're with her—

RAY: It's not the same.

GRACE: As what?

RAY: As what I feel when I'm with you, what I feel when I look at you, what I feel when I hold you, what I feel.

GRACE: Ray?

RAY: Hmm?

GRACE: I'll tell her.

RAY: No.

GRACE: Yes, I'll tell her.

RAY: Don't joke.

GRACE: Am I joking?

RAY: Of course you're joking. You won't tell her. You know you won't.

GRACE: If you won't—

RAY: You know you won't tell her, so why speak of it?

GRACE: Ray?

RAY: Hmm?

GRACE: She invited me to tea.

RAY: She what?

GRACE: She sent a note and invited me to tea. I accepted.

RAY: You shouldn't have accepted.

GRACE: What could I do?

RAY: Decline.

GRACE: It would be rude—

RAY: Rude?

GRACE: Rude if I declined.

RAY: I'll tell her you can't.

GRACE: I want to.

(As Ruth speaks from her home, Grace joins her. In the home there is a table

flanked by two chairs. A teapot and cups sit on the table. Ray remains visible in another area.)

RUTH: Thank you for coming.

GRACE: Thank you for asking.

RUTH: *(Pause, as they observe each other.)* Well. How are you?

GRACE: Well.

RUTH: Well, good.

GRACE: *(Pause.)* And you?

RUTH: Well. *(Picks up teapot.)* Tea?

GRACE: Yes, please. *(Ruth pours.)* Is Dr. Garrison here?

RUTH: No.

GRACE: Oh.

RUTH: Raymond's not home.

GRACE: Oh.

RUTH: He's out.

GRACE: Oh.

RUTH: Walking.

GRACE: Ah.

RUTH: How do you take your tea?

GRACE: Sugar.

RUTH: He was fortunate to find you. I've noticed a difference in him since Miss Springle retired and you took over. A difference. She was an excellent worker, though a morose and lumpish woman. I never asked her to tea. You have a better quality entirely.

GRACE: Thank you.

RUTH: I believe she depressed him. But, now, with you, things are…things are better all around.

GRACE: Really?

RUTH: Oh, yes. *(Pause.)* Lovely day, isn't it?

GRACE: Yes, isn't it?

RUTH: A graceful season, this, while it lasts.

GRACE: Yes.

RUTH: So quickly gone.

GRACE: Yes.

RUTH: Then brutal winter.

GRACE: Yes.

RUTH: Brushing against us as we sleep.

GRACE: Keep a fire burning.

RUTH: Oh, dear, I'm talking about the weather. Engaging in small talk at which I'm not very good.

GRACE: I'm not either.

RUTH: *(Pause.)* He met you…?

GRACE: Who?

RUTH: Raymond. Where was it?

GRACE: On the train.

RUTH: Oh, now I remember. You traveled on the same train.

GRACE: Sometimes we talked. I was looking for work and as it happened—

RUTH: As it happened, he hired you.

GRACE: I hope…I hope I am satisfactory.

RUTH: I'm sure you are. I'm sure you're more than satisfactory.

GRACE: I want to please.

RUTH: You do. You do. You're the sort of woman who…

GRACE: Who what?

RUTH: Well, I suppose I mean…well, I don't know what I mean exactly. How is the tea?

GRACE: Excellent.

RUTH: Nothing happens over a cup of tea. Or do you prefer something stronger?

GRACE: Actually, I do.

RUTH: Something stronger then.

GRACE: I prefer something stronger.

RUTH: Brandy?

GRACE: Gin?

RUTH: Gin, yes. Anything with it?

GRACE: A glass.

RUTH: A glass? Of course. *(Pours drinks.)* Do you enjoy working for my husband?

GRACE: Yes.

RUTH: I used to work for him, you know.

GRACE: I didn't know.

RUTH: Before our marriage.

GRACE: *(Looking around.)* You have a nice home.

RUTH: I grew up here.

GRACE: Roots.

RUTH: The kind that won't let go.

GRACE: I have no roots.

RUTH: Everybody has roots.

GRACE: They aren't what they used to be.

RUTH: What is?

GRACE: I wish I had roots. You know, a family.

RUTH: Raymond is my family. We have no children. He wants all the attention. Selfish man. A selfish man. Perhaps you have found him so?

GRACE: I'm selfish too.

RUTH: Are you?

GRACE: Very.

RUTH: So am I.

(Ray speaks from another. He is present in the minds of both women.)

RAY: That night...that night, that first night I saw you, that first time, I saw...

GRACE: Saw what?

RUTH: What did you see?

RAY: I saw something...

RUTH: What?

GRACE: You could have looked away.

RAY: Something...

RUTH: You could have turned away if you'd wanted.

RAY: Something...

GRACE: You could have moved on.

RAY: I saw something in your eyes, something I had never known, something that eluded me, excluded me, turned its back on me.

RUTH: We both saw it.

RAY: I wanted it.

RUTH: I wanted it too.

GRACE: (Interrupting presence of Ray in their minds, goes to window.) Interesting landscape.

RUTH: What?

GRACE: Out there.

RUTH: Oh.

GRACE: The landscape.

RUTH: (Joins Grace at window.) Seductive.

GRACE: You're high up.

RUTH: Very high up. Grace? May I call you Grace?

GRACE: Of course.

RUTH: A lovely name.

GRACE: So I've been told.

RUTH: I'm sure you have. You must have many admirers.

GRACE: Only one.

RUTH: Lucky man. Tell me about him. No. I am too forward. Forgive me.

GRACE: Okay.

RUTH: Later, if you wish.

GRACE: You are so high up. So very high up. A pleasure to be high up. High up with an untamed view.

RUTH: A fence would inhibit…inhibit the wildness of the site, compromise it, don't you agree?

GRACE: Yes.

RUTH: Natural but violent beauty appeals to me.

GRACE: So very high up.

RAY: *(Speaks from another area. He is present in the mind of Ruth.)* Perhaps it was the dress.

RUTH: Perhaps.

RAY: Or something else. Who's to say?

RUTH: Who's to say?

RAY: I wanted to touch—

RUTH: You did.

RAY: Did I?

RUTH: You were nervous.

RAY: Yes, I was.

RUTH: Eager. Both of us, eager.

GRACE: *(Interrupts presence of Ray in Ruth's mind.)* You have a lovely garden.

RUTH: Yes. Lovely.

GRACE: Do you care for it yourself?

RUTH: Yes.

RAY: *(In Ruth's mind.)* We had the same thought.

RUTH: I waited to see what you would do. To see what was next.

RAY: You whispered something.

RUTH: I never kissed a man before. Only boys.

RAY: I am a boy.

RUTH: You whispered something.

RAY: Take off your dress.

RUTH: I did.

RAY: It fell to the floor.

RUTH: I stood quietly before you in my white slip.

RAY: On your shoulder, a committee of freckles.

RUTH: And you?

RAY: Me?

RUTH: It isn't fair that you're fully dressed.

RAY: No. It isn't fair.

RUTH: *(Interrupting presence of Ray in her mind.)* More gin?

GRACE: Well, a little.

RAY: *(In Ruth's mind.)* Not fair at all.

RUTH: I won't let you go.

RAY: You don't have to.

RUTH: Ever.

RAY: Ever.

RUTH: *(Interrupting presence of Ray in her mind.)* Gin in the afternoon. A woman to talk to.

GRACE: What shall we talk about?

RUTH: When we know each other, we'll share our secrets.

GRACE: If we share our secrets, we'll know each other.

RUTH: Have you many secrets?

GRACE: One.

RUTH: Only one?

GRACE: Only one.

RUTH: I have one. Or two. *(Pause.)* Grace?

GRACE: Hmm?

RUTH: It's good to have a woman to talk to. I don't have many visitors.

GRACE: I know.

RUTH: I suppose my husband told you?

GRACE: Yes.

RUTH: What did he tell you?

GRACE: That you don't have many visitors.

RUTH: Visitors don't interest me. Usually. But you...you interest me.

GRACE: You interest me.

RUTH: A little more gin?

GRACE: Well...

RUTH: Well?

GRACE: Well, a little.

RUTH: *(Pours.)* A little goes a long way.

GRACE: A little more goes a longer way.
     (Ruth pours.)

RUTH: It's good to talk to a woman.

GRACE: Mrs. Garrison—

RUTH: Call me Ruth.

GRACE: Ruth.

RUTH: You must visit often. I will tell Raymond to give you time off from your duties.

GRACE: We should speak to him.

RUTH: He won't deny me.

GRACE: Mrs. Garrison—

RUTH: Leave him to me. And you must call me Ruth. I won't have it any other way.

GRACE: Ruth.

RUTH: That's better.

GRACE: Ruth—

RUTH: I enjoy talking to you. You have…a quality. A quality…I can't think how to describe it. Some have it. Some don't. A very few, like you…

(Ray speaks from another area. He is present in the minds of both women.)

RAY: You began it.

RUTH: You began it.

GRACE: You began it with your eyes. Looking at me, the way you looked at me. You began it.

RAY: You spoke first.

GRACE: You spoke with your eyes.

RUTH: It had already begun. *(Interrupting presence of Ray in their minds.)* Grace?

GRACE: Hmm?

RUTH: There was something you wanted to tell me.

GRACE: Another time.

RUTH: Something you wanted to say.

GRACE: Another time.

RUTH: Well, then, we'll look forward to…to another time.

GRACE: Yes, we'll look forward. *(To Ray, but remains with Ruth.)* Ray?

RAY: Hmm?

GRACE: She asked me…

RAY: To do what?

GRACE: To return.

RAY: Don't.

GRACE: Selfish man.

RAY: You don't have to…to do what she asks.

GRACE: I want to.

RAY: *(To Ruth.)* I wish you wouldn't

RUTH: What?

RAY: You know what.

RUTH: What?

RAY: Invite Grace to tea.

RUTH: I like her.

RAY: I wish you wouldn't.

RUTH: She likes me.

RAY: She's being polite.

RUTH: She's someone...someone...well, she has a quality. You know what I mean. Besides, you're away so often.

RAY: My work—

RUTH: Yes, I know.

RAY: When I'm here, I don't want to share you.

RUTH: Selfish man.

RAY: I thought...I thought that's what you wanted.

RUTH: In the beginning it was.

RAY: And later?

RUTH: We didn't think about later, did we?

RAY: Thinking wasn't what I wanted to do when I was with you.

RUTH: A man of action.

RAY: You inspired me. You inspired me to action.

RUTH: *(Pause.)* When we were young...

RAY: We were very young.

RUTH: In the beginning.

RAY: In the very beginning.

RUTH: When you first looked at me.

RAY: And you said, "What are you looking at?"

RUTH: And you said, "Looking for, not at."

RAY: And you said, "You won't find it here."

RUTH: And you said, "Yes, I will."

RAY: And I did.

RUTH: Because I know what you want.

RAY: You don't know what I want.

RUTH: I know.

RAY: I can't help what I want.

RUTH: Neither can I.

    (Returns to Grace as Grace speaks.)

GRACE: *(At window.)* High up, with the world spread out below, high up the way we are here...

RUTH: What?

GRACE: I feel...

RUTH: What?

GRACE: Spellbound.

RUTH: *(Indicating tea things.)* Tea?

GRACE: Please.

RUTH: *(Pours tea.)* He'll be home soon.

GRACE: What does he think of…of our friendship?

RAY: *(To Ruth, but remains in other area.)* Is everything all right?

RUTH: What makes you ask?

RAY: Nothing.

RUTH: Is everything all right with you?

RAY: Fine.

RUTH: Good.

RAY: Fine.

RUTH: Everything's all right.

RAY: Because if it's not…if it's not, what would be the point?

RUTH: No point. *(To Grace.)* He says, "Meet people. Do things."

GRACE: Do things?

RUTH: "Do things. Get out and about. Do things," he says. Do things? What? What things? "You're too dependent," he says.

GRACE: Are you?

RUTH: He prefers it.

GRACE: Do you?

RUTH: He needs me to be dependent.

GRACE: What do you need?

RUTH: Come, sit, talk to me. He'll be home soon and then I will have to share you.

GRACE: All right.

RUTH: Come, sit and talk. Shall we forget tea and go straight to the gin?

GRACE: Straight to the gin.

RUTH: Agreed. *(Pours gin.)*

GRACE: That first afternoon, that first afternoon, here, when we…when we became friends…well, you weren't what I expected.

RUTH: What was I?

GRACE: Not what I expected

RUTH: You weren't what I expected.

GRACE: Wasn't I?

RUTH: What did we talk about?

GRACE: This, and that. The view. You said it was—

RUTH: Seductive.

GRACE: It was.

RUTH: You seemed to want to tell me something.

GRACE: I wanted to.

RUTH: Why didn't you?

GRACE: A change of plans.

RUTH: Do you want to tell me now?

GRACE: I don't recall what it was.

RUTH: Ah. *(Pause.)* Is your boyfriend—?

GRACE: Boyfriend?

RUTH: The man you mentioned. Is he good to you?

GRACE: Usually.

RUTH: When he isn't?

GRACE: I tell him I will leave him.

RUTH: Will you?

GRACE: If he's not good to me.

RUTH: If he thought you were…were unfaithful to him, if he thought that, what would he do?

GRACE: I don't know.

RUTH: Would he leave you?

GRACE: I wouldn't let him.

RUTH: Could you stop him?

GRACE: I'd stop him.

RUTH: How?

GRACE: I'd stop him.

RUTH: *(Pause.)* When he's with you…

GRACE: What?

RUTH: What do you do?

GRACE: Do?

RUTH: To pass the time. Or does time slip away without your noticing?

GRACE: We dance.

RUTH: Dance!

GRACE: He's a good dancer.

RUTH: Is he?

GRACE: A very good dancer.

RUTH: Raymond's a good dancer.

GRACE: Is he?

RUTH: I met him at a summer dance. At Crooked Lake.

GRACE: Crooked Lake?

RUTH: I was seventeen. He was attracted by my red silk dress. The other girls wore pastels—organdy and taffeta and chiffon, like bridesmaids.

GRACE: Why red?

RUTH: Red is my color.

GRACE: Mine too.

RUTH: He whispered words I hadn't heard before. I blushed red as my dress. "All boys want to do is put their hands up girls' skirts," I said. "What's wrong

with that?" he asked. Yes, he's a very good dancer. *(Pause.)* In the beginning, with your boyfriend, where did you dance?

GRACE: On the train.

RUTH: On the train!

GRACE: In the bar car. No one was there. Not even the waiter.

RUTH: Was it dangerous?

GRACE: Dangerous?

RUTH: The movement of the train.

GRACE: We didn't think of danger.

RUTH: No. Of course not. *(Pause.)* This man...this man is married?

GRACE: Yes.

RUTH: Will he abandon his wife?

GRACE: He says he will.

RUTH: He hasn't, has he?

GRACE: No

RUTH: They say things that aren't true.

GRACE: Who?

RUTH: Men.

GRACE: And women?

RUTH: Women too.

GRACE: A man, or a woman, will sometimes say things that are true.

RUTH: True for the moment.

GRACE: That's all there is.

RUTH: Forgive me. I am too inquisitive. You must forgive me.

GRACE: *(Pause.)* That afternoon...that first afternoon, why did you invite me to
tea?

RUTH: It was the thing to do. No. That's a lie. Raymond spoke of you.
Obliquely, of course, but he spoke of you. When he told me Miss Springle
retired, he spoke of you. Something about the way he spoke of you...I
wanted to see for myself. I went to the office and looked in the window. I
watched you at your desk.

GRACE: You watched me?

RUTH: I was drawn to...to something in you...to you. I sent an invitation to tea.

GRACE: I accepted.

RUTH: An invitation.

GRACE: Proper and polite.

RUTH: I was brought up to follow rules.

GRACE: So was I.

RUTH: Do you follow rules?

GRACE: My own.

RUTH: Lucky you.

GRACE: I get what I want.

RUTH: Because you make your own rules?

GRACE: Yes.

RUTH: If only I could.

GRACE: You do. I see it in your eyes. I recognize it. The untamed view.

RUTH: In my eyes?

GRACE: Does he see it? The untamed view?

RUTH: We have no secrets.

GRACE: None at all?

RUTH: Well, perhaps one.

GRACE: At least one.

RUTH: More gin?

GRACE: More.

RUTH: *(Pours gin.)* More it is

GRACE: Gin improves my vision.

RUTH: Good.

GRACE: How about you?

RUTH: I am not usually intemperate.

GRACE: I'm not either.

RUTH: One shouldn't go too far. One shouldn't.

GRACE: One should.

RUTH: All right.

    (They sip their drinks.)

RUTH: You have beautiful hair.

GRACE: Thank you.

RUTH: Does he brush your hair?

GRACE: Brush my hair? No.

RUTH: May I? May I brush your hair?

GRACE: If that's what you want.

RUTH: Come. Sit by the window in the light. I will brush your hair in the light.

    (Grace sits by window.)

RUTH: Wonderful hair.

GRACE: Be gentle.

RUTH: Yes.

GRACE: Ah.

RUTH: Yes.

GRACE: Don't hurt me.

RUTH: I won't. *(Beat.)* How is that?

GRACE: Good.

RUTH: And that?

GRACE: Very good.

RUTH: Yes.

GRACE: Oh, very, very good.

RUTH: Yes.

GRACE: Yes.

RUTH: Wonderful.

GRACE: *(Pause.)* That first afternoon…That afternoon, here, when we had our tea…That afternoon—

RUTH: Something happened.

GRACE: I wasn't looking for it.

RUTH: Nor I.

GRACE: I didn't want it.

RUTH: Yes, you did.

GRACE: Did I? Perhaps I did.

RUTH: Oh, yes.

GRACE: It surprised me.

RUTH: Me too.

GRACE: Were you ever…surprised before?

RUTH: Once.

GRACE: Tell me.

RUTH: It was long ago.

GRACE: Tell me.

RUTH: I didn't know it would happen again.

GRACE: Tell me.

RUTH: It was on our honeymoon.

(Pause. Ray enters during speech.)

RUTH: Raymond and I were at a small hotel on a point overlooking the sea. One night there was a gathering. A crowded room. I was by a window looking out into the night. I saw the room reflected in the window. A woman watched me. I had seen her on other evenings playing cards. I watched her watching me. I was afraid to turn around, afraid to see, afraid of what she would see. She crossed the room and stood behind me. Our eyes met in the glass, caught. She whispered something. Her breath was warm. It was a foreign country.

RAY: What foreign country?

(END OF ACT I)

ACT II

Scene: Same as end of Act I.

RAY: What foreign country?

RUTH: Raymond.

RAY: What are you up to?

RUTH: Up to?

GRACE/RUTH: Talking.

RAY: Talking. Ah, talking. I envy you. Women know how to talk to each other.

GRACE: *(Starts to exit.)* I ought to go.

RUTH: No. Stay. We'll have a drink. The three of us. Raymond, fix her a drink.

RAY: If Grace doesn't want—

RUTH: Raymond! *(To Grace.)* You don't have to run out.

GRACE: I wasn't—

RUTH: Raymond will think you don't like him.

GRACE: That's not true.

RAY: Please stay.

RUTH: We want you to stay *(To Ray.)* Isn't that right?

RAY: That's right.

GRACE: Well, if that's what you want, well, then, well, I'll stay.

RAY: *(Pours drinks, pause.)* What foreign country?

RUTH: Shall I go to the kitchen and bring back some food?

RAY: Yes. I'm hungry. Hungry in the extreme. Must be the walking. Works up a hunger. For something substantial. Something meaningful. Something of that nature. Walking works up a hunger.

GRACE: Like dancing.

RAY: Like dancing. *(To Ruth.)* What about that food?

GRACE: *(To Ray.)* Why don't you get it?

RUTH: I'll get it.

RAY: I'll get it.

RUTH: I don't mind.

RAY: *(Gets up.)* I will get it.

RUTH: No, I will.

RAY: I said I would.

RUTH: Really, Raymond—

RAY: I don't want Grace thinking I'm a man who—

RUTH: Who what?

RAY: Expects women to wait on him.

GRACE: I'll tell you what: I'll get it.

RAY: You're the guest.

RUTH: She's more than the guest.

(Ruth exits. Grace and Ray sip their drinks.)

RAY: She didn't...?

GRACE: Didn't what?

RAY: She's not...?

GRACE: What?

RAY: She's not...taking up your time?

GRACE: No.

RAY: I don't want her taking up your time.

GRACE: She isn't.

RAY: Making you do things you hadn't thought of doing.

GRACE: She couldn't.

RAY: I suppose not.

GRACE: *(They sip their drinks.)* Well?

RAY: I don't know.

GRACE: Think of something.

RAY: Yes.

GRACE: Or I will.

RAY: Please, Grace, nothing rash.

GRACE: Rash?

RAY: Regarding Ruth.

GRACE: Nothing rash.

RAY: Good.

GRACE: We can't just spring it on her.

RAY: True.

GRACE: We have to consider...to consider the consequences.

RAY: True.

GRACE: I mean, well, I know I've been...I've been pushing you—

RAY: Pushing, yes.

GRACE: Pushing you to tell her. I mean, I even said I would tell her. But telling her in a sudden manner, just like that, without preparation, dropping it on her, well, it would be cruel, wouldn't it?

RAY: You changed your tune.

GRACE: I'm not a cruel woman.

RAY: I told you I would tell her and I will.

GRACE: You will?

RAY: I will.

GRACE: Nothing rash, Ray. You said so yourself. It would serve no purpose.

RAY: No purpose at all.

GRACE: Nothing rash.

RAY: We'll work it out.

RUTH: *(Enters with tray of food.)* Work what out?

RAY: Ah, cheese and bread, pâté.

GRACE: Delicious.

(They eat.)

RUTH: Work what out?

RAY: What?

RUTH: You said, "We'll work it out."

RAY: Did I?

GRACE/RUTH: You did.

RAY: Ah, well, we were speaking of things that go on in my office.

RUTH: Oh.

(They eat, pause.)

RUTH: *(To Ray.)* I was telling Grace about our honeymoon.

RAY: Grace doesn't want to hear about our honeymoon.

RUTH: Oh, I'm sorry.

GRACE: I do.

RUTH: *(To Ray.)* She does.

RAY: She doesn't want to hear about us.

GRACE: I do.

RUTH: *(To Ray.)* See?

RAY: *(Tasting cheese.)* Something off about this.

RUTH: Off?

RAY: A bit off.

RUTH: Try the other one.

RAY: What were you telling her?

RUTH: This, and that. *(To Grace.)* We had quite a time. Though not what we expected. We were at a small hotel. On a point overlooking the sea.

RAY: A point? It was a cliff, a precipice.

RUTH: Spectacular.

RAY: A point? You make it sound timid. It was anything but timid. One false step…

RUTH: You have no sense of adventure.

RAY: I have a sense of adventure, but it doesn't include walking along a precipice.

RUTH: Do you remember that woman?

RAY: What?

RUTH: You know—

RAY: What woman?

RUTH: At the hotel. The one with the cards? Always at a table by the window with a deck of cards. A fortune-teller.

GRACE: Or a gambler.

RUTH: Always turning over the cards. Looking at us—

RAY: Looking at you. *(To Grace.)* She was charmed by Ruth.

GRACE: Who wouldn't be?

RAY: Bewitched.

RUTH: On my breakfast tray one morning I found the Queen of Hearts beside the grapefruit. *(To Ray.)* You thought it amusing. You laughed.

RAY: No, I didn't.

RUTH: *(To Grace.)* He did.

RAY: *(To Grace.)* She remembers what she wants to remember, even things that didn't happen.

RUTH: I remember your laughing. Squinting your eyes together, your head thrown back, mouth open, laughing, a man's laugh, loud, a pulse visible in your neck. I wanted to touch it.

GRACE: *(To Ruth.)* Did you? Touch it?

RUTH: *(To Ray.)* Did I?

RAY: Possibly.

RUTH: The Queen of Hearts on the breakfast tray.

RAY: I don't remember the Queen of Hearts on the breakfast tray.

RUTH: Oh, yes.

GRACE: How was the dancing?

RAY: Dancing?

RUTH: Grace's boyfriend is a good dancer.

RAY: Is he?

RUTH: We were talking about him before you came in.

GRACE: He's a good dancer.

RAY: Really?

GRACE: Very good.

RAY: You dance well together, do you?

GRACE: We're meant for each other.

RUTH: Raymond's a good dancer.

GRACE: Is he?

RAY: Ruth.

RUTH: You are.

GRACE: We could go dancing together.

RUTH: We could. *(To Ray.)* We could go to Crooked Lake.

RAY: Ah, well, some day.

GRACE: Crooked Lake?

RUTH: Do you know it?

GRACE: Yes.

RUTH: Charming place.

GRACE: Yes, charming.

RUTH: Raymond took me there, not long ago.

GRACE: Did he?

RUTH: He said, "Ruth, let's go dancing."

GRACE: He did?

RUTH: What a surprise! We hadn't been dancing in years.

RAY: My work—

RUTH: I know, I know. *(To Grace.)* I can't imagine what caused him to suddenly want to go dancing.

GRACE: *(To Ray.)* What was it?

RUTH: Whatever the cause, it's a pleasure to once again be dancing.

GRACE: Oh, yes.

RUTH: We'll all go.

GRACE: I'll wear my red dress.

RUTH: *(To Ray.)* She's magnificent in red.

RAY: You've seen her in red?

RUTH: They danced on the train.

RAY: Who?

RUTH: Grace and her boyfriend.

GRACE: *(To Ray.)* We didn't think of danger.

RAY: Of course not.

GRACE: It was the bar car. No one was there.

RAY: Not even the waiter?

RUTH: I imagine it.

RAY: I imagine it, too.

GRACE: In my red dress.

RUTH: Yes, that's how I imagine you. What about him? Raymond, how is he dressed?

RAY: I don't know.

RUTH: Imagine it.

RAY: I don't know.

GRACE: Come on.

RUTH: How?

RAY: All right. A dark suit.

GRACE: With tiny almost invisible stripes.

RUTH: His hand on your back.

GRACE: Warm.

RUTH: Insistent.

RAY: Searching.

RUTH: The little lamps on the tables swaying, spilling light.

GRACE: It's after midnight.

RAY: A cigarette burning in an ash tray.

RUTH: Smoke hanging in the air.

RAY: He whispers something.

RUTH: He asks you to go to his compartment.

RAY: It's more comfortable there.

GRACE: Oh, how we danced! Get up. I'll show you.

RAY: What? No. I don't feel like dancing.

RUTH: No one asked you to.

RAY: Who's she going to dance with?

RUTH: Me.

GRACE: *(To Ray.)* I'll dance with Ruth while you watch.

RAY: You want me to watch?

GRACE: Does that bother you?

RAY: Bother me? No, of course not.

RUTH: What's the problem?

RAY: There's no music. You can't dance without music.

RUTH: The radio. *(Turns on radio. Dance music.)*

GRACE: *(To Ruth.)* Shall we dance?
    (They dance.)

RAY: Why would it bother me?

RUTH: *(To Grace, while dancing.)* Did you go to his compartment?

GRACE: That night?

RUTH: Did you?

GRACE: I may have.

RUTH: Ah.

RAY: Ah?

RUTH: Just ah.

RAY: Oh.

GRACE: *(To Ray.)* She's a good dancer.

RAY: That's enough. *(Turns off radio.)*
    (Grace and Ruth stop dancing.)

RUTH: Don't turn off the music.

RAY: That's enough!

GRACE: We were just getting started.

RUTH: Dance with us.

RAY: What?

GRACE: Dance with us.

RAY: All together?

GRACE: We'll make our own dance.

RAY: No.

GRACE: Dance with us.

RAY: No, thank you.

RUTH: *(To Grace.)* He's conventional.

RAY: I am not.

RUTH: It's all right, dear.

RAY: I am not conventional.

RUTH: It's all right.

RAY: I'm open-minded.

RUTH: Not at all.

RAY: Very open-minded.

GRACE: An open-minded man.

RAY: Did you go to his compartment?

RUTH: *(To Grace.)* He's trying to show how open-minded he is.

RAY: *(To Grace.)* She's teasing.

GRACE: I see.

RAY: I'm more open-minded than most.

RUTH: You are. *(To Grace.)* It's one of the things that drew me to him. *(To Ray.)* Something beyond the obvious.

RAY: *(To Grace.)* Did you go to his compartment?

GRACE: I may have.

RAY: Perhaps you did. Perhaps you both were thinking the same thing. Or perhaps it was your idea.

GRACE: Thinking had nothing to do with it.

RAY: Perhaps he saw something in you that reminded him of...that reminded him. Perhaps he saw...He saw something he...He saw you.

RUTH: How's the pâté?

GRACE: He was persuasive, impossible to resist.

RUTH: *(To Ray.)* Do you like the pâté?

RAY: *(To Grace.)* You didn't resist.

RUTH: Do you like it?

GRACE: I wanted to.

RAY: Resist?

GRACE: Go to his compartment.

RUTH: I said, how is the pâté?!

RAY: Pâté?

RUTH: How is it!?

RAY: What are you getting upset about?

RUTH: I am not upset!

RAY: You're shouting.

RUTH: Shouting? I am not shouting. *(To Grace.)* Am I shouting?

RAY: All right, you're not shouting.

RUTH: I asked a question.

RAY: What?

RUTH: *(To Grace.)* He does that, you know, avoids the question, puts you off by not answering.

RAY: The pâté is excellent.

RUTH: *(To Grace.)* Perhaps you've noticed that he puts you off.

RAY: I said, the pâté is excellent.

RUTH: *(To Grace.)* Where does he live?

RAY: Who?

RUTH: Grace's boyfriend.

RAY: Don't put Grace on the spot.

RUTH: *(To Grace.)* What's his name? Your boyfriend. No. Don't tell me. I mean, he could be anyone.

RAY: *(To Ruth.)* You're too inquisitive.

RUTH: He could be anyone.

GRACE: He could be.

RUTH: I'm curious.

RAY: You're putting Grace on the spot.

RUTH: Grace enjoys being put on the spot.

GRACE: What makes you say that?

RUTH: A hunch.

GRACE: I'll tell you about my boyfriend.

RAY: You don't have to.

GRACE: I want to. *(Pause.)* My boyfriend loves two women.

RUTH: *(To Ray.)* What do you think of that?

RAY: Two women?

RUTH: Grace's boyfriend loves two women. What do you think of that? A theoretical question.

RAY: What do I think, theoretically, of Grace's boyfriend loving two women?

RUTH: What do you think?

RAY: It's possible.

RUTH: To love two women?

RAY: Yes.

GRACE: Equally?

RAY: Equally.

RUTH: Exactly the same?

RAY: I didn't say exactly the same. I said equally.

GRACE: It happens, I suppose.

RAY: You can't predict it but—

RUTH: It happens.

GRACE: Love is limitless.

RAY: It's not as though there's a certain amount and it gets used up.

GRACE: It's inexhaustible.

RUTH: Enough for everybody.

RAY: Enough to go around. More gin?

GRACE: Please.

RUTH: Someone suffers.

RAY: Someone doesn't have to.

RUTH: But someone does.

RAY: It's between Grace and her boyfriend.

RUTH: Leave him.

GRACE: Leave him?

RUTH: That's my advice. Leave him.

RAY: Leave him?

RUTH: He's not going to abandon his wife.

RAY: He might. I'm not saying he would. He probably wouldn't. I don't know.

RUTH: What should she do?

RAY: Who?

RUTH: His wife.

RAY: I thought you meant Grace.

RUTH: I feel sorry for his wife.

GRACE: I'm the one making sacrifices.

RUTH: We all make sacrifices.

GRACE: I'm the one alone most of the time. I'm the one with the half life, waiting for calls, sneaking around, hoping.

RUTH: She probably loves him.

GRACE: Who?

RUTH: His wife.

GRACE: I thought you meant me.

RAY: You'd have left him by now if you didn't love him.

RUTH: What about his wife?

RAY: What about his wife?

RUTH: What if she left him?

RAY: She won't.

RUTH: She might.

GRACE: You're assuming she knows. She may know. Or she may not.

RAY: She'd have left if she wanted to.

RUTH: Something keeps his wife from leaving. Habit. Or need. Or comfort. Or she has nowhere to go. Or…or it's love.

GRACE: Does she know?

RUTH: His wife?

GRACE: Does she?

RUTH: She knows him.

GRACE: If she knew, what would she do?

RUTH: Kill him.

RAY: Kill him?

RUTH: She ought to.

RAY: Kill him?

RUTH: It's quite natural.

GRACE: It's extreme.

RAY: He deserves to be killed, that's true. But he's only a man trying to live his life the best way he can. I'm not making excuses. Well, yes, I am. He's only a man who—

RUTH: You amuse me.

RAY: Why?

RUTH: Because you do.

RAY: You amuse me.

RUTH: Why?

RAY: Because you do.

GRACE: You both amuse me.

RUTH: His wife knows.

RAY: What makes you say that?

RUTH: A hunch.

RAY: I feel sorry for him.

GRACE: Why?

RUTH: *(To Ray.)* What if Grace moved in with them?

GRACE: What?!

RAY: Ruth!

GRACE: That would be something, wouldn't it?

RAY: *(To Ruth.)* You're embarrassing Grace.

RUTH: Grace is friends with his wife.

GRACE: Close friends.

RUTH: If Grace moved in with them, his wife would have someone to...to talk to. Someone to keep her company when he goes away. *(To Grace.)* He travels, you said.

GRACE: Yes.

RAY: Ah.

RUTH: Plenty of room in the house. *(To Ray.)* It's a big house, she said.

RAY: Did she?

GRACE: Yes.

RUTH: What if Grace moved in with them?

RAY: Ridiculous. Absurd. Impossible. Unthinkable. Completely unthinkable. Totally and completely unthinkable. Would his wife agree?

RUTH: Yes! What an idea. His wife suggests it.

GRACE: What an idea.

RUTH: Let's say the arrangement falls into place and Grace is living with them. *(To Ray.)* Is that what he wants?

RAY: It's...it's unusual...intriguing.

GRACE: There's one thing, though.

RAY: What?

GRACE: Well, I mean, well, all right, maybe his wife knows about...knows... well, she knows. Maybe she does. Let's say she does and seems to—

RUTH: To accept it?

GRACE: To accept it, yes. To let it be...for various reasons, for her reasons, and well, what I want to know is what happens when he finds out—

RAY: Finds out what?

GRACE: He thinks of the arrangement as his. His double marriage.

RUTH: His wives?

GRACE: At first it doesn't occur to him.

RAY: What doesn't occur to him?

GRACE: As they sit on the porch and read the evening paper and sip their gin and talk. As they listen to the frogs and crickets, the crunch of gravel as cars pass by. The whistle of the night train. It doesn't occur to him.

RAY: What?

GRACE: When he gets up from his wife's bed and quietly searches for his slippers.

RUTH: Brown leather slippers.

GRACE: When he tiptoes across the room—

RUTH: Trying not to wake his wife.

GRACE: Into the hall.

RUTH: Careful of creaking floorboards.

GRACE: Down the passage to my room. He doesn't realize that his wife and I...his wife and I...He doesn't realize.

RAY: Realize what?

GRACE: One night he arrives home early.

RUTH: To enjoy his double marriage.

GRACE: He pushes open the front door. Where are they? He hears something. Dance music. He follows the music to its source.

RUTH: *(To Ray, indicating glass.)* Pour a little more gin in here, will you?

RAY: Certainly. *(He does.)*

GRACE: A white curtain at the window, translucent, the garden beyond, late after-noon, the buzz and hum of nature, a breeze from the open window stirs the perfumes, blending them, his wife's and mine. He sees us, and knows.

RAY: What if he already knows?

RUTH: Raymond, don't.

RAY: Where's your spirit of adventure?

GRACE: He already knows?

RUTH: *(To Ray.)* He wouldn't let on that he knows. Would he?

RAY: He and his wife have no secrets.

RUTH: He wouldn't let on because it might endanger the arrangement.

GRACE: He and his wife have no secrets?

RAY: No secrets. None at all. Some. One or two.

RUTH: He might be making a mistake by letting on.

GRACE: He knows about his wife and me?

RUTH: Perhaps he should shut up.

GRACE: Did his wife tell him?

RUTH: *(To Ray.)* Now you've done it.

RAY: His wife didn't tell him, but he knows.

GRACE: How?

RAY: He sees it in their eyes, the way they look at each other. The way they look at him.

RUTH: Not the same.

RAY: Not exactly.

GRACE: What you're saying is, he had come home early and seen them? Perhaps he stood outside the window—

RUTH: Stop.

GRACE: With the moon at his back, he watched them dancing in their red dresses.

RUTH: Please stop.

GRACE: Stop?

RUTH: We're getting carried away.

GRACE: What if I asked him to make a choice?
   (No response from Ray.)

GRACE: *(To Ruth.)* What if I asked her?
   (No response from Ruth.)

GRACE: What if I made a choice? *(She considers this.)* If a choice had to be made…who would be chosen and who not, if a choice had to be made?

RAY: Grace.

GRACE: Of course my boyfriend and his wife are nothing like that. I'm not either. Still it's amusing to imagine…well, to imagine. But they're nothing like that. I'm nothing like that.

RUTH: *(To Ray.)* You want both of them, but you don't want them to have each other.

GRACE: *(Getting up.)* It's getting late.

RUTH: No, please.

RAY: I'm sorry.

GRACE: Thanks for the gin. And the food. Thanks for everything.

RUTH: Grace

GRACE: *(Hearing the train whistle.)* Listen.

RUTH: Yes.

GRACE: The train.

RAY: The night train.

RUTH: Yes.

GRACE: No. Don't see me out. I know the way. Good-bye. I had a lovely time. Good-bye.

RAY: Wait!

RUTH: Don't go.

GRACE: Something of a surprise to be in…in this position. Between them, so to speak. No, not a surprise because I knew where I was, what I thought I was doing, but I didn't know…didn't know…well, you understand, don't you? *(Grace exits. Ruth turns to Ray.)*

RUTH: Now you've really done it.

RAY: Ruth, I'm sorry.

RUTH: What are we going to do?

RAY: I don't know.

(Grace returns to the train. Ruth joins her at a table by the window.)

RUTH: Is this where you met?

GRACE: It is.

RUTH: Who spoke first?

GRACE: He did.

RUTH: He spoke first?

GRACE: No. I spoke.

RUTH: Which?

GRACE: I spoke.

RUTH: Saying?

GRACE: "Do you always stare that way? Or is it me?"

RUTH: "It's you." That's what I would have said. "It's you."

GRACE: He did.

RUTH: What happened next? No. Don't tell me. He asked if he could join you. And you said—

GRACE: Yes.

RUTH: You said yes and he bought you a drink—

GRACE: Gin.

RUTH: Gin.

GRACE: He asked my name.

RUTH: Grace.

GRACE: "Grace who?"

RUTH: "You don't need to know my last name."

GRACE: Yes, that's what he said, and then, "I don't usually pursue women on trains."

RUTH: He's a shy man.

GRACE: Shy?

RUTH: In a way.

GRACE: The waiter brought my drink.

RUTH: And that's how it began.

GRACE: How did it begin with us?

RUTH: With tea.

GRACE: Tea?

RUTH: Or was it something stronger?

GRACE: Something stronger.

RAY: *(Enters bar car, approaches table.)* May I join you?

GRACE: *(To Ray.)* We were talking about the time we met.

RAY: *(Sits.)* The time you met me?

GRACE: It was winter.

RAY: Or the time you met Ruth?

GRACE: In the spring I met Ruth.

RUTH: *(To Ray.)* It was winter when she met you.

RAY: I thought it was spring.

GRACE: *(To Ray.)* Winter.

RAY: Ah.

RUTH: *(To Ray.)* In the spring, I invited Grace to tea.

RAY: Ah, yes.

GRACE: *(To Ray.)* We argued about my going. You didn't want me to.

RAY: You went anyway.

GRACE: Tulips at the front of the house in a neat row.

RUTH: I was at the window looking out.

GRACE: Your gaze…*(Turning to Ray.)* Your gaze affected me.

RUTH: And me.

RAY: And me.

GRACE: *(To Ruth.)* You stepped behind the curtain.

RUTH: When I opened the door, we pretended that gaze had not taken place.

RAY: You could pretend such a thing?

GRACE: Almost.

RUTH: The gaze was in the room with us.

GRACE: Though we averted our eyes.

RAY: A bold look.

GRACE: We sat down behind the teapot. *(To Ray.)* I asked if you were home.

RUTH: "Raymond's not home. He's out."

RAY: Walking.

RUTH: "How do you take your tea?"

GRACE: "Sweet."

RUTH: We talked.

GRACE: Awkward at first.

RUTH: Only at first.

GRACE: We talked about the weather.

RUTH: Small talk.

GRACE: And other things.

RUTH: We were fortunate to find you.

GRACE: Thank you.

RUTH: *(To Ray.)* But I'm thinking of another time, before that, a January night when the moon reflected on the snow, when you walked up the path, your shadow gliding on ahead, toward me. Out I ran to greet you, slipping on the steps, falling forward at your feet.

RAY: I picked you up.

RUTH: And I saw... I saw—

GRACE: Saw what?

RUTH: A change. *(To Ray.)* You were not the same.

GRACE: *(To Ruth.)* How was he different?

RUTH: An elemental difference. *(To Ray.)* I felt it when you picked me up and I leaned against the bulk of your body, feeling your body—new, unknown. *(To Grace.)* He was more...more...more. *(To Ray.)* A man I didn't know.

RAY: A man you wanted to know?

RUTH: *(To Grace.)* Then, in the spring, I met you. And I knew what had changed.

RAY: *(To Ruth.)* You changed too.

RUTH: Yes.

GRACE: And all that summer, we three, we...we...

RUTH: We did, didn't we?

GRACE: Because of that thing that binds people together, that keeps them bound, that catches them so irrevocably, catches them in each other.

RAY: Are you sorry?

GRACE: No.

RAY: In spite of everything, all that's happened, all that?

RUTH: No.

GRACE: *(To Ray.)* Are *you* sorry?

RAY: I'm not sorry about love.

RUTH: Well, there you are.

    (Grace, Ruth, and Ray turn to audience.)

RAY: *(To audience.)* There you are.

GRACE: *(To audience.)* There you are.

END OF PLAY

Emma's Child

Kristine Thatcher

for Corey Matthew Greminger

BIOGRAPHY

Emma's Child was commissioned and nurtured under the auspices of Cynthia White's Play Development Program, at the Oregon Shakespeare Festival. It was one of three winners of the Susan Smith Blackburn Prize for Best Plays of 1995. It will have its midwest premiere at Victory Gardens in the fall of 1996, where Ms. Thatcher is a member of the Playwrights Ensemble. Her first Play, *Niedecker,* opened to critical acclaim in New York City, at the Women's Project and Productions in 1989. *Niedecker* was nominated for the National Arts Club's Joseph Kesselring Award in 1987 and was a finalist for the Susan Smith Blackburn Prize in 1986. *Waiting for Tina Meyer,* her one-act, opened at New York's West Bank Cafe in 1989. *Under Glass* is a companion play to *Emma's Child* and was also a Susan Smith Blackburn finalist. Her latest play, *Apparitions,* was commissioned by Peninsula Players and received its premiere production in Door County in the summer of 1995. Ms. Thatcher is also an actress and most recently appeared as Hannah Jarvis in the Goodman Theatre's production of Tom Stoppard's *Arcadia*. She makes her home in Chicago with her husband, actor David Darlow, and their daughter, Kerry Miriam.

ORIGINAL PRODUCTION

Emma's Child was first produced at the Black Swan Theatre of the Oregon Shakespeare Festival, on April 1, 1995. It was directed by Cynthia White, with scenic design by Curt Endlerle, costume design by Alvin Perry, and lighting design by Robert Peterson. The music director was Todd Barton. The cast was as follows:

Jean Farrell	Linda Emond
Henry Farrell	Dan Kremer
Tess McGarrett	Debra Wicks
Franny Stornant	Kirsten Giroux
Emma Miller	Christine Williams
Laurence	Ray Porter
Mary Jo	Cindy Basco
Vivien Rademacher	Judith Sanford
Dr. Helen Arbaugh	Debra Wicks
Sam Stornant	Mark Murphey
Michelle	Christine Williams

CAST OF CHARACTERS*

JEAN FARRELL: The adoptive mother, age 40.
HENRY FARRELL: Her husband, age 46.

TESS MCGARRETT: A social worker, any age.

FRANNY STORNANT: Jean's best friend, age 40.

EMMA MILLER: A birth mother, age 19.

LAURENCE: A male nurse, age 30 to 40.

MARY JO: A nurse's aide, middle 20s.

VIVIEN RADEMACHER: Hospital administration, any age.

HELEN ARBAUGH: Neurosurgeon, any age.

SAM STORNANT: Franny's husband, 40s.

MICHELLE: A birthmother, early 20s.

TIME

The action of the play takes place between the fall of 1990, and the summer of 1991.

PLACE

Chicago. There is a permanent area upstage center that is Christ Hospital, Robin's world. Surrounding his isolette are the machines that monitor his progress, the rocking chair, the table. These few pieces make up the only world he knows. All other locales exist in the corners downstage right, center, or left. Set pieces need only be suggested.

EMMA'S CHILD

PART I
ACT I
Scene I

October, 1990. Place: A suggestion of the comfortable, but modest, home of Jean and Henry Farrell. There are bay windows, beyond which are shade trees in full autumn colors. A calico cat sleeps in a patch of sunlight. There are vases filled with the treasures of a backyard garden: roses, mums, dahlias, cosmos, catchfly, asters, and lime green grape vines. It is moments before Jean and Henry are to face an important interview. They are coming unglued. They burst into the room. Jean carries a tall vase filled with flowers.

HENRY: I think it's better if you don't!

JEAN: Well, what am I gonna say, then?

HENRY: Tell them she died of natural causes.

JEAN: But, she didn't! Henry, don't move that vase. I just put it there.

HENRY: Jean, we'll be sitting around this coffee table. We won't be able to see her.

JEAN: *(He's right.)* Dammit!

HENRY: I know you spent a lot of time on this stuff, but come on, I want a little eye contact with this woman. We never have this many flowers. She's going to wonder where we're keeping the deceased.

JEAN: Well, thanks a lot!

HENRY: Just calm down, will you?

JEAN: *You* calm down.

HENRY: Can I move the vase?

JEAN: Move it!

HENRY: Where were we?

JEAN: What natural causes?

HENRY: Just say old age.

JEAN: She was sixty-three. She didn't go peacefully in her sleep.

HENRY: Can't you fudge it a little?

JEAN: Are you going to "fudge" when they ask about *your* health?

HENRY: All they have to do, Jean, is dig up a few medical records. I've been cancer-free for five years. What's the big deal?

JEAN: Then don't ask me to mess with my mother's liver!

HENRY: Oh, come on, it's not the same thing.

JEAN: My mother won't be raising this child! You will! You are not actually going to wear that sweater, are you?

HENRY: What's wrong with it?

JEAN: It's too small! What about the powder blue I gave you for Christmas?

HENRY: It won't go with these pants.

JEAN: Yes, it will!

HENRY: No, it won't! These pants are green!

JEAN: They're dark blue, Henry.

HENRY: No, they're not!

JEAN: Which of the two of us is color-blind!

HENRY: The powder blue itches. It makes my neck sweat.

JEAN: Go *away!* What did you want to ask me? You came in here to ask me something?

HENRY: Where's the scouring powder?

JEAN: Don't tell me!

HENRY: Well, if you'd stop bitching for two minutes—

JEAN: Jesus. Jesus God.

HENRY: It's just the sink and the toilet! The floor is done!

JEAN: Give me one.

HENRY: No! Absolutely not!

JEAN: I may have to kill you, then.

HENRY: When the caseworker asks whether we smoke, how would you like to answer?

JEAN: Do you still have them?

HENRY: No.

JEAN: You *destroyed* them!

HENRY: Five minutes after you surrendered them!

JEAN: I'm going down to the corner. I'll be back.

HENRY: The hell you are! This person is due here any minute.

JEAN: Then what about the sink and the toilet!

HENRY: And how you can talk about cigarettes, when we've just had a conversation about my cancer is beyond me! It's unconscionable!

JEAN: I've kept my smoke away from you. What I do in the backyard does not harm you. It is not your business!

HENRY: When you knowingly tamper with the well-being of my wife, it *does* harm me! It *is* my business! You have *quit*, Jean. It's been eleven days. Just *stay* quit!

JEAN: I want a divorce.

HENRY: You can have a divorce. What you can't have is a cigarette.

(*The doorbell rings. They take a covert moment as everything between them changes.*)

HENRY: Come on, Jean.

JEAN: I can't make up a story, Hal.

HENRY: Neither can I.

JEAN: Fine.

HENRY: Do you really want a cigarette? I could—

JEAN: No. I'm just talking.

HENRY: Good.

JEAN: Maybe later.

HENRY: Should I change?

JEAN: What?

HENRY: If these pants are blue—

JEAN: They *are* blue, but never mind. You look great. Open the door.

HENRY: You're ready?

JEAN: Yes.

(*Cross-fade to Emma.*)

HENRY AND EMMA: Are you sure?

JEAN: (*Focused on Henry, but addressing Emma.*) I'm sure.

(*Henry exits.*)

Scene II

June, 1991. Place: The Newborn Special Care Unit at Christ Hospital. Upstage center is Robin's home, an isolette with solid sides, so he is in no danger of rolling out. These also hide him from audience view. He lies at the waist level of an adult. Attached to the upstage side of the isolette is a pole about six feet tall, and from that pole spreading out over the isolette is a roof or hood, containing temperature and light controls. We never see this child. He is always covered or swaddled. Nearby is a small machine that monitors his vital signs. Stage right center is a comfortable rocking chair and a small table.

EMMA: Henry couldn't make it?

JEAN: (*Jean turns to Emma.*) I beg your pardon?

EMMA: Henry flaked out?

JEAN: He had to work.

EMMA: Right.

JEAN: He really did have to work, Emma.

EMMA: Are you ready?

JEAN: Yes.

EMMA: He's right here.

(They approach and peer into the crib.)

EMMA: Hi, Blue Bear. There's the guy! Hi, Blueberry.

JEAN: *(Drinking him in, which takes a neutral second.)* Hello, Robin.

EMMA: Whatchoo doin' today? Whatchoo doin'? *(To Jean.)* Do you see?

JEAN: Yes.

EMMA: I think old Larry must have wondered what happened to me.

JEAN: Larry?

EMMA: Laurence. The nurse. He may be a fruit loop, I don't know.

JEAN: Oh.

EMMA: I think he's pissed because I haven't been here. He gives me these looks.

JEAN: Oh, no. I'm sure he—

EMMA: It's hard to get away. It's over an hour from Joliet. And I got a summer job with the Park District now.

JEAN: I'm sure he understands.

EMMA: I don't have my own car.

JEAN: He understands.

EMMA: Plus, Michael's walkin' and climbin'. He's a tornado. Yesterday he pulled a chest of drawers down on himself. I like to be with him when he's awake, because he could just croak himself any minute now. He don't understand about gravity yet. My dad keeps sayin', "He's got a date with Mr. Gravity!" So I kinda wanna be around when the introductions are made, you know?

JEAN: *(Intensely focused on the baby.)* Is he okay? Does he—?

EMMA: He does that when he's sleepy. It's spooky, but he don't really have a grip on his eyes.

JEAN: Oh. So he's—

EMMA: It's just a sign he's gettin' sleepy. *(To Jean.)* They already told me he's not gonna make it.

JEAN: Who told you?

EMMA: Doctor Arbaugh. Somethin' about the stuff in his head. I said it was okay not to revive him if something should happen. Do you think that was smart? I don't know.

JEAN: I don't know either, Emma. They've told me a little, but I still have so many questions. Does the doctor come by often?

EMMA: I don't know. I talked to her on the phone. This is only the third time I've been here.

JEAN: Oh.

EMMA: I *want* to come. I had to borrow my dad's truck to meet you here today.

JEAN: It's okay, Emma.

EMMA: He don't have no clothes or nothin'. I brought him some of Michael's baby stuff, but I just didn't keep that much. They're all dirty now, and—it don't look like anybody around here does personal laundry. His diapers are always clean when I come. Still, he's got a pretty bad rash. *(Hopefully.)* Do you want to hold him?

JEAN: No, not yet.

(One of Robin's machines starts to beep.)

JEAN: What's that?

EMMA: It's one of his monitors. I've seen 'em flip it off here. *(She swats at a switch and the sound stops.)* There.

JEAN: Should we call someone?

EMMA: If there's a real problem, it makes another sound.

JEAN: What does it monitor?

EMMA: I can't figure it out. *(To the baby.)* But, you're okay, aren't ya, Baby Bear? He looks like his father. Funny how he turned out. Jamie is so smart. He was always doin' the kind of math that didn't even look like numbers, know what I mean? Just, all these crazy squiggles on the page? And it's not just math; he was always after me about how bad I spoke. I probably should have paid more attention to it when I had the chance. And he has these blue-ice eyes, that smack out of his face. He is *good lookin'*, *(To the baby.)* just like you, Blue Bear. *(To Jean.)* I never thought I'd see Jamie again. Somebody from the bar said they saw him out with my mother a while ago. But, I don't believe that.

JEAN: Your mother?

EMMA: On a date.

JEAN: I'm sorry?

EMMA: The guy who told me is full of crap. I mean, she probably would, she *would*. But she's the last thing in the world Jamie would go for. She's thirty-five years old, okay? 'Member that cold snap about a week ago? I ran into him about that time. Just walkin' the street, his arms full of books. He invited me for a beer. It was like some weird dream. We sat there, at the same table. The music was the same, the people was the same. I could see that look in his eyes, and hear that thing in his voice. The only difference—I was in stitches. No joke! I mean, I really was—I was in—

JEAN: They hadn't removed your stitches.

EMMA: I still *had* 'em. So, at the bar, that night, I let him come on in the same old way. I didn't hear nothin' new, but, I was *seein'* for the first time since he dumped me. He was *some* frat rat, and I was just a local nuthin'. It was cold, and I was wearin' cutoffs, and, I don't know, he pissed me off. So, for no reason, alls a sudden, I open my bag and take out a xerox of Robin's footprints, and I put the paper down—bang—right there on the table. Jamie looked at it, and he stopped breathin', just like that. I told him I wasn't comin after nuthin'. And I told him what a poor condition his little boy was in. He listened, and he listened, and when he finally talked, he asked a lot of questions. I told him about you guys. I told him about the monitors, and the tubes, and the sirens. So, he starts snifflin' and cryin'. Give me a break! And he goes, "Can I come up with you some time and seeee little Robin?" And I'm like, you're kiddin' me! So, I say to him, I go, "No way. No way in this wide world will you ever lay eyes on that boy." I know he's the father, and he's probably got rights, but I don't want him near this child. And I don't think he'll sue me or nuthin'. But, even if he does, I won't have him around. Okay?

JEAN: It's fine by me.

EMMA: *(Looking down at Robin.)* Hey, Fellah. *(She reaches for a jar under the isolette.)* This is the stuff they put on his rash.

JEAN: That's good.

(There is a silence.)

EMMA: You know how the agency shows those family album deals?

JEAN: Yah.

EMMA: I had it narrowed down to you and one other couple. They had a seven-year-old boy, and I thought it might be nice for the baby to have an older brother. But that night I had a dream, and I saw you. My dad thinks dreams are God talkin' in your ear, tellin' you what to do. I like that. Course, at the time I had this dream, I thought Robin was gonna be healthy. I thought he was gonna be some great gift. *(Beat.)* He needs clothes.

JEAN: *(Silence.)* I have clothes.

EMMA: I thought you might.

JEAN: They were meant for him.

EMMA: He needs clean things.

JEAN: I'll bring them.

EMMA: He needs cuddlin' or somethin'. You want to hold him?

JEAN: Not yet.

EMMA: I'm supposed to have the truck back by four. My dad's gotta go to work.

JEAN: You're leaving?

EMMA: I'd better get goin'.

JEAN: Oh.

EMMA: He's no trouble. My dad's gotta work, and…Michael has that date with Mr. Gravity.

JEAN: Right.

EMMA: I kinda gotta be there for that. *(She smiles hard at the baby.)* Blueberry! Baby Bear! Don't be shy now. *(She turns to go.)*

JEAN: Emma!

EMMA: Yeah?

JEAN: *(Changing her mind.)* Keep in touch.

(Emma gives a cynical wave, and goes. Jean looks down at the child.)

JEAN: So, Robin. Well, now. *(A beat.)* I hear you've got some kind of crazy diaper rash. *(Calculating how one goes about it, she picks up a towel and slings it over her shoulder. She awkwardly locates and gathers the things she'll need for the change, then turns her attention to Robin.)* Now, how do we, uh—? Oh, these—right, these tabby things—*(She opens the diaper, and peers at its contents.)* Whoa. Whoa! *(She looks around for a nurse, then back to Robin. She looks around again.)* Nurse?

(Cross-fade begins. Tess enters the Farrell living room.)

Scene III

Tess and Henry have just finished a tour of the house. They are four hours into the homestudy. In the shadows around the isolette, Jean tackles the diaper change on her own under the ensuing dialogue.

TESS: That about wraps up the tour of the house. Oh, yes, one more thing. Do you have any smoke detectors or fire alarms?

HENRY: *(Who is coming in just behind her.)* What? Uh, no. No. Nothing like that.

TESS: No?

HENRY: No. We don't believe in them.

TESS: *(Pause.)* May I ask why not?

HENRY: We don't think they're necessary.

TESS: They save lives, Mr. Farrell.

HENRY: I'm sorry?

TESS: They save lives.

HENRY: *(Pause.)* Frankly, I won't have one in my home.

TESS: The state requires them.

HENRY: You're kidding. No, they don't.

TESS: *(Pause.)* Why—why are you so opposed to them? Is it the cost?

HENRY: It's the principle.

TESS: Because they're quite inexpensive. You can pick them up at any discount store.

HENRY: I realize that.

TESS: If you want to be licensed to adopt, you'll have to get one.

HENRY: *(Beat.)* Are we, by any chance, having the same conversation?

TESS: Boy, you know, that's what I'm wondering.

HENRY: I'm talking about guns. What are you talking about?

TESS: Guns!

HENRY: Right. Fire arms. Didn't you say fire arms?

TESS: I said smoke detectors or fire alarms.

HENRY: Oh!

TESS: Ohh!

HENRY: Fire *alarms!*

TESS: Yes.

HENRY: I thought you were going to make me get a pistol or something. It made no sense.

TESS: *(Laughing.)* And it was going so well up until then.

HENRY: It was, wasn't it?
   (They chuckle.)

TESS: I guess I don't need to ask you about guns now, do I?
   (They laugh.)

HENRY: I'm sorry. I get hard of hearing when I'm nervous.

TESS: You're not nervous, are you?

HENRY: Oh, we've been—we have been a little nuts.

JEAN: *(Entering with the towel, wiping her hands.)* How was the tour? Did we pass?

HENRY: *(Rising.)* Why don't you take over?

TESS: Henry thinks he blew it.

JEAN: He does, does he?...*(A trifle dangerously.)* Did he?

TESS: No, he's doing fine.

JEAN: You told her about my politics, eh?

HENRY: No, I told her about our sex life.

JEAN: What's that?

HENRY: A joke, honey.

TESS: He told me about your smoke detectors.

JEAN: Are the batteries dead?

HENRY: No. Never mind.

TESS: Lunch was excellent. We should have helped you with the dishes.

JEAN: No trouble at all.

TESS: I have one more question, and then I'll be out of your way. How are you holding up?

JEAN: Fine.

HENRY: Great.

TESS: This one is sometimes the most difficult. I should probably start with it, but—

JEAN: Go ahead. Fire away.

TESS: What kind of baby do you want?

JEAN: What do we want?

TESS: What kind?

JEAN: *(Laughs.)* Any old kind.

TESS: I mean, what are your limits? I think you made it clear earlier you want an infant, no older than eight months?

JEAN: Does that limit us? It's just that we don't want to miss out on parenting an infant. Chances are, this will be our only child.

TESS: It's fine. It's your choice. What else? Would you be willing to take a child of color?

JEAN: Yes.

HENRY: I don't know.

TESS: *(Focusing on Henry, but without judgment.)* Mixed-race? Caucasian-Hispanic?

JEAN: Yes.

HENRY: Uh—yeah, I guess.

TESS: Asian-Caucasian?

HENRY: Mm-hmm.

JEAN: Yes.

TESS: Caucasian-black?

JEAN: Yes.

HENRY: Um—if you want to know what my ideal child would be like—it would be—uh, Caucasian.

TESS: That's fine. Boy, girl?

JEAN: Either.

HENRY: A girl is my preference, though, I'd take a boy, too.

TESS: Would you be willing to take a child with mental or emotional disabilities?

HENRY: No.

JEAN: I don't know. Our *ideal* child would be healthy.

TESS: What about physical disabilities?

JEAN: I can't say no, just like that. I very well might.

HENRY: I would consider taking a child with correctable or minor physical problems.

TESS: Cleft palate, club foot, along those lines?

HENRY: Yes. But nothing major. I'm not cut out to be—I know what I can do.

TESS: *(Reassuring him.)* That's fine, Henry. We want the clearest possible picture of the child you want. Where Jean is concerned, a child of color or mixed heritage would be fine. She would also be willing to consider a child with disabilities. Where you are concerned, a healthy, Caucasian infant girl would do the trick, though you would accept a boy. Is this right?

HENRY: It's rigid, probably.

TESS: It's specific. We want to find these children the parents they were meant to have. It may mean you'll wait a bit longer.

HENRY: That's fine. We've waited a long time already. We're good at waiting.

TESS: Your patience will pay. Listen, I hate to eat and run. I have another home-study tonight at six, and I need to get to my own home first.

JEAN: It's over? That was it?

TESS: It wasn't so bad, was it?

JEAN: No.

HENRY: It was fine.

TESS: *(Gathering her things.)* You should be hearing from the agency in a couple of weeks.

JEAN: That's—two weeks.

TESS: Fourteen days.

HENRY: Thank you.

TESS: No problem. My pleasure, actually. What did you do with my coat, Henry?

HENRY: I'll get it.

TESS: Nice meeting you, Jean. The flowers are great.

JEAN: Yes.

TESS: Take it easy.

JEAN: I will. I *do.*

TESS: Bye, now.

JEAN: Bye. Thank you. *(After Tess is gone, and to no one in particular.)* Thank you.

(Lights cross-fade. The dialogue does not stop.)

ACT II
Scene I

Time: June, 1991. Place: The Farrell living room. The shade trees through the window bear the green leaves of summer. A vase of peonies sits on the table. A large canvas tote bag sits in the middle of the floor. Franny stands close by.

FRANNY: Where did he go?

JEAN: No doubt he dumped the bags in your room, and made a bee-line for his office.

FRANNY: Novel?

JEAN: No, he's paying the bills today. He's doing a feature for the Trib on the pros and cons of riverboat gambling. Unfortunately, he's having a little trouble focusing.

(Lights up full.)

JEAN: Thank you for coming, Fran.

FRANNY: *(Removing her jacket.)* I wouldn't have missed the birth of this child for the world, are you kidding?

JEAN: God, woman, how much weight have you lost?

FRANNY: Fifteen, maybe.

JEAN: I don't think I've ever seen you with your hair so long. *(Or short, depending.)* Franny, you look fabulous. Are you in love, or what?

FRANNY: You know, I was trying to figure out on the plane how long you've waited for this baby. You stopped using birth control, when? Seventy-seven?

JEAN: Seventy-six. The bicentennial.

FRANNY: That's fifteen years ago.

JEAN: A helluva long pregnancy.

FRANNY: I believe only the pterodactyl takes longer to reproduce itself.

JEAN: I believe you're right.

FRANNY: Are you stunned? You seem kind of—

JEAN: It's a little like getting hit by an ice cream truck. Fairly shocking, but still, you're lying in a puddle of Haagen Das.

FRANNY: Might as well grab a spoon.

JEAN: Precisely.

FRANNY: Show me this birthing kit you've put together.

JEAN: I have an expert on the scene, at last. You're my salvation.

FRANNY: I don't know how expert I am. Every birth is different.

JEAN: The birth-partnering books, Franny. They're driving me insane! Why I ever agreed to coach her through labor, I will never know.

FRANNY: One thing at a time.

JEAN: Okay. The birthing kit: *(She grabs the tote bag and starts tossing things out of it.)* Hal made me these charts to keep track of the time between contractions. Massage oil, unscented, in case she's feeling nauseous.

FRANNY: Pay attention to the lower back.

JEAN: Right. A cold pack for chipped ice, in case she wants to suck. Bubble bath, a manicure kit, moisturizers, a deck of cards.

FRANNY: Are you planning to be there a few days?

JEAN: I thought if the labor is long, we'd just have some fun.

(Franny hoots.)

JEAN: Is this, like, too stupid?

FRANNY: Not at all. Keep going.

JEAN: My favorite blue ice skating socks. I read somewhere their feet get cold.

FRANNY: Nice touch.

JEAN: Champagne, three glasses. A dozen roses—that's Hal's job, on the day.

FRANNY: Excellent.

JEAN: I want her to know how grateful we are. She couldn't be doing more for us if she was donating a vital organ: her lungs. Her heart.

FRANNY: Tell me about the books.

JEAN: They're making me nuts!

FRANNY: So you said.

JEAN: The way they breathe is important. That's the main thing, right?

FRANNY: Just go.

JEAN: Okay. During the early stages of labor, when a contraction hits, I'm supposed to encourage her to take a deep, cleansing breath, followed by six to nine chest inhalation-exhalations. We conclude with another cleansing breath. During the accelerated phase, she takes a cleansing breath, and then I encourage her to pant as the wave rises.

FRANNY: Jean?

JEAN: What?

FRANNY: The way they breathe ain't diddly.

JEAN: What? No!

FRANNY: That's the trouble with book learning, okay? I've been there hundreds of times, and I'm telling you: the breathing stuff is basically bullshit.

JEAN: Then, I'm lost.

FRANNY: Breathing is important when a woman gets nervous, or scared. It's important when the baby's head is crowning, and they don't want him to come out too fast. So, they tell her to blow—like she's blowing out a candle. Yes?

JEAN: Yes.

FRANNY: A good birth partner is someone who can keep a sense of humor. She knows when to leave you alone if you want to shut down, and she can lead you with a clear, rational mind when yours is full of obscenities.

JEAN: Great. I've met this woman twice.

FRANNY: So what? Even if you screw up, what choice will Emma have? I've seen birth partners hyperventilate and pass out on the floor. I've heard them crying for their own mothers. The woman who is giving birth still finds a way to get that baby out, no matter what kind of blithering idiot is holding her hand.

JEAN: The upshot is that any moron can be a birth partner, is that right?

FRANNY: I'm glad to see you're following me here. Just be sensitive to when she wants your touch and when she loathes it. The same thing goes for the sound of your voice.

JEAN: This is something you can describe for a million years, but a woman like me will never get it.

FRANNY: Sort out the little things for her.

(The phone rings.)

FRANNY: Feed her chipped ice. Shall I pick up?

JEAN: Maybe it's the hospital. *(She quickly repacks the bag.)*

FRANNY: Hello?...Relax. It's for me. Henry?...No, I've got it...Go back to work. It's not the hospital. It's for me...Yeah. Try to relax. *(She returns to the phone.)* Hi, there...Very nice voice. He's...Yes, I made it...It wasn't too bad.

JEAN: Yo, Sam.

FRANNY: I don't think so. Not tonight.

JEAN: Tell him Henry got the cigars.

FRANNY: Tomorrow afternoon maybe...There's a lot going on around here...I know...No, I haven't...I will, I will...

JEAN: Let me talk to him when you're done.

FRANNY: I have to go...Yes, I have the number...I miss you, too.

JEAN: Let me talk to him.

FRANNY: Me, too...Me, too. Bye. *(She hangs up.)*

JEAN: *(Surprised.)* Franny! I wanted to talk to him.

FRANNY: Jean—

JEAN: *(After a second.)* That wasn't Sam, was it?

FRANNY: No.

JEAN: Who was that?

FRANNY: It wasn't Sam.

JEAN: *(Beat.)* Who was it?

FRANNY: Scott.

JEAN: *(Cautiously.)* Old friend?

FRANNY: New. I've wanted to tell you. I couldn't do it long distance.
    (The phone rings again.)

FRANNY: I needed your face.
    (Silence, as priorities shift, and they make certain it doesn't ring again. Henry has grabbed it. Finally:.)

JEAN: Lives here in Chicago, does he?

FRANNY: No. He—followed me here.

JEAN: He…followed you?

FRANNY: This probably isn't the best time to talk about it.

JEAN: Franny—

FRANNY: You've got other concerns.

JEAN: Are you leaving Sam?

FRANNY: Sam left me. It took me years to see it, because we still shared the same house, two amiable souls who never really connected. He won't talk to me. He watches television, or plays with his damned computer. He won't even leave the house any more, Jean, except to go to work.

JEAN: You're leaving Sam.

FRANNY: I'm going to take a month away, just to think things through. If I can't stay here, I'll go to my sister in Evanston.

JEAN: Won't it be rather difficult to think rationally with this Scott person following you around?

FRANNY: Jean, I want you to meet him. He's wonderful.

JEAN: Franny, Sam has been my friend for seventeen years.

FRANNY: I know.

JEAN: *(Beat.)* I need something. You want something? An iced tea? Soda?

FRANNY: Wait, Jean.

JEAN: Just give me a *minute*, okay?

HENRY: *(Headlong.)* Jean, that was Tess on the phone.

JEAN: Tess.

HENRY: She says our son is on his way.

JEAN: What?

HENRY: A son. Our son.

JEAN: But—how do they know it's a boy?

HENRY: Emma's been at the hospital for the last hour. They've been doing ultrasounds. There's some—

JEAN: Where's the—um. I've got the diaper bag. Do you have the—?

HENRY: They don't want us to come, yet.

JEAN: What do you mean they don't want us to come? It's seventy miles to Silver Cross—

HENRY: Even so, they want us to stay right here for the moment. Tess'll call within the hour.

FRANNY: A son.

JEAN: *(Slightly giddy.)* God, Franny, I bought everything pink! Everything is pink and green!

HENRY: There may be some problem, honey.

JEAN: No. It's not a problem!

HENRY: No, Jean. They may have to deliver by C-section.

JEAN: Why?

HENRY: She didn't say.

FRANNY: Maybe they can't get him to turn.

HENRY: She says we should still get ready. If they decide to let her deliver naturally, they expect it will be a long labor. We'll have plenty of time to get there.

FRANNY: This is it, Jean! What do you want to do? What should we do?

HENRY: We're packed. We just need to kill some time until the phone rings again.

FRANNY: Maybe get into comfortable clothing. Sneakers.

HENRY: I need to find my cigars.

JEAN: *(To Henry.)* Where's the hammer?

HENRY: The hammer?

JEAN: The hammer! The hammer! How many times do I have to say it? Hammer!

HENRY: Basement stairwell. On the hook. Same as always.

JEAN: *(She grabs up the birthing kit bag.)* I'll be back. Oh my God, it's a boy. *(Jean exits.)*

HENRY: What is she doing?

(Cross-fade begins.)

FRANNY: My best guess is that she's going to go chip some ice.

(The cross-fade is complete.)

Scene II

End of June, 1991, the hospital. Jean crosses quickly and ties on her robe.

JEAN: *(At the isolette, beaming down at Robin.)* Don't look at me like that, I told you I'd be back. What've we got today? *(She rummages in her bag.)* Look at this: a music box! It plays "Let me Call You Sweetheart." My Grandparents gave it to me after a certain trip to Las Vegas that looms legendary in family lore. It had something to do with forgetting where they parked their Buick, and having to wire home for money. They lost their car, but they remembered to bring me this. I've been saving it all these years for my own child. I thought maybe you could—well, here it is. It's an insistent little tune, but, it will give you a break from these crazy sirens. There is such a thing as music, Robin. *(She winds it up, opens the lid, and places it next to his ear.)* You like that? *(He does.)* And this is nothing. There is a corporation called Muzak that does a whole lot better than this. Okay, what else have we got? *(Into her bag again, she pulls out a stuffed doll.)* Ah, yes. Humpty Dumpty. This guy could be your brother, no kidding—look at that noggin. I'm gonna tuck him in with you, because, when I'm not around, I figure you can use a friend, right? So just—you know, talk to him. Ask him stuff. *(Going right for the diaper, we hear the tabs.)*

JEAN: I gotta tell ya, kiddo, I hate this part. *(She peels it back.)* Whoa—still pretty bad. Does it hurt? Does it sting? *(Looking up and around, but proceeding to change him rather awkwardly.)* Do these sirens get on your nerves, or what?

LAURENCE: Mrs. Farrell? You asked for me?

JEAN: Laurence. Have I taken you away from somebody?

LAURENCE: No, no. What can I do for you? You've got it on backwards.

JEAN: What?

LAURENCE: His diaper. Teddy bears in front.

JEAN: I'm new at this.

LAURENCE: It's okay.

JEAN: I have a bunch of questions.

LAURENCE: I'm not surprised.

JEAN: Good.

LAURENCE: Shoot.

JEAN: First, I would like to know where I am. Most of these babies are pretty small.

LAURENCE: Preemie-R-Us, yes.

JEAN: This little one over here—he—she?—will go home? I saw the mother here the other day—they'll go home together?

LAURENCE: That's right. That's baby Angela. She's a twin. Her sister Letitia is down the way there.

JEAN: They'll go home?

LAURENCE: That's what we're hoping. Mom is in drug rehab.

JEAN: Oh, I see.

LAURENCE: Keep your fingers crossed.
(Robin's machine whines. Laurence flips the switch.)

JEAN: Why did it beep? What does it mean?

LAURENCE: Time to change his IV, that's all. *(He proceeds to do so during the course of their conversation.)* If there's a real emergency, you'll know it. More questions?

JEAN: Boy, it makes me nuts, that sound.

LAURENCE: You get used to it.

JEAN: So, is there anybody else here like Robin? Same problems? Similar problems?

LAURENCE: No, 'fraid not.

JEAN: *(Disappointed.)* Oh. *(To the baby.)* You're a trailblazer, Kid.

LAURENCE: Not exactly. We've seen little guys like Robin in the past. What else?

JEAN: The diaper rash, what is that? I mean, come on—can't we—?

LAURENCE: His medication is harsh. We're understaffed. Emergencies crop up. It means that every once in a while he has to lie in it. We do our best, Mrs. Farrell.

JEAN: I'm sure you do, but he—

LAURENCE: Are you going to be around during visitor's hours?

JEAN: Yes.

LAURENCE: You've located the diapers and ointment. Very good. When you help us, you're helping him.

JEAN: I see. All right. Now, it's about this nose-tube.

LAURENCE: Yes?

JEAN: He keeps trying to pull it out. It must be very irritating.

LAURENCE: That's a safe assumption.

JEAN: He wants it gone. He wants to be treated like a person. He wants to try the bottle again.

LAURENCE: He told you this?

JEAN: Yeah, he wants to belly up to the bar like the midgets over there.

LAURENCE: He won't suck. He's deficient in the sucking area.

JEAN: *(To the baby.)* Are you gonna lie there and listen to this? *(To Laurence.)* He sucks the tip of my little finger.

LAURENCE: *(Mildly appalled.)* You put your finger in his mouth?

JEAN: I cut my nails; there's no polish. It's clean.

LAURENCE: And he sucks it?

JEAN: Like a leach.

LAURENCE: Mrs. Farrell—

JEAN: Jean.

LAURENCE: Jean, you may be getting your hopes up for—

JEAN: If he doesn't eat, we put the hose right back.

LAURENCE: *(Beat.)* Sounds good to me.

JEAN: Simple.

LAURENCE: I'll speak to the doctor.

JEAN: So, tell me about the machinery.

LAURENCE: We're monitoring his lungs and his heart, among other things. Blood pressure pops up here. This little gizmo tells me what the temperature of his environment is. *(He pats the machine.)*

JEAN: Should I be careful about exciting him? His heart and his lungs are weak?

LAURENCE: Actually, no, this is all standard procedure for a newborn like Robin.

JEAN: Then, I can give him a little exercise?

LAURENCE: I don't know what you have in mind, but, if we're talking baby aerobics, he's probably game.

JEAN: How often does his doctor come along? Dr. Arbaugh? I would like to catch her.

LAURENCE: Once a day, about seven in the morning.

JEAN: That's before visiting hours.

LAURENCE: Right, but I could set up an appointment for you later in the day, if you want.

JEAN: I do want.

LAURENCE: Stop by the desk on your way out, and we'll give her office a call.

JEAN: Great.

LAURENCE: I like his outfit.

JEAN: Well, we're trying to create some excitement around here.

LAURENCE: The socks do it. I'm a sucker for argyle. What else?

JEAN: Can one—maybe—?

LAURENCE: What?

JEAN: Pick him up? Hold him? I see that rocking thing there. Would he like to change his environment, or do you think that would be—? That's probably a bit much, huh?

LAURENCE: Oh, that would be fabulous.

JEAN: Well, yeah, but—we're talking a—water balloon here!

LAURENCE: Sit down. *(Grabbing up the bed pillow that lies on the seat of the chair.)* Take this pillow for your arm, and make yourself comfy.

JEAN: Really?

LAURENCE: Have a seat.

JEAN: He won't mind?

LAURENCE: I'd say, it will be the equivalent of—oh—pick any ride at Disneyland.

JEAN: Okay.

LAURENCE: It's better if two of us do it; I'm going to get Mary Jo. I'll be right back. *(He exits.)*

JEAN: *(She gets up and leans into the isolette.)* We're going to try something here, Baby. "Pirates of the Caribbean" coming up. If you don't panic, I won't. If, at any point, you hate this, however, just call out, all right? Boom! Back in the old isolette, okay? *(She looks for Laurence.)* What a name for a bed. "Isolette." *(To the baby.)* You needn't look so all alone, Gummy. We do have a certain amount of experience on which to draw. You're not the first. I met someone like you once before. It was during a field trip with Mr. Garchow *(Pronounced "Gar-shaw".)* Tenth-grade social studies—to the Coldwater State Hospital. *(As she speaks she takes brand-new clothing out of a bag, and puts it away. She rips price tags from a few items. Then she takes Robin's dirty laundry from under the isolette, and stuffs it into her bag.)* My mother used to say they had "no business taking a bus full of children to that awful place." We went in single file from one ward to the next. My classmates and I were introduced to mongoloid babies, with their high-pitched cries; young women, tearing their hair and skins; and old men, deserted, wailing, clad only in diapers. To think she lived with those sounds day and night. By the time we bottlenecked, just outside her room, I couldn't keep my limbs still, or catch a decent breath. Just ahead, my friend, Bev Tucker, class vice-president and future homecoming queen, turned to me with a sharp whisper: "My God, you won't believe this. Nine years old, and lying in a baby's crib. Wisps of hair, on a *horse's* head. Her eyes must be five inches apart. Pass it on. They have to turn her twice a day. Her name is Debbie. Pass it on." *(Beat.)* The sunlight streamed into her quiet bed as I came near. Out of the corner of my eye, I saw her awesome shape. *(She gently touches the child.)* Not unlike yours, my boy. I also saw she kept her eyes cast down as Bev went by. I decided I wouldn't look, either, as I took my turn before her. And, then, we both surprised ourselves: she looked up, and I looked down. In that one moment, I saw her daring! I saw her humor, her sweet, forgiving soul. Never before had I seen a face so loving and open. I wonder, if she could see you now, what she would say to you. What wonderful thing would she say?

HENRY: *(A voice from the dark, barely entering, with a large tray which he deposits on the coffee table.)* Pot stickers.

JEAN: I want to say it.

Scene III

It is mid-June, three days after Robin's birth, 11:30 at night in the Farrell living room. Exhausted, but engaged, Henry hunches over white cartons on the coffee table. Jean returns with a fresh glass of wine.

HENRY: Your favorite. And lemon chicken, for Chrissake.

JEAN: What's that?

HENRY: Would you at least try the watermelon? It's from the Oak Street Market.

JEAN: Since when? I was there yesterday.

HENRY: Six o'clock this morning. That clerk you like—

JEAN: Isabel.

HENRY: She told me herself: the first shipment of the season came in this morning at six.

JEAN: It looks good.

HENRY: You've been saying that since nine o'clock.

JEAN: It's looked good since nine o'clock.

HENRY: Then put down the wine glass, and eat some of it.

JEAN: Sing your part by yourself one more time, and then I'll add the harmony. "O, Come All Ye Faithful": here we go.

HENRY: Why do you torture me?

JEAN: You've almost got it.

HENRY: Please. I have a five-note range.

JEAN: You exaggerate.

HENRY: Then why, in God's name, do you want to hear me sing Christmas carols?

JEAN: I love it when you sing.

HENRY: In the middle of June, no less.

JEAN: I can conjure you at age thirteen when you sing. It's just possible I married you for your singing voice. Stop looking at me like you're the last sane person on earth. Sanity shouldn't flaunt itself. Come on. "Oh Come All Ye Faithful "All" and "ful"—same note.

HENRY: Shh!

JEAN: What?

HENRY: Franny's sleeping.

JEAN: And where was she all afternoon and evening, that's what I want to know! Why does she feel she has to go sneaking around with that Todd-person?

HENRY: When you can handle the information without referring to the man as "that Todd-person," I'm sure she'll tell you.

JEAN: Okay. I'm sorry. Todd. Simply Todd. I'm sure Todd is a fine, decent—

HENRY: His name is Scott, Jean.

JEAN: *(Beat.)* Let's try "Joy to the World" again. You've got that pretty good. Just remember: *(She sings.)*
>   "Joy To The World
>   The Lord (Go down on Lord.) Is Come"

HENRY: No.

JEAN: Do it! Just let loose. Set yourself free.

HENRY: Not until you give equal time to Hanukkah. Let's do "The Dreidel Song."

JEAN: Far be it from me to slam your heritage, but "The Dreidel Song" is a bore, Henry.

HENRY: It is not a bore!

(He sings it. She joins him after a line or two, rather dispassionately.)

HENRY: Ohhh, Dreidel, Dreidel, Dreidel
   I Made It Out Of Clay
   And When It's Dry And Ready
   Oh, Dreidel I Will Play
   Oh, Dreidel, Dreidel, Dreidel...

(They stop and look at each other.)

HENRY: Okay, it's a bore.

(One last attempt at feeding her.)

HENRY: You got a nice piece of fruit there. Fresh off the vine, I swear. Any nutrition is better than no—

JEAN: "Nice piece of fruit?" I "got a nice piece of fruit?"

HENRY: I sound like my mother, is that what you're saying?

JEAN: I didn't say it.

HENRY: But that's what you're thinking.

JEAN: I'm glad you asked. You know what I'm thinking, honey?

HENRY: Oh, Christ.

JEAN: No, go ahead. You know what I'm really thinking?

HENRY: Okay, let me see. You are silently musing on Molière's astute observation that "It's good food and not fine words" that keeps us alive.

JEAN: Nice try, but no.

HENRY: *(Beat.)* Then you agree with Fielding that there is at least one fool in every married couple.

JEAN: *(Beat.)* I don't want to hurt your feelings, Hal, but I really wasn't thinking about you.

HENRY: At this particular point in time.

JEAN: Not at this time, no.

HENRY: Then—what first occurred to me, and I don't know why the hell I didn't say it right off—

JEAN: Go ahead.

HENRY: You're about to suggest that if we save the seeds from this rotting watermelon, we can make a fortune manufacturing maracas.

JEAN: *(Beat.)* You amaze me.

HENRY: I got it right?

JEAN: No!

HENRY: If that isn't it, then, gosh, I give up. I really can't imagine what you're thinking. I'm afraid you're going to have to tell me.

JEAN: I'm thinking I'd like to call Tess, and try to get Emma's last name and telephone number.

HENRY: That's confidential information, Jean. We don't have any right to it.

JEAN: Under the circumstances, don't you think they'd make an exception? They could call Emma first, find out if it's okay with her.

HENRY: Why do you want—? Why do you think it's necessary to—?

JEAN: I'd like to meet with her, make sure she's okay, and that she understands why we didn't take the baby.

HENRY: I'm sure she understands that.

JEAN: Don't you think, though, that we ought to finish it with her?

HENRY: Maybe. What about the child?

JEAN: They would never let me see him, Henry. It's intensive care, honey. Besides, I don't think I *want* to meet him. How could I look into his face and tell him we had someone else in mind. I can't do that. How's that for cowardice?

HENRY: No.

JEAN: He's just waiting for someone. Lying there, looking around, waiting for the pay-off.

HENRY: It's not—

(*She puts her head down. Henry pulls her into his arms. He is quiet. He feels her grief before he hears it. He looks miserably at the ceiling. Then in an unsteady bass, he sings.*)

HENRY: "O, Come All Ye Faithful
    Joyful And Triumphant
    O, Come Ye, O, Come Ye
    To Bethlehem
    Come and Behold Him
(*His voice trails off.*)
    Born The...."
(*There is a silence, and then the lights fade to silhouette.*)

ACT III
SCENE I

July, 1991. Dr. Helen Arbaugh's tasteful inner office. There is a desk and a few chairs. As the dialogue continues and the scene is being set, Mary Jo, moves into place at the isolette. During the course of the following action, she unobtrusively dresses Robin, if necessary, and stands by his crib, with her back to us, quietly giving him medication.

DOCTOR: Sorry I'm late. *(She picks up the phone.)*

RADEMACHER: I just got here myself.

DOCTOR: Hello, Laurence.

LAURENCE: How are ya, Doc?

RADEMACHER: Helen, we need about—

DOCTOR: Hang on a second, Viv. *(Into the phone, as the lights come up.)* Effie, send them in.

RADEMACHER: Not yet, Helen.

LAURENCE: They've been waiting forty-five minutes, Viv.

RADEMACHER: A three-minute discussion, Helen. Let's put up a united front.

DOCTOR: Oh, I think we can sort through it without a plan, Viv. This woman seems really rather extraordinary. Have you been reading Laurence's reports?

RADEMACHER: I have. And, I see all kinds of red flags, Helen.

DOCTOR: What are they?

RADEMACHER: She visits every day. This child does not belong to her. He has a severe—

(Jean, Henry, and Franny enter.)

JEAN: I'm sorry. Am I interrupting? She told us we could come in.

LAURENCE: Is she interrupting, Viv?

RADEMACHER: Not at all. Hello there.

DOCTOR: *(Turning to the three newcomers.)* Come in. I'm Helen Arbaugh, Robin's physician.

JEAN: I'm Jean Farrell.

DOCTOR: Nice meeting you, Jean. I know you and Laurence have met. Do you know Mrs. Rademacher?

JEAN: No, I don't.

RADEMACHER: Vivien Rademacher, administration.

JEAN: Oh! *(She shakes Viv's hand.)* Nice to meet you.

DOCTOR: If you don't mind, Vivien asked if she could join us this morning.

JEAN: Not at all. This is my husband, Henry, and our friend, Franny Stornant. *(Henry and Franny shake hands with the doctor.)*

DOCTOR: A pleasure. Vivien Rademacher.

RADEMACHER: Hello.

DOCTOR: And Laurence Ray, who is responsible for Robin's primary care.

LAURENCE: How do.

JEAN: I was hoping—

DOCTOR: *(Picks up the phone again.)* Did Effie offer you a cup of coffee?

JEAN: She did. No thanks.

DOCTOR: Forgive me. I'm useless without that second cup.

MRS. RADEMACHER: Mrs. Farrell—

DOCTOR: *(Into the phone.)* Coffee. Ten minutes ago.

MRS. RADEMACHER: Mrs. Farrell, you have—you've set a certain precedent, Mrs. Farrell. Much as we admire what seems to be your intent, we just need to get a few things clear. There are some legal matters that come into question concerning your visits.

LAURENCE: Which don't necessarily take into account what's best for the child.

MRS. RADEMACHER: I'm certain that's not so, but nonetheless—

DOCTOR: Mrs. Farrell, first, you wanted to ask me some questions about the baby's condition?

JEAN: Yes, I did.

DOCTOR: What do you want to know?

JEAN: He seems so uncomfortable. Isn't there anything more you can do for him?

DOCTOR: I'm afraid not much.

HENRY: We've been told he's not going to make it.

DOCTOR: The prognosis is extremely poor.

JEAN: There's supposed to be some kind of surgery you can do in cases like his?

DOCTOR: We did it.

JEAN: It didn't work?

DOCTOR: Robin was born via emergency C-section on the morning of June 6th, correct?

JEAN: Yes.

DOCTOR: His physicians at Silver Cross Hospital diagnosed severe hydrocephalia. He was flown from Joliet to Chicago that same afternoon.

JEAN: Right.

DOCTOR: We confirmed the original diagnosis. Hydrocephalia is caused by a defect in the membrane that is supposed to absorb cerebrospinal fluid. As a result, fluid collects in the cranium. This condition can also be caused by a tumor, and sometimes we see it happen after surgery to correct spina bifida.

JEAN: Yes.

DOCTOR: I operated on Robin to determine one thing. If the fluid in his head had been clean, then I would have installed a small tube under the skin, called a shunt. The tube is designed to carry excess water from the brain to the abdominal cavity, a place where the body may get rid of it. In Robin's case, the fluid was contaminated with debris. We did not implant the shunt. All that was left for us to do was to close him up, and make him as comfortable as possible.

JEAN: Debris? What does that mean? What are you talking about—debris—?

DOCTOR: Foreign material.

JEAN: What kind of foreign material?

DOCTOR: Bone splinters from the cranium, and brain matter.

JEAN: I see.

HENRY: Chances are he's severely retarded, then?

DOCTOR: Yes.

JEAN: So you can't install a—what did you say? A shunt?

DOCTOR: Correct.

JEAN: It would get clogged.

DOCTOR: That's right. In order to keep the tube clear, we'd have had to perform surgery every couple of weeks. There would certainly be infection, and other complications too numerous to mention.

JEAN: I see. Would you may have attempted to put in the shunt if a parent had insisted?

DOCTOR: It's possible, though it wouldn't have—

JEAN: (Suddenly up close and personal.) That's what I meant, Hal. He fell through the cracks in the transfer from Emma to us.

MRS. RADEMACHER: We do not allow our patients to fall through cracks, Mrs. Farrell. Dr. Arbaugh and the staff at the hospital are engaged in saving lives. We do everything in our power to—

LAURENCE: Relax, Vivien.

MRS. RADEMACHER: I beg your pardon?

LAURENCE: Relax. Nobody's gonna sue.

MRS. RADEMACHER: Laurence, you were invited to this meeting as a courtesy—

DOCTOR: Have you been designated his next of kin, Mrs. Farrell?

JEAN: No.

MRS. RADEMACHER: Are you trying to gain custody of the child?

HENRY: No. Our agency has advised us to drop the adoption proceedings.

MRS. RADEMACHER: Then Emma Miller will remain the legal guardian?

HENRY: Yes.

MRS. RADEMACHER: (Disappointed.) I see. Mrs. Farrell, if that's the case, I'm not sure that it's right for you to have access to this baby. It could be harmful to both of you.

HENRY: That's what I'm wondering, too.

LAURENCE: Vivien, you're not on the floor. It won't do any harm. It's only for another couple of weeks.

JEAN: Why? What happens in a couple of weeks?

LAURENCE: They're trying to find a bed for him at Misericordia, Jean. They think it will be about two more weeks before they can get him in.

MRS. RADEMACHER: The expenses of a special care unit are phenomenal, I'm sure you understand. Miss Miller, the legal guardian, is relying on state funds, which makes Robin's stay here untenable.

JEAN: What's Misericordia?

LAURENCE: It's a home for individuals with special needs, run by the Sisters of Mercy.

MRS. RADEMACHER: It's a wonderful place, Mrs. Farrell. The sisters stress giving each child or adult the most normal life possible.

JEAN: Where is it?

LAURENCE: About thirty miles south of here.

JEAN: South?

LAURENCE: So, what's the harm, Vivien? Give them two more weeks.

MRS. RADEMACHER: I understand, believe me, Laurence, but, technically, Mrs. Farrell had permission to visit the baby only once, over a week ago, on June 22nd. She's been back every day since. Your charts say that she cycles his arms and legs, and massages him.

LAURENCE: Yeah. It's pretty abusive stuff.

MRS. RADEMACHER: He is attached to a heart and lung monitor, is he not?

DR. ARBAUGH: It's standard procedure, Viv. I see no harm in a little exercise or massage.

MRS. RADEMACHER: Emma Miller could come down mighty hard on this hospital if anything should—

JEAN: She won't.

LAURENCE: She doesn't come around anymore, Vivien. She wants Mrs. Farrell here.

HENRY: If something does go wrong, and you're at fault, Jean, she could take us to court.

JEAN: Henry, you met Emma! What are you talking about?

HENRY: I met her twice. She's sweet, but she told us herself she has no money, and no means of support.

JEAN: Jesus Christ.

LAURENCE: Vivien, cut to the chase. Are you going to terminate Mrs. Farrell's visiting privileges, or what?

MRS. RADEMACHER: Mrs. Farrell, we do have volunteers who come to rock the babies three evenings a week, but they go through a training course, which you have not had.

LAURENCE: She doesn't need it. And the volunteers won't go near a baby like Robin. *(To Jean.)* They like the midgets.

RADEMACHER: According to our insurance underwriters—I mean, I hate to be the one here who—

JEAN: Robin needs more than three evenings—

MRS. RADEMACHER: I know he does. I know he does, dear. So does every baby on the floor. But it's my job to protect both the children and this hospital. I know how you must feel. I know you've come to care for Robin, but we have the welfare of many children to consider. You do understand if there was anything more we could do for Robin, we'd bend every effort to it, don't you?

JEAN: Yes.

MRS. RADEMACHER: And you do understand that procedure here is strictly regulated by federal and state law, by private insurance carriers, by the board of directors—

JEAN: Yes. I do. Can I see him, or not?

MRS. RADEMACHER: Helen?

DOCTOR: Don't look at me, Viv. It's fine with me.

LAURENCE: And I'm game.

(Rademacher shoots him a look.)

LAURENCE: Not that anyone is asking.

MRS. RADEMACHER: *(At last, to Jean.)* You can see him this morning, but I have to take this issue to committee. It's possible I may need to bring it before the board. As I said, we're in new territory. We need to take it slowly.

LAURENCE: Naturally, since time is of the essence.

(Vivien opens her mouth to speak again.)

DR. ARBAUGH: Okay, thanks, Vivien. You can go ahead. Laurence, thank you, you'd better get back to the floor.

MRS. RADEMACHER: I'm sorry, Mr. and Mrs. Farrell. *(She exits.)*

HENRY: We understand. You've been very kind.

LAURENCE: *(To Jean.)* I'll see you in a few minutes, then.

JEAN: Yes.

LAURENCE: Wanna hold him?

JEAN: Sure

LAURENCE: I'll find Mary Jo. I have a surprise for you.

JEAN: What?

LAURENCE: *(Touching Henry's shoulder.)* See you upstairs. *(He exits.)*

DR. ARBAUGH: Is there anything else you wanted to ask me?

JEAN: I was going to ask if my husband and my friend could meet Robin this morning, just for a few minutes. Maybe I'd better not press it.

DR. ARBAUGH: It's fine with me. I'll waylay Vivien, and see if I can get her to go along with it.

HENRY: I don't know, Jean. Maybe it would be better if we didn't.

JEAN: Henry, just for a few minutes.

HENRY: I really don't want to get into legal difficulties with this hospital.

DR. ARBAUGH: *(Looks from Jean to Henry.)* I don't sense a united front here.

HENRY: No, you don't.

DR. ARBAUGH: If you want me to intervene on your behalf, just say the word. Why don't you just take a few minutes here to talk it over in private? Let me know what you want to do. In the meantime, I'll hunt down Effie and that cup of coffee, okay?

JEAN: Thank you.

MARY JO: *(Lights come slowly up on Mary Jo, at the isolette, as they go down on the office.)* You're late.

DR. ARBAUGH: Take your time. Whatever you decide to do is fine.

JEAN: Thanks.

(The doctor exits. Jean senses the resistance around her.)

JEAN: So, now what?

HENRY: I don't know what to say to you. I am at a total loss.

MARY JO: I probably shouldn't tell you.

HENRY: What is going on with you, Jean?

(Jean picks up her bag, and heads for the isolette.)

MARY JO: I'll be dead meat, but I don't care. I'm gonna tell you anyway.

Scene II

The hospital. Later that morning.

JEAN: That's the spirit.

MARY JO: Major victory.

JEAN: What is?

MARY JO: They're putting him on the bottle.

JEAN: When?

MARY JO: Eleven o'clock.

JEAN: All right! *(She approaches the crib quietly.)* Now, steady on, Babe, it's just me. How are you today? *(She peers into the crib.)* Whoa, my little short stop. It fits, what do you know! Wait a minute. Where is it?

MARY JO: It's ancient history.

JEAN: The dreaded tube is gone! *(To Robin.)* Hey, there's a profile for ya. Zowie.

MARY JO: Laurence took it out at 8:30. He's waiting for you, too.

JEAN: He said he had a surprise.

MARY JO: The eleven o'clock feeding is yours.

JEAN: You're kidding.

MARY JO: I'm straight.

JEAN: Yay, Robin! How about that? He looks happy.

MARY JO: How can you tell?

JEAN: I don't know, really. That's a good question. His face is relaxed. You're doing great today, pal. *(Jean turns to her bag and rummages.)*

MARY JO: He usually throws up when he first sees her. He gets those little arms and legs wheeling, and the next thing you know, barf city. You're Franny?

FRANNY: Yes.

JEAN: I'm sorry, Mary Jo. Sorry. Yes, this is my friend, Franny Stornant.

MARY JO: *(Extending her hand, Franny takes it.)* It's good to see you. I've heard a lot about you.

FRANNY: Nice to meet you, too.

JEAN: She may have permission to be here, I don't know.

MARY JO: And I don't care. I'm just glad you made it. *(To Jean.)* Laurence wasn't sure. We thought Henry might—we put him in the Cubs uniform just in case—

JEAN: *(To Franny.)* Don't be shy. Come on. Come over here. *(Pulling back the covers.)* There he is. There's my pal.

FRANNY: *(In her years at the birthing center, she has not been privy to this.)* Sweet God.

JEAN: Say hello. Here's Franny, babe. Isn't she pretty?

FRANNY: *(Still looking at the baby.)* Oh, Jean.

JEAN: What?

FRANNY: He's little.

JEAN: I know.

FRANNY: He's—he's just—

JEAN: *(Proudly.)* I told you.

FRANNY: Hello, little baby.

(Jean produces a walkman.)

MARY JO: What are you gonna do?

JEAN: I thought I'd play him some music.

MARY JO: No, come on.

JEAN: These sirens must drive him nuts.

FRANNY: Jean, do you think that's a good idea?

MARY JO: What've you got?

JEAN: I wanted something lyrical and simple. After due consideration, I think I'm going to go with Perlman and Domingo.

MARY JO: *(As she looks at the cassette cover.)* These are two geeks in open collars and sports jackets. Are you sure?

JEAN: I'm sure, Mary Jo.

MARY JO: They look like a couple of Tony Bennett wanna-bes.

JEAN: *(Turning to the baby.)* All right now, look. See this? Walkman. What you are about to hear is food for your soul.

MARY JO: You should get him some Nirvana. "Smells Like Teen Spirit."

JEAN: Thanks for your input, Mary Jo, but I think it's crucial we limit it to music that won't fry the few brains they say he has left.

MARY JO: He's a kid. He's gonna hate this stuff. Trust me.

JEAN: Let's find out.

FRANNY: Jean, he may be too fragile for something like this.

JEAN: Franny's not the first person to underestimate you, Robin. Don't take it personally. *(To Robin.)* I'm going to adjust this over your ears. *(She reaches in, and immediately encounters a problem she hadn't anticipated.)* Oh, no. Mama's an idiot.

MARY JO: Put it under his chin.

JEAN: And Mary Jo is a genius.

MARY JO: Tell Laurence.

JEAN: Now, holler, kiddo, if it's too much. Raise a hand, kick a leg, spit up; I don't know. Give a sign, okay? *(She turns it on, and waits, watching him with intent.)*
(Sound: The audience finally gets a break from the beeps and whines. They hear the first strains of Toselli's "Serenata." The women cannot hear, so they watch. Mary Jo leans in.)

MARY JO: Is he dead?

JEAN: Robin?

MARY JO: Wow!

JEAN: Do you think he's okay?
(They see something in his manner, a sigh or an intake of breath.)
(Simultaneously.)

MARY JO: Holy smokes!

JEAN: Good God!

FRANNY: I don't believe it.

MARY JO: Zone, baby, zone.

JEAN: That Perlman and Domingo, huh?

MARY JO: Jean, I went to the hospital library. I was looking around, and I found this. *(She hands Jean a photocopy of an article. Jean sits in the rocker, and begins to read. Mary Jo turns back to Franny at the crib.)* It's probably not my business, but I know she's not getting much support. I mean, as long as she comes anyway, somebody ought to be holding out a little hope.

FRANNY: Yes.

MARY JO: *(To the baby.)* Whuz up, Gee? How's my bud? That's right. Go with the beat, Babe. *(To Franny.)* How's Tom?

FRANNY: *(Staring at her for a moment.)* I beg your pardon?

MARY JO: You have a son Tom? Stockbroker? Six-foot something?

FRANNY: Yes.

MARY JO: I could do with a six-foot stockbroker, let me tell you. I suppose he's also a nice guy.

FRANNY: He's swell.

JEAN: *(Glancing up from her reading.)* I guess I talk about you a little.

FRANNY: I guess you do.

MARY JO: *(To the baby.)* Are you lookin' at me, goomba-loomba? Smile, Robin. Smile. *(She reaches in and tickles him.)* Geech, geech, geech, geech. geech! *(Nothing.)* You're hopeless, you know that?

JEAN: *(Finishing the article.)* This is incredible.

MARY JO: I thought you'd like it.

JEAN: *(Transfixed, she reads aloud.)* Listen to this, Franny: "While many hydro-cephalic children have neurological problems, some are normal. Recently, British neurosurgeon John Lorber examined a number of people with severe untreated hydrocephalus—up to 95% of their brain tissue had been replaced by fluid. He reported startling findings: over half of the severely hydrocephalic individuals he examined had normal IQ's and were func-tioning well in society. One man was a university honors graduate in math-ematics!" *(She is excited.)* That's him. That's Robin.

FRANNY: Severe, *un*treated hydrocephalus?

JEAN: There's a chance his IQ is normal?

MARY JO: Fifty-fifty, according to the Brit.

JEAN: Wow.

MARY JO: I thought you'd like it.

JEAN: Why didn't Arbaugh tell me about this study?

MARY JO: Maybe she doesn't know. I had to do a little digging. Besides, most people see a child like this, and think it would be a mercy if he died.

FRANNY: Surely not the child's surgeon.

MARY JO: Well. You wouldn't think so.

JEAN: Thank you, Mary Jo, thank you.

MARY JO: Consider me your spin doctor.

JEAN: *(To Franny.)* What do you think?

FRANNY: I'd want to talk it over with Doctor Arbaugh.

JEAN: So, I will. *(She joins Franny at the crib.)* You should have seen him a few days ago. He's improved.

FRANNY: He's awfully content at the moment.

MARY JO: The kid don't smile.

JEAN: The kid don't have much to smile about. Now, Mary Jo, I want to learn how to pick him up. Just me. Like you guys do.

MARY JO: No. Not me. I don't.

JEAN: I thought—

MARY JO: Oh, no. I'm a notch above a candystriper, okay? Nurse's aide: I do diapers and *some* medication.

JEAN: Who *does* pick him up? Laurence?

MARY JO: He prefers two of us, but I've seen him do it by himself. I'll get Laurence. *(Mary Jo starts to go, but thinks better of it.)* Don't do anything. I'll be right back.

JEAN: Trust me.

(Enter Laurence.)

LAURENCE: *(Addressing Mary Jo.)* Where *are* you? Why can I never *find* you?

MARY JO: I was just looking for you.

LAURENCE: What a marvelous coincidence, then! Lucky us! Kelly Davis needs aspirating.

MARY JO: Okay.

LAURENCE: She stopped breathing ten minutes ago.

MARY JO: *(To Jean.)* He's kidding. Though she *is* stuffed up. Mrs. Farrell would like a lesson in picking up the baby. Like you do, sometimes, alone.

LAURENCE: Okay. I'll see to it. Chop, chop, Mary Jo.

(Mary Jo exits.)

LAURENCE: There goes the most indolent creature on the face of the earth. "Beulah, peel me a grape," doesn't begin to describe it.

JEAN: I wouldn't say so.

LAURENCE: You know something I don't?

JEAN: She keeps herself busy.

LAURENCE: Mrs. Stornant! How lovely. Your follow-through is admirable. Where's the mister?

FRANNY: He had to go back to work.

LAURENCE: He's a free-lance writer, isn't he?

JEAN: That's the party line, Laurence, okay?

LAURENCE: I love a party. We do have clearance for this little visit?

JEAN: From Doctor Arbaugh. We weren't able to locate Mrs. Rademacher.

LAURENCE: I didn't hear that second part, okay?

JEAN: What second part?

LAURENCE: As long as we understand each other. Now, what? You want to pick the kid up?

JEAN: And make it to the rocker, each of us in one piece.

LAURENCE: Okay. Here's what you do. Get your right hand under his back and hips.

JEAN: Now?

LAURENCE: Or I could meet you here a week from Tuesday.

JEAN: Okay, okay. *(She moves to the isolette.)*

LAURENCE: Wait. Let me disconnect the monitors. *(He looks into the crib for the first time.)* What the hell is that?

JEAN: It's a walkman.

LAURENCE: *(Truly stumped, he lets out a breath, and scratches the back of his neck.)* "Peter, Paul & Mommy?"

JEAN: Would that be better?

LAURENCE: It's good. I can't believe you found it necessary to hook him up to yet another machine.

JEAN: This one is different.

LAURENCE: What are you playing for him?

JEAN: Perlman and Domingo.

LAURENCE: "Danny Boy?"

JEAN: Toselli's "Serenata."

LAURENCE: Nice. Get it off him.

JEAN: Okay.

LAURENCE: Lovely choice, though. All right. Take the fingers of your left hand, and start exploring the nape of his neck.

(Jean starts maneuvering.)

JEAN: Oh, God.

LAURENCE: Stop imagining things, okay? Just follow my directions.

JEAN: Right. So, I'm exploring the nape of his neck with my fingers.

LAURENCE: Move them up his head til you feel the bones of his skull. There's sort of a rigid bowl there.

JEAN: Got it.

LAURENCE: And you've got his back and hips?

JEAN: Yes, I think so.

LAURENCE: If your chair is ready—

FRANNY: *(Making quick adjustments.)* It is.

LAURENCE: More pressure on the bone of his head than on his back. Lift away.

JEAN: Jesus!

LAURENCE: I'm right here. Lift away.

JEAN: *(Trusting him, she lifts the child, and makes her way toward the rocker.)* Jesus God.

FRANNY: You're doing fine.

LAURENCE: He's top-heavy, but you knew that.

JEAN: I can't sit.

LAURENCE: You can.

JEAN: I'll drop him.

LAURENCE: Sit!

JEAN: I'm going to drop him.

FRANNY: No, you're not.

LAURENCE: You're going to sit. *(Quietly.)* Sit down, Jean.

> *(She does. They look at one another, full of triumph.)*

LAURENCE: Ta-dah! That's all there is to it.

JEAN: My life passed before my eyes, do you know that?

LAURENCE: Think how he must have felt.

JEAN: Poor gummy.

LAURENCE: You're okay.

JEAN: What's that?

LAURENCE: You're good.

JEAN: Okay. Good.

LAURENCE: I've got an enema to attend to.

JEAN: By all means—

LAURENCE: *(To the baby.)* Well, you're the cat that got the cream, aren't you? *(To Jean.)* Holler when you want to make the return trip.

JEAN: Yeah, well, don't go too far.

LAURENCE: Aisle Three, kiddo. *(He starts to go, and remembers.)* Did she tell you? She told you, didn't she?

JEAN: Yes!

LAURENCE: The bitch!

JEAN: And the feeding tube is gone.

LAURENCE: Of course. Silly me. I'll meet you at eleven.

> *(He's gone.)*

JEAN: You there, Fran?

FRANNY: Just pulling up a chair. *(A beat.)* Sorry.

JEAN: What?

FRANNY: I apologize.

JEAN: Why?

FRANNY: Never mind. I'm here now.

JEAN: Oh. *(Beat.)* You might want to bring Scott out of hiding. I'll roast a chicken or something.

FRANNY: You don't have to—

JEAN: A roast chicken doesn't necessarily mean I'll be his bosom buddy. Just an attempt at objectivity.

FRANNY: Thank you.

JEAN: I'm holding my child, Fran.

FRANNY: I see.

JEAN: *(Turning her attention to the baby.)* Let's see now, Robin, you've made some progress with the rash from hell. And, the feeding tube is gone! How about that? You're going to have an unparalleled feast at eleven. When the time comes, suck, Robin just like you do with Mommy's finger. Laurence won't take any guff, and he'll be up your nose with the dreaded rubber hose, if you don't suck. I mean it! I'm gonna start with your head instead of your feet today, okay? And here's what I want you to think about: since they're not going to do any more for you, by way of surgery, to relieve this pressure, you're going to have to start doing for yourself, darlin'. *(Massaging his head, she takes a moment to frame her message, and invents a late-night campfire story.)* My dad was a pack rat, too. He managed to save every bit of saran wrap, string, and aluminum foil from the time my grandmother first started packing his lunches back in 1932. He had every knickknack anybody ever gave him, including four mugs depicting women in evening gowns; the more you drank, the less they were wearing, okay?—just to give you an idea of the "debris and foreign material" that was in Grandpa's head?

FRANNY: Surely, you jest.

JEAN: *(To Franny.)* His hall closet bulged with tax returns, and tennis rackets, and rolls of toilet paper he got on sale at K-Mart. *(Back to the story.)* Only the truly brave descended the cellar stairs, for the basement was so burdened that one could only make it to the washer-dryer by negotiating a treacherous path that wound its way under towers of yellowing newspapers, past the rusting teeth of antique chain saws, and around bamboo hat racks, whose arms reached out to snag at your clothes, and clutch at your hair. People went into that basement to add the fabric softener, and were never heard from again. We pleaded with your Grandpa to get help, to call Am-Vet, or the Salvation Army. But, he refused to listen. Time and again, he admonished us with one simple phrase, that left us bewildered and silent: "Waste not, want not," he would say. Then, just when we thought it was too late, a miracle happened. He retired, and decided to move to Florida. In one all-out, ride-it-to-hell rummage sale, over five consecutive afternoons, he made forty-seven hundred dollars, Robin. And as he bid farewell to the last of the Tupperware, and the lava lamps, and the car-vacs; when his house was clear, and clean, and empty; we watched one magical afternoon in autumn, as he turned into a beautiful snow bird with white wings, a set of golf clubs, and a T-shirt that read: "Nixon's the one, and Agnew's another one." And he flew up into the pale, gray sky, turned south, and soared from view. The moral of this story is: if you don't need it, chuck it. You're like Grandpa, only you save water. The children of Israel could profit by your example. But, take it easy. You're still very small. No need to take on our sins just yet. You're a baby. *(With deeper intent.)* You're my Robin. If you're thirsty, if you need water, I'll know it, and I'll give you a drink, okay? Let it go. Let it go for Mama.

HENRY: *(As lights begin to cross-fade.)* It would take everything you've got to raise an absolutely perfect baby. This boy lies flat on his back twenty-four hours a day.

FRANNY: *(Slipping from the chair.)* Maybe I should leave you two alone for a while.

JEAN: Take a deep breath, little one. Here we go. *(She rises and returns the child to his crib, covers him, and kisses him.)*

HENRY: What would you do about the university? You can't leave a child like Robin with some teenaged baby-sitter. You can't put him in a normal day-care setting.

(Franny crosses into Arbaugh's office.)

Scene III

Return to the doctor's office.

FRANNY: Maybe it would be best if I waited in the hall, Henry.

HENRY: No, Franny, stay a minute.

FRANNY: Henry, I think—

HENRY: This baby needs round the clock care.

JEAN: *(From the crib.)* Honey, I know that.

HENRY: He needs a trained nurse on the scene. He needs special handling, and special medication.

JEAN: *(Coming into the light of the doctor's office.)* When did I ever say I was going to bring him home?

HENRY: You don't have to say it.

JEAN: Maybe Emma would help. Maybe she'd take room and board, in exchange for—

HENRY: You've lost your mind. Emma lives on welfare with her alcoholic father and her two-year-old son. Look, the agency is still in our corner. They'll find us another child. It means waiting again, that's all.

JEAN: I don't want to wait any more. I don't have to wait. I have a child right here to look after. Okay, Emma is out. I know it's crazy. But, I can find a way to make it work, if you will just give me a chance. Don't you trust me, Hal?

HENRY: It's not a question of—

JEAN: Do you *trust* me? Do you think I will look after our best interest? I'm not saying bring him home and raise him. I know you're against that idea.

HENRY: But, you're not, Jean. You'll figure out a way.

JEAN: So, now I'm a conniver?

HENRY: I don't know.

JEAN: Well, that's interesting.

HENRY: Just get yourself above the situation. Have the courage to mourn.

JEAN: He's not dead! He's alive and kicking about fifty yards from here.

HENRY: You just heard the doctor say the boy is dying.

JEAN: She did *not* say that. She never said that! She said the prognosis is poor.

HENRY: Extremely poor.

JEAN: I don't care what she said.

HENRY: Honey, they can't even put the shunt in—

JEAN: Stop it!

HENRY: Jean, you've got to listen to—

JEAN: No, I don't. *(Beat.)* You're afraid of him, Hal.

HENRY: What?

JEAN: He won't contaminate you.

HENRY: *Wait* a minute.

JEAN: We made a commitment to Emma that we would look after him from the moment he was born.

HENRY: Don't you dare do this to me! I *never* committed to this child! It was always understood I would only accept a healthy infant.

JEAN: And if I had given birth to him, what then? Would you still be walking away?

HENRY: You did not give birth to him, Jean. I can't tell you what my reaction would be if you had. I really don't know.

FRANNY: He's thinking of *you*, Jean, of what your life will be like—

JEAN: Well, cut it out. Do me a favor, and stop thinking of me. I don't want you to think of me.

FRANNY: He needs a mother's care. It's up to his mother—

JEAN: Who is mother now, Franny? Who's his mother?

HENRY: Emma!

JEAN: Emma's out of the picture. That's not the legality, I know, but it's the reality. He doesn't have one soul to care for him, or to intercede on his behalf.

HENRY: Don't you remember how it was? I thought we were losing our minds the day he was born.

JEAN: We did lose them, but we got them back. Minds are like boomerangs.

HENRY: Don't you remember the pain we felt?

JEAN: Look, I'll keep you out of it.

HENRY: There is no future for us here. The boy is dying.

JEAN: *(She finds her position.)* I'm going to visit him today, and again tomorrow, and the day after that, until they send him to Misericordia. Then I will visit him at Misericordia. Henry, you talk about the pain we felt, and it's true, we did. It's pain I gather you're still feeling. I'm not. Haven't you noticed? All gone. *He* did it. You're right, you do have a choice: you can come with me, and meet him, or you can go home, and hang on to your precious pain. I'd like your blessing, Hal, but if I don't get it, that's fine, too.

HENRY: My best judgment is that you have no *idea* what you're doing. *If* Robin survives, he'll languish his whole life, and I will watch you struggle to fulfill some kind of promise that no one in the world expects you keep: not me, not our family, not our friends, not the agency, not even Emma. If he *dies*, we'll have another round of misery like we've had for the last month. And Jean? I don't know how you imagine you are capable of taking it. Even if you *can* take it, and believe me, I'm *not* thinking of you at the moment, *I* can't take it! Although you don't remember, I'm part of this. I'm the one who picks up the pieces. I'm the one who held you, and heard you, and fed you, and coaxed you to bed for nights on end…You've asked for my blessing? Well, you can't have it. You can't have it. *(He exits.)*

JEAN: We'll take a bus home.

FRANNY: What do you think you're doing?

JEAN: I'm sorry?

FRANNY: Jean. You can't expect Henry to want to support Robin. The man is forty-six years old. He has one shot at being a father, and he wants it to be a joyful experience.

JEAN: Yes? And?

FRANNY: You don't seriously believe raising Robin would be a joyful experience?

JEAN: Well, you don't, that's clear.

FRANNY: Not everyone is cut out to raise a child with special needs. To force Henry to do something against his nature is a betrayal.

JEAN: How can you stand there and talk to *me* about—

FRANNY: What's more, you're betraying yourself!

JEAN: Ah. This is good. How so?

FRANNY: Dammit, Jean, over the years, I've heard in minute detail what you want from motherhood. I'm privy to every secret wish in your head. None of it has anything to do with this boy. This boy will never read. Never chase a cat, or run downstairs on Christmas morning. There will be no idle chat around the kitchen table. He'll never know a woman, never bounce a child on his knee. I am your friend. It seems to me the only thing I can *do* at this point is try to stop you from making a terrible mistake.

JEAN: Once, do you remember—when I was going through all the surgeries and in vitros, when I was exhausted, and we didn't know where else to look for money or support, in an attempt to comfort me, you said, Franny, and I quote: "If you think the journey has been difficult for you, think what it must be like for the child who is trying to get to you." I laughed when you said it; it sounded so New Age. But, the terrible thing is, you were right! I look at Robin, and see evidence of a harrowing journey.

FRANNY: You don't think I meant this! I only meant to comfort. I never meant for you to chain yourself to the first—

JEAN: Of course you didn't mean this! What kind of idiot would wish for a child with Robin's problems? I wish to God he was healthy! No one ever dreams of this! But, sometimes, this is what comes. In fifteen years of doing every-thing I can think of to bring a child into my life, this child is the one I've been given. And much to my surprise, he's better than anything I *ever* dreamt. I know you think that's crazy, and so does Henry. Because you won't *look,* and if you *don't* look, you won't *get* it. You're afraid of Robin because you think he *is* "his problem." If you come with me, you will see past the deformity, I assure you, to the tremendous person he has had to become in one short month. I am so certain of this, that if you still don't get it, after you've spent one morning with him, I'll walk out of here, away from him for the last time, without one backward glance.

FRANNY: *(Beat.)* Okay.

(Franny and Jean stand blinking at one another.)

JEAN: What?

FRANNY: I said okay. Lead on. Let's go meet Robin.

(Without further ado, Jean picks up her things and leads Franny out of the room. Blackout.)

PART II
ACT IV
Scene I

Place: Michigan's Asolbo River. It is a dark and stormy night. Dripping woods loom above, and a gray, sullen lake lies in the distance. Henry and Sam are miserable. Their camping gear lies nearby. Sam is attempting to light a fire with no success. Henry illuminates his pitiful attempts with a flashlight. Together the men have killed half a bottle of vodka.

SAM: Birch bark, that's what we need.

(He attempts to light another wet match. Henry looks on with a mixture of thinly veiled pity and contempt.)

HENRY: What's that you say?

SAM: We could get this fire going if we had birch bark. In a wet woods, you can always start a fire with birch bark. The Indians used it for everything. You can write letters on it. You can sew with it, lace up your moccasins with it. You can even build a canoe. The bark has petroleum in its skin, which makes it not only waterproof, but also flammable. It's a natural accelerant.

HENRY: That's wonderful.

SAM: Oh, yeah. Find yourself a piece of drenched birch bark, set a match to it, and you've got yourself a fire.

HENRY: It's white, isn't it, Sam? Birch bark?

SAM: That's right.

HENRY: *(He shines his flashlight on something in the distance.)* Is that a birch over there?

SAM: *(Sam looks up.)* Yes, it is. That's a yellow birch. The Irish considered that particular kind of birch to be a bewitching tree. I think they called it the white lady of death. They actually believed the top branches could reach down and touch your soul. If it did that, you were a goner.

HENRY: Lots of birch bark right there, then.

SAM: That's a live tree, Henry. We'll pay a five hundred dollar fine if they catch us messing with a live tree. A birch is fragile; if it has open places in the skin, the insects get inside and kill it.

HENRY: Oh.

SAM: The wind plays havoc with it, too.

HENRY: Too bad.

SAM: But, even if that *was* a dead tree?

HENRY: Yeah?

SAM: We've got a helluva a lot of soggy matches here. Birch bark doesn't ignite all by itself.

HENRY: So, the subject of birch bark is pretty much a moot one.

SAM: Pretty moot. A doggone waste of breath, actually. Now, if I'd thought to bring along some steel wool, we could unravel a piece of it, and together with the flashlight batteries, get a spark going.

HENRY: But, you didn't think to bring steel wool?

SAM: No, I didn't. Even if I had, we'd still need a heck of a lot of—

TOGETHER: Birch bark.

SAM: It's your basic Catch 22. *(Indicating a bottle of vodka that Henry clutches to his side.)* Don't bogey that bottle.

HENRY: *(Surrendering it.)* I'm going to remember what I've learned tonight. You never know when you'll get yourself stuck in the middle of a wet woods, in freezing weather, with night coming on.

SAM: It's handy information.

HENRY: It is. *(Beat.)* However, strictly speaking, a Catch-22 it is not, Sam. If you're in the mood to split hairs, and what the fuck else have we got to do on a night like this? A Catch-22 is a situation where something desirable is unattainable because one of its requirements can never exist in the presence of some other of its requirements.

SAM: Say again?

HENRY: The lack of fire-making tools is only really a Catch-22, if the necessary birch bark isn't available precisely because steel wool is, or vice versa.

SAM: Ah. I see. *(Silence.)* Would the term *snafu* be more applicable?

HENRY: I believe I can allow it, yes.

SAM: Fine. Tell me this—

HENRY: Yes?

SAM: Jean puts up with you every day and every night, is that right?

HENRY: Essentially.

SAM: Wonderful woman.

HENRY: Patient woman, yes. Might I add it is my sincere hope that the tranquility of your marriage to Franny did not rest on your fire-building abilities.

SAM: It did not.

HENRY: Good.

SAM: Goddamn Mount Pinatubo. It'll warm up tomorrow. But, hell, if it's warm, if it's cold, if we freeze our butts off, I'll still take the woods every time. I can finally breathe! Can you breathe?

HENRY: No problem so far.

SAM: How I ever came to believe a transfer to the New York office of Arthur

Anderson was my destiny calling, I will never know. Anyway, my kid is married, my wife has fled the scene, and I am thinking about coming back here for good.

HENRY: Back to Michigan? What would you do?

SAM: Start my own accounting firm. I was raised in the woods.

HENRY: Around here?

SAM: Hell, yes. My folks owned a lodge in Gaylord. This is home to me. I've come home! God! I love it here. There's no duplicity here. There's no room for liars here. You've gotta tough it out, know what I mean?

HENRY: Not exactly, Sam. My definition of roughing it has always involved a screen door of some kind.

SAM: You've never been camping?

HENRY: I'm a Jew. Hotels and boardwalks come strongly into play when I'm defining a really swell vacation. Give me white sand, a mai tai, and some sun tan oil, and I am on vacation!

SAM: Why did you suggest camping, then?

HENRY: Was this my idea?

SAM: If memory serves.

HENRY: I don't know. I thought I could get you to meet me here. I know you like to camp.

SAM: Well, next time suggest the mai tai, sun tan oil thing.

HENRY: You got it.

SAM: *(He shakes his head. Humiliated.)* It's the kindness that's killing me. All the mushroom soup and tuna casseroles from the neighbor ladies, the endless analysis over drinks with well-meaning pals, and now this: Deliverance 2.

HENRY: It wasn't just for you. I needed to get away.

SAM: Yeah?

HENRY: Yeah.

SAM: I heard you guys are in trouble.

HENRY: It's a mess.

SAM: She really wants to bring that kid home?

HENRY: She really does.

SAM: If she does, then what? Will you leave?

HENRY: She wouldn't. She won't.

SAM: There's no telling what a woman will do, especially one who knows she's suckered your trust. You're a writer.

HENRY: Sometimes.

SAM: Then you know about the weakness in human nature. Women are the worst. Tell me about Franny, for example.

HENRY: I beg your pardon?

SAM: Quote somebody. Tell me I'm not crazy. Tell me the worst thing anybody ever wrote about a woman.

HENRY: Why would you want—?

SAM: Or women, in general. Let's throw caution to the wind, and just lump 'em all together, what do you say? Because, after seventeen years, I never thought I could hate her, but I do. I financed that fucking birthing center of hers. It was the biggest mistake of my life. Once it took off, we were stuck. There was no considering a transfer out of that hell hole. She was in paradise. She was always so—lah-de-dah, off to the theatre, galleries in Soho, concerts in Central Park. "Let's step over this inert body to get a better view of the Chrysler Building." Jesus Christ, if I'd had to hear her wax sentimental one more time about the fucking Chrysler building—have you been to New York lately?

HENRY: What are you talking about?

SAM: Calcutta without the cows, that's what I'm talking about. Mass psychosis! I can hardly leave the house any more. From an airplane, it looks exactly like a malignant skin tumor.

HENRY: But I thought—

SAM: After all the years I suffocated in that pit for her sake, I lose my mind when I think of her with that jerk—I think up tortures. I dream of murder. If one other person has hated a woman the way I hate Franny, I might survive. So tell me the worst. It was probably Shakespeare, wasn't it? Shakespeare could hate a woman, couldn't he?

HENRY: What?

SAM: Shakespeare could hate a woman.

HENRY: Yes.

SAM: Couldn't he?

HENRY: He could be venomous on the subject, yes.

SAM: What'd he say? Hit me with it! No holds barred!

HENRY: That's good. "No holds Bard." I like that.

SAM: Go ahead.

HENRY: Well, there's *King Lear*. Let me think…
     (Scanning beautifully.)
          Behold yond simp'ring dame,
          Something, something
          Down from the waist they are something,
          Something, something
          But to the waist do the gods inherit,

Beneath is all the fiend's.
There's hell, there's darkness, there is the
sulphurous pit,
Burning, scalding, something, something; fie, fie, fie!

SAM: "The sulphurous pit?" He actually said that?

HENRY: Takes your breath away, doesn't it?

SAM: That's some memory you got there. Something, something.

HENRY: Does that do it for you?

SAM: It comes pretty damn close. Doesn't quite say it, but it comes close.

HENRY: Then there's Yeats, who wrote about forgiveness.

SAM: Fuck him.

HENRY: Right.

(Cross-fade.)

Scene II

The hospital. Jean makes her way to the side of the isolette, where Mary Jo waits for her.

MARY JO: Jean!

JEAN: Mary Jo, how's it going?

MARY JO: Fine!

JEAN: *(Looking into the crib.)* What's he plugged into?

MARY JO: Green Chili Jam.

JEAN: Where's Humpty?

MARY JO: He hurled all over Humpty. Humpty pissed him off, that's all I can figure.

JEAN: *(To Mary Jo.)* So, he's eating, then?

MARY JO: A record four ounces.

JEAN: Good boy.

MARY JO: Jean, we've got a situation on our hands.

JEAN: What's that? What do we have?

MARY JO: A bit of a situation. That's what I would call it: a situation. I can't say what kind of a situation until the L-man gets here. He'll come down on me like a ton of bricks if I explain about...

JEAN: The situation.

MARY JO: Right.

JEAN: Go get him.

MARY JO: Okay.

JEAN: I want to know.

MARY JO: Okay. *(Colliding with Laurence.)*

LAURENCE: Did you tell her? Mary Jo, if you told her—

MARY JO: No, no, no. Go! Talk.

LAURENCE: Because if you told her—

MARY JO: Talk. Go.

JEAN: What is wrong with you people?

LAURENCE: Sit down.

JEAN: *(Sitting.)* What is it? Tell me.

LAURENCE: Jean, something peculiar is going on, and, we're excited, which takes the Charles Grodin Understatement of the Week Award.

JEAN: What? What is it? What's going on?

LAURENCE: As you know, every Monday and Thursday morning, I weigh Robin, and measure the circumference of his head.

JEAN: Yes?

LAURENCE: This morning, I noticed he'd dropped six ounces when I weighed him, and I thought, here's an oddity. Then, when I measured his head, he'd lost seven centimeters. Somehow, between last Monday and today, he has found a way to rid himself of seven centimeters.

JEAN: Is that a lot?

LAURENCE: About three inches. A little fluctuation is normal, but this is—a lot, yes. So, I looked up his birth records, and all told, he's lost eight and a half centimeters since he first came here a month and a half ago.

JEAN: What's happening to it? Where is it going?

LAURENCE: We're not sure. Somehow he's managing to flush it away.

MARY JO: Let's call a spade a spade. He's pissing it into his diapers.

JEAN: Is he?

LAURENCE: *(With a glance at Mary Jo.)* That appears to be the case, yes.

JEAN: What does Arbaugh say?

LAURENCE: She can't really explain it, either. It should not be happening.

MARY JO: It's a miracle!

LAURENCE: Mary Jo, let's try to stay on the same page!

MARY JO: How else do you explain it?

LAURENCE: I'll be happy to set you up with Arbaugh.

MARY JO: But, she can't explain it either.

JEAN: Is that true?

(Laurence nods. Jean is careful, but obviously radiant.)

JEAN: I knew he was smart…I knew he was clever, but, I really had no idea he was a prodigy.

MARY JO: This proves it.

LAURENCE: Look, I can tell you that I haven't seen anything like this, but it's important for you to know—

JEAN: Can I pick him up?

LAURENCE: Uh—sure. Mary Jo, you want to help me—?

JEAN: No, no. I'll get him. *(She rises, goes to the crib, and easily takes up the child.)* You clever, clever boy! You amazing shrinking thing, you! Are you practicing voodoo when I'm not here? *(She sits with him, and rubs his head tenderly.)* It's important that I know what?

LAURENCE: Well, it's important that you grasp the fact that, although we are stumped, it is what it is. It is only what it is. That's it. It's nothing more.

JEAN: Have you been reading Camus?

LAURENCE: What I mean to say is that it doesn't necessarily prove he's on the road to recovery. He could gain back this water any time.

JEAN: He could, but he won't.

LAURENCE: But, the other thing, Jean, is that they've found a bed for him at Misericordia.

JEAN: When?

LAURENCE: Three days from now.

JEAN: Tell me exactly where this place is.

LAURENCE: Just off 57, in Harvey.

JEAN: Shit. It's the construction on Lake Shore Drive.

LAURENCE: So, we're talking two hours to Misericordia, and two hours back.

MARY JO: The train is faster.

LAURENCE: What about your job?

JEAN: I'll take a sabbatical.

LAURENCE: You don't need to see him every day, either, Jean. You could come two or three times a week.

JEAN: I *do* need to see him every day, and he has to see me. We can't afford a set back.

LAURENCE: I can try to convince Arbaugh to hold off on the release. But, he's travel-worthy, and as long as the state is picking up the bill, old Viv will be breathing down my neck.

JEAN: This is absurd. Why are we discussing the empty bed at Misericordia. He has a bed at home, with bumpers, and soft quilts, and a zoo of stuffed animals that are fading with the wait. Why should I drive four hours every day, when I need only walk up a flight of stairs? The money I would save on gas alone will pay for someone to come in and help me part-time. Why are we talking like all of that does not exist?

LAURENCE: You tell me.

JEAN: Robin's coming home, that's all there is to it.

LAURENCE: And Henry? You gonna get him lobotomized or what?

JEAN: He has to agree. That's it.

LAURENCE: Not just for your sake, either. DCFS won't place even a child as needy as Robin in a home where there is strife.

MARY JO: Leave your husband.

JEAN: What?

MARY JO: Leave the bastard.

LAURENCE: Mary Jo!

MARY JO: DCFS places with lots of single parents.

LAURENCE: That's hardly the point!

MARY JO: He sounds like an ogre. I say leave him.

JEAN: Have I made him out to be an ogre?

MARY JO: Authentic dweeb.

LAURENCE: Mary Jo, are you on some sort of medication that I as your immediate supervisor ought to know about?

JEAN: Have I really made him out to be so bad?

MARY JO: The "iceman cometh." Some snowman guy.

LAURENCE: Mary Jo, are you, by any chance, and I shudder to think, referring to the play by Eugene O'Neill, entitled *The Iceman Cometh?*

MARY JO: Maybe.

LAURENCE: I have a certain admiration for you, Mary Jo. You smack up against great literature the way Jerry Ford used to hit doorways. In Eugene O'Neill's classic, *The Iceman Cometh*, Hickey is a notorious womanizer, who repeatedly cheats on his wife, and eventually kills her to spare her the pain of his indiscretions. Do you honestly see a parallel here!

MARY JO: Before I answer that?

LAURENCE: Yes?

MARY JO: Who's Jerry Ford?

LAURENCE: Shoot me.

JEAN: Laurence.

LAURENCE: Somebody pull the trigger.

JEAN: The problem is with me, do you understand?

MARY JO: No, it's not.

JEAN: Yes, it is.

LAURENCE: What? What are we talking about now?

JEAN: He could have had children of his own if it weren't for me. He's never complained. If I've mislead you, Mary Jo, I'm sorry. My slightest wish has been his command. He's given me every single thing I ever wanted.

LAURENCE: Except Robin.

JEAN: Yes.

LAURENCE: Do you want to call him?

JEAN: I can't. He's fishing with a friend in Michigan.

MARY JO: Call the State Police.

JEAN: No, M.J. It wouldn't matter.

LAURENCE: There's not the slightest chance he'll change his mind, is there?

JEAN: He's not ready, yet, no.

LAURENCE: We can get the wheels in motion around here if you want Robin to come home with you. But understand this: Misericordia is a fine place. You needn't worry about the kind of care he'll get there. You can see him as often as you like. Why not save yourself some time in hell? Let him go.

JEAN: I can't do that.

LAURENCE: He can't live here forever. And do understand, Jean, you'll never win this one. I know you think you will, but you only win this one somewhere in the back of your head, in some little corner where everybody is Mother Theresa. There is nothing in the real world to support your fantasy. Let him go to Misericordia. Ten tons will come right up off your shoulders if you do.

JEAN: No.

LAURENCE: Do it.

JEAN: *(Rabid.)* I'm telling you, no! He's family, now.

LAURENCE: Then Henry will be packing his bags, I assume?

JEAN: I will keep them both. I don't how, but I will. I will "connive" until Robin shows his true colors, or until Henry does. *(Beat.)* I have not misjudged Hal. I have not.

(The baby blows a raspberry. After a moment.)

LAURENCE: I think he just gave you the Bronx cheer.

JEAN: What's the matter, gummy? What is it?

MARY JO: Looks like he's taking a dump.

LAURENCE: Un Petit editorial comment, perhaps?

JEAN: No doubt.

MARY JO: It's a record breaker. Go, baby, go.

(They laugh at the expression on his face.)

MARY JO: Such relief! Have you ever seen such relief?

LAURENCE: Audrey Hepburn in *Charade.*

MARY JO: Audrey—what?

LAURENCE: When she finds the stamps, remember? She gives these priceless stamps to the little kid, thinking they're nothing, and the little kid goes to a dealer, and—

MARY JO: The kid goes to some drug guy? Some junkie?

LAURENCE: *(Pearls before swine.)* Yes. Some junkie, Mary Jo. Exactly. Some drug guy. It's tragic.

(Mary Jo is slightly offended, but doesn't know why.)

JEAN: That's better, isn't it? Diaper time? *(She offers the bottle to him.)* Are you done with this bottle? Do you want any more of—? Oh, my God.

MARY JO: Dimples!

(Mary Jo does some sort of Happy Feet Dance. Jean throws her head back and crows. Laurence, who is kneeling next to the chair, grabs Jean by the knees, and shouts encouragement. They have never before, not one of them, seen him smile.)

(Blackout.)

Scene III

The woods. The clearing night sky reveals various constellations in full bloom. Sam has managed a puny little fire and is resting on his sleeping bag. Henry pokes at the fire with a stick.

SAM: That's funny. With me, it was always a catcher's mitt.

HENRY: No, pink ballet slippers.

SAM: What else?

HENRY: Pony rides. Trips to the orthodontist. Father-daughter banquets. Sizing up her boyfriends, making them feel just a little uncomfortable. But, eventually, walking her down the aisle.

SAM: Basically, it boils down to Jean. You check out okay?

HENRY: Yeah.

SAM: That means you don't even have to go through this adoption bullshit. If she wants to bring this kid home, fine. It's her choice. But, you tell her what it means.

HENRY: I have too much invested.

SAM: Money well-spent. It taught you a lesson. Life is short. Apply the brakes. Put your foot down.

HENRY: My foot is down. My foot has been down. It's made a hole in the floor boards. My heel is throwing up sparks from the pavement. She hasn't noticed. Besides, I'm not talking about money. I'm talking about Jean.

SAM: Hell, I invested seventeen years, and look what it got me.

HENRY: Sam, it's over between you and Franny because you decided it was over.

SAM: *(Flaming.)* I didn't go sneaking around with somebody else. I didn't call the lawyer. I didn't flee to fucking Chicago.

HENRY: And during that time when things were falling apart, did you feel there was nothing you could do to fix them up again? Did you ever go after her? Did you say, "Let's try again?" Did you ask her to stop seeing him?

SAM: I won't live with a cheat.

HENRY: We're not talking about some floozy, Sam. We are not talking about a woman who was faithful for seventeen years. You won't live with a cheat? Is that what you said?

SAM: I was a good husband, Hal! Come on, for Chrissake! *She* left me.

HENRY: You didn't really think invective was going to lure her back home, did you? You got what you wanted.

SAM: And what would that be?

HENRY: Escape from the city, the freedom to come back to the woods, to open your own business and start over—along with the added bonus of sympathy from the neighbor ladies, and drinks from all your pals.

SAM: What a twisted view of adultery. You ought to be a divorce lawyer.

HENRY: Just don't tell me you had no say in the matter. Because I know you did! We never achieve what we think we want. We get what we ask for. We create our own—*(Henry stops, and shakes his head.)* What the fuck am I saying?

SAM: It's your feminine side coming out. Just take a deep breath, think of Chuck Norris, and it will go away.

(Sam stares at Henry. Henry laughs.)

SAM: If what you say is true, what about the bouncing baby boy who is currently slam-dunking your marriage?

HENRY: You're not serious?

SAM: You brought it up. What is it you were "creating" when you brought him into the picture?

HENRY: *(Beat.)* You misunderstood me.

SAM: Goddammit, I did not misunderstand you. I've been listening very carefully. You said we create our own lives. We are responsible for what happens to us.

HENRY: For our reaction to what happens to us.

SAM: I got what I wanted when Franny made it with a stranger. For the moment, I'll choke it down. It's your turn. You said your heel is through the floorboards, throwing up sparks from the pavement. You can't even face a five-minute visit with the little son of a bitch. Why?

HENRY: You're ruthless, you know that, man?

SAM: And you're not? Shit!

HENRY: *(Silence.)* Six years ago, they said I had tumors along my spine and on two of my ribs. This punk-kid surgeon told me what he and his buddies were gonna do to fix me up. Two holes front and back, collapse a lung, move the heart to one side, cut away two vertebrae, and reconstruct the spine with three titanium rods and a few bear claws. He'd yank the two ribs at the last minute, move the heart back, inflate the lung, and staple me back together. The odds were one in twenty I'd bleed to death on the table. If the spinal cord coiled, or if he cut a feeder along the way, then, he said, the odds were one in ten I'd live the rest of my life paraplegic. We knew he was the best in his field, so Jean and I listened politely, then hurried right home to examine our other options. Turned out, there were none. I went to a lawyer, and made out a will. She delivered me to the hospital on the appointed day, and we said good-bye without ever using the word. They drugged me to the gills. Even so, I trembled on the table as the anesthesiologist began his prep. I comforted myself by thinking about that tunnel they talk about. I was gonna fly through the tunnel, toward the light, and over some little bridge, into a garden where I would throw a little frisbee with all my former pets. They're supposed to be the ones who meet you first: the pets. After a little workout I'd find the nearest B&B that would take me and five or six dogs. I might nap, get in a shower, and go out on the town with my dad. I've missed my dad. I was thinking he'd be dressed in white linen, with a dry martini in his right hand, and the cigarette that killed him in his left, but—

SAM: Macabre little evening.

HENRY: Still, pleasant enough. Enough to see me through. However, much to my surprise, I woke up in a room full of red eyes and florescent lights, wondering why they had stuffed a garden hose down my throat. I swiped at it, and these huge hands came out of nowhere, and pinned my arms back. These hands belonged to a hag in white, Elsie, I will never forget *her* name—old Elsie kept calling me Harry. "Harry, don't pull at that tube. Harry, lie still." For three days she tortured me. She stabbed me with needles, pinched at the bags, and the tubes, which held me together. She probed my wounds with her heavy fingers. I thought to myself, if she'll only go away, I'll do anything. I will happily suffocate. The red eyes overhead rescued me and spun me away from her into nothing, nothing at all, a black vacuum. I waited there alone until I coughed, and awoke to a shower of blood that spattered my chin and the sheets that covered me. Elsie hissed in my ear, "Good sign, Harry, you're expectorating." Then she stuffed the garden hose further down my throat. I willed myself into my father's arms, but, couldn't find him. And, so, I sought refuge whenever I could in the void. No place. No time. No pain. *(Pause.)* Intensive care. There's no place like it. Robin is how old? *Six weeks?* On medication so strong it burns his skin. He can't turn his head to see who's coming to prod and poke at him. The pressure in his skull makes his eyes roll back in his head. She thinks I'm not listening. She thinks because I court the wheel-chair every time I go in for a routine check-up, that I'm afraid of him. Combination by association, or some damn thing. But, I know what she's up to with that kid, and she's wrong. The difference between that child's experience and mine is this, and it's a crucial difference: There is no hot-shot surgeon who's gonna rescue him. Jean can stand at that bedside for-ever, and nothing will change. *(Beat.)* I'm a grown man, and I couldn't abide it! A baby like that should not be made to suffer. I say, please, God, have a little mercy. Don't keep dragging him back. Let him go.

SAM: She can't.

HENRY: What do you mean, she can't!

SAM: The kid ambushed her when she wasn't looking. Now, she's hooked. Same thing happened to me when I first met Tom. Franny and I had been going out for about three weeks before she introduced me to him. It was Easter Sunday. We'd gone to church, all three of us, and I was going to spring for a big breakfast. She said he liked waffles. We were walking toward the front door of Uncle John's Pancake House. I had just taken her hand, when the little shit, all of seven years old, suddenly raced between us, in a fucking rage. He screamed, "I break your love!" Then, he smashed his arm across our fingers, broke our hands apart, and burst into tears. Franny stooped to talk to him—she was twenty-two years old, and so God Almighty beauti-ful—I thought, "If I can win this jealous little bugger, I can win her." So that's what I decided to do. I bought him presents. I took him to amuse-ment parks, and circuses. We went fishing, we went to basketball games. I'm the one who brought him home the Harley.

HENRY: The Harley?

SAM: Remember that night?

HENRY: Vividly.

SAM: If you're a parent, there's nothing worse, than when your teenager is not home yet, and the phone rings after midnight. They brought us to where he was. We sat next to his bed holding hands. She was thinking—whatev-er the hell she was thinking, I never knew. But, I was thinking back to the day I first met him. All the bribes, all those years, were nothing but a plea to him to let me stay close to his mother. Until the night of the accident, honest to God, I never realized, it was the little bugger who had the hammerlock on me. I would have done anything, *anything* to keep him alive. Scotch-tape him back together, I don't care. You know, I didn't have a thing to do with bringing that kid into this world, but, I was the only father he was ever going to know, and he, sure as hell, was my only son. I'd be goddamned if I was going to let him go without a fight. At the time I married her, everybody thought she was so lucky. I was this white knight, who'd made an honest woman of her at last, who had taken on the support of the bastard son; but that night in the hospital, looking down at him, I realized for the first time what I must have known all along: From that Easter morning on, he had been my little boy. I was the lucky one.

(Silence.)

HENRY: I see.

SAM: Is she living with this guy yet?

HENRY: No

SAM: Any plans to?

HENRY: Not that I know of.

SAM: *(A beat.)* I never would have left her, no matter how...

HENRY: No

SAM: The status quo was bearable, sometimes comfortable.

HENRY: Women don't like things comfortable. They pretend they want it cozy, with their afghans and their throw pillows, but just as you settle in for a nap, they're in your fuckin' face, have you ever noticed that?

SAM: Hell, yes. The phone rings: Somebody's in crisis, they gotta go. Or maybe—maybe they don't like the way you looked at 'em when you got up that morning, so they have to sit up all night and *talk.* Or company's coming, so they have to *clean.* Not only do they have to clean, but if you want any peace at all, *you* have to clean.

HENRY: Yup. Yup.

SAM: Well, shit.

HENRY: Take this. Cut me off.

(He tosses the bottle of vodka to Sam.)

SAM: Shit, man.

HENRY: Knock yourself out.

SAM: Did you bring aspirin, by any chance?

HENRY: *(Henry tosses him his knapsack.)* In the front pocket.

(Sam goes for the small bottle, opens it, swallows two, and swigs. He replaces the bottle and then settles back. Henry looks out at the clearing sky.)

HENRY: Every thing we look upon is blest.

"I am content to follow to its source
Every event in action or in thought
Measure the lot; forgive myself the lot!
When such as I cast out remorse
So great a sweetness flows into the breast
We must laugh and we must sing,
We are blessed by everything,
Every thing we look upon is blest.

SAM: *(Moved.)* Keats?
HENRY: Yeats, Sam.
SAM: Okay, so. Yeats.
     (Cross-fade.)

ACT V
Scene I
   The hospital. Rademacher, Laurence, and Mary Jo stand a certain distance from the crib.

RADEMACHER: Have you tried to reach her?
LAURENCE: I called her father's place. That's where she's living, yes?
RADEMACHER: As far as I know.
LAURENCE: The line's been disconnected.
RADEMACHER: Are you sure?
LAURENCE: Show me the number you've got.
     (Lights up as Rademacher does.)
LAURENCE: Six-seven-two-two. That's the number I've been calling. It's no longer in service.
RADEMACHER: Well, now what?
MARY JO: Have you tried Jean?
LAURENCE: Since eight o'clock. Nobody's there.
MARY JO: She's on her way, then.
RADEMACHER: Mrs. Farrell cannot sign the releases.
LAURENCE: *(Irritated.)* We know that, Viv. We'll keep trying Emma Miller, okay?
RADEMACHER: What about the mother?

LAURENCE: Which mother?

RADEMACHER: Emma's mother. The mother of the mother.

LAURENCE: She is listed on my chart as deceased.

RADEMACHER: According to the DCFS report, she's very much alive. She has an address and telephone number.

LAURENCE: That's not what I've got.

RADEMACHER: I have a phone number here. Let's try it. Try it!

LAURENCE: Would you get out of my face with the goddamned paper, Viv? I've had a rotten night. Enough already. *(Beat.)* Yes, give it to me.

RADEMACHER: *(Showing him.)* Right there.

(Jean walks in.)

JEAN: Good morning.

LAURENCE: *(Replacing the phone in its cradle.)* Hello.

MARY JO: Hello, Jean.

RADEMACHER: Mrs. Farrell.

JEAN: Here's clean laundry. *(She drops a plastic bag at her feet. She holds a brown paper parcel in her arms.)* And, don't tell the adults on the floor, because we don't want any carnage, a genuine Barney doll. What a coup!

LAURENCE: I tried to call you.

JEAN: *(He has never called before.)* You did? What for?

LAURENCE: Come here. Come sit with me.

JEAN: No.

LAURENCE: Come on, Jean, sit with me for a minute.

JEAN: Where is he?

LAURENCE: He's in his crib.

JEAN: What's he doing?

LAURENCE: Let me tell you what happened. *(Laurence extends his hands to her.)*

JEAN: *(The beginning of a wail.)* Wait a minute. Wait. Wait!

(Cross-fade.)

Scene II

The offices of Family Resources. A young pregnant woman waits by herself. She looks at the posters on the walls, paces. Tess McGarrett enters.

TESS: Michelle? How are you doing?

MICHELLE: I wouldn't mind stepping out for a smoke.

TESS: They're here. They're in Alan's office. It'll be just another minute or two. Can you wait?

MICHELLE: Sure.

TESS: Are you nervous?

MICHELLE: *(Laughing.)* I'm just thinking about how I got myself into all this.

TESS: Michelle, if you have any doubts, won't you please tell me now? You are, of course, free to change your mind any time up to three days after the birth, but I have to tell you, if you're not sure, you'd be doing this couple a big favor by saying so now.

MICHELLE: I won't change my mind. I just want to meet them, and get on with it. *(There is a gentle knock.)*

TESS: Now's your chance. *(She opens the door.)* Hi. Come on in. *(Henry and Jean enter.)*

MICHELLE: Hi.

HENRY: Hello.

TESS: This is Michelle. Michelle, this is Henry and Jean.

HENRY: It's nice meeting you.

MICHELLE: You, too.

JEAN: *(Tight.)* Hello.

MICHELLE: *(There is an awkward silence, and then Michelle laughs.)* I've been reading about you.

HENRY: You saw the album?

MICHELLE: I liked the family reunion, and Tenth Annual Softball Game.

TESS: Why don't we sit down?

MICHELLE: Okay.

HENRY: *(After a moment.)* How are you feeling?

MICHELLE: Big as a barn, and my feet hurt all the time, but they say she's in good shape.

HENRY: It's a little girl?

MICHELLE: Oh, yeah, didn't they tell you?

HENRY: No.

MICHELLE: Due December 9th.

HENRY: That's soon.

MICHELLE: Yes. Pretty soon.

TESS: I can't help but notice the resemblance between you and Jean, Michelle.

MICHELLE: You look like my Aunt Carol. She was an ice-skater.

JEAN: Oh. Thank you.

MICHELLE: I also liked the fact that you were from different religious backgrounds. *(To Henry.)* And you're in the arts?

HENRY: Yes.

MICHELLE: I always wanted to be a dancer. *(To Henry.)* I know you're a writer, but I don't guess I've ever read anything you've written.

HENRY: You're among the vast majority, then. Don't feel bad.

MICHELLE: I have lots of questions to ask you. I hope you don't mind.

JEAN: *(Reserved.)* No. That's good. I have some questions, too.

MICHELLE: Should I just start?

TESS: Why not?

MICHELLE: Okay. These are stupid, some of them, but just to get the conversation going—*(She clears her throat.)* Henry, how do you feel your life has prepared you for fatherhood?

HENRY: That's not at all a stupid question. Huh. When we tried to have a baby of our own—I don't know if they told you—

MICHELLE: A little. I know you tried for a long time.

HENRY: When it didn't work out, we felt deprived of something that most people take for granted. I know I wouldn't have been a good father if it had happened when I was twenty, or even thirty. It's been a long, wanting time, during which I've been able to think, and to decide what kind of father I want to be.

MICHELLE: I see.

HENRY: But, for me, it's not so much about fatherhood. It's about parenting. The two of us together. Stronger than we were.

MICHELLE: Two. That's important. If things work out between us, Jean, what can you give to this child?

JEAN: What can I give?

MICHELLE: What can you offer, as a mother

JEAN: I don't know.

HENRY: *(Beat.)* Time?

JEAN: What?

HENRY: Your time.

JEAN: Time, effort, yes.

(Henry takes Jean's hand.)

JEAN: My hands. My voice. My lap. Stories. Music. I have a music box that my grandparents brought me when I was a kid—We have a wonderful home, and a great big garden. I want to go on my hands and knees across that garden with my child. We like to go places: the beach, the aquarium.

MICHELLE: *(Rising, and coming close to them.)* This may sound awful, but—ever since I got pregnant, I feel like I've been baby-sitting. Watching over this child for somebody else. She isn't mine.

(Cross-fade begins.)

LAURENCE: Can I call Henry for you?

MICHELLE: I've taken care of her for somebody else.

Scene III
The Hospital.

LAURENCE: Where's Henry? Is Henry near a phone?

JEAN: Not until Tuesday.

LAURENCE: What about your friend, Mrs. Stornant?

JEAN: She went back to New York. Yesterday. How's that for impeccable timing?

LAURENCE: I'll get someone to drive you home.

JEAN: *(Her eyes fall on the child.)* Why is the side of his face purple?

LAURENCE: The blood has stopped flowing, you understand? It stops, and settles.

JEAN: It's a hell of a time to ask, but was he baptized?

LAURENCE: Emma had him baptized the first time she came up, but, you're not gonna like it: He's a Methodist, kiddo.

JEAN: *(Laughs, in spite of herself.)* No, that's fine. He's so little. So little.

LAURENCE: I've looked after babies like Robin in the past. They're usually irritable. You can understand it, because of the pressure on the skull and the spine. But, he never complained.

MARY JO: He was champ material.

JEAN: And, yesterday!

MARY JO: I know!

LAURENCE: That was incredible!

JEAN: My Grandma always said a baby's smile was a sure sign of gas.

LAURENCE: With all due respect, your Grandma didn't know bupkis.

JEAN: What happens, now?

LAURENCE: Rademacher just talked to Emma's mother, and there's an all out search. Her mother never knew about Robin, never even knew she was pregnant.

JEAN: I'm not surprised.

LAURENCE: Emma will tell us what she wants done with him.

JEAN: I was pushing him. I should have told him to take it in gradual stages.

LAURENCE: So, you were a nudge. Every good mother is a bit of a nudge. This kid was going to get better, and that's all there was to it. So, he did! I think he hung on just to see what crazy massage technique you were gonna bring in next. He was getting stronger. He was taking food on his own. He was figuring out his own little shunt system.

JEAN: If he was doing all that—then why?

MARY JO: Maybe he didn't want to cause trouble at home.

LAURENCE: We knew from the beginning, Jean.

JEAN: Did you try to resuscitate?

LAURENCE: Emma left instructions not to.

JEAN: *(A lifelong regret is born.)* Of course.

LAURENCE: *(Gently.)* You remember I told you about the apnea monitor?

JEAN: No.

LAURENCE: The gauge we have for his lungs?

JEAN: Oh, yes. Yes.

LAURENCE: His lungs were strong. So was his heart. It happens sometimes that, in spite of that, babies will—his brain stopped telling his body to breathe around eight o'clock last night. I had no right to hook him up to oxygen, you understand?

JEAN: Yes.

LAURENCE: I could not use extraordinary means. I could only touch his cheek, shake him, talk to him. Sing songs. Wind up the music box. Okay?

JEAN: Okay.

LAURENCE: He persisted.

JEAN: I see.

LAURENCE: About four this morning—I could no longer, in all good conscience— *(Silence.)*

JEAN: Stubborn cuss.

MARY JO: Yes.

JEAN: *(Beat.)* Where's Emma? We wait for Emma?

MARY JO: There are a few things we can do in the meantime.

JEAN: What?

MARY JO: Why don't we get him dressed? Should we dress him, Laurence?

LAURENCE: Yes. What do you think he would like to be wearing?

JEAN: The Cubs uniform.

MARY JO: Cubs, definitely.

LAURENCE: We all agree for once. With the argyles?

JEAN: Are they clean?

LAURENCE: Got 'em right here. Would you like to do it?

JEAN: You do the uniform, and I'll do the socks.

LAURENCE: Good thinking.
(They dress the child.)

MARY JO: What about his possessions? Would you like them?

JEAN: No, leave the doll. Is it clean?

MARY JO: He only spit up on it a hundred and sixty-two times, but miraculously, today it's clean.

JEAN: Humpty was his whipping boy, I'm afraid. Let's put in the A&D ointment, too, just in case. And the walkman. He'll need the tapes, of course.

MARY JO: And the music box?

JEAN: He never had shoes, did he?

MARY JO: The music box, Jean?

JEAN: I should have brought him some sneakers. Black hightops.

(Mary Jo tucks the music box beside him.)

LAURENCE: Do you want to say anything?

JEAN: Say anything?

LAURENCE: To him. Some final words.

JEAN: *(Simply.)* I will blow kisses heavenward, shooting stars that will fall on your tummy, and your cheeks, and the soles of your feet. When you least expect them, they will rain down on you, and they will warm you, when you need warming, and they will make you laugh, when you feel alone, and they will remind you, when you need to remember. I will always love you, and I will always remember.

LAURENCE: *(Waiting, and then.)* You want to say anything, Mary Jo?

MARY JO: *(Honored.)* Oh, yes.

LAURENCE: By all means.

MARY JO: I just wanna say that he was an awesome kid, and I'm sorry Jean never got a chance to spring him. Go, Bud! Find the beat, Babe!

LAURENCE: *(Reverently waiting for more, he suddenly realizes she's done.)* Is that it?

MARY JO: Go. Talk.

LAURENCE: Thank you, Mary Jo. How eloquent. *(He looks down at Robin's face.)* Dear Heavenly Father, take Jean's child, Robin, in Your Arms. He has had a tremendous journey, however brief. He stands before you, a spiffy little character, in a baseball jacket and argyle socks. Please note: The dreaded tube is gone, no mean achievement. He is a child of valor and of heart. There is a trinity here on earth that stretches loving arms to You in the fervent hope that You will nourish and encourage this brave boy forever. Bring comfort to his grieving mother. May we four meet again in joyful reunion. Eternal rest grant unto him, O Lord. And let perpetual light shine upon him. May he rest in peace. Amen.

MARY JO: Amen.

LAURENCE: Stay as long as you like.

(Laurence and Mary Jo leave silently. Jean looks down at Robin for a while. She picks up the music box, winds it, and listens for less than three seconds. She

snaps it shut, and like some guilty thief, puts it in her purse. She returns to his side. Henry appears in the door. He is equipped with a teddy bear. He stands rather awkwardly with a smile on his face. She turns, sees him. She walks toward him.)
(Blackout.)

END OF PLAY

THE BABY
Robin Andrew Miller

Naturally, Robin is a problem for the properties department. What follows is a rather technical description of the child. He would have weighed a little over eleven pounds at birth. He should weigh approximately thirteen pounds as the play opens. His body is fourteen inches long, from his toes to his shoulders, and this expanse contains a little under half of his total body weight. From his shoulders to the top of his head, he measures approximately fourteen inches. The circumference of his head measures approximately twenty-two inches. It is bulbous, and, from the browline to the crown, full of water. It is crucial that moving with this baby in one's arms is an off-center, slightly terrifying experience. He is always cloaked from audience view by the isolette, or by blankets. The absolute realism that would require George Lucas's hand is to be avoided, as is the other extreme: pantomime.

Green Icebergs

Cecilia Fannon

for John Glore, teacher and friend
David Emmes, il mio regista
and
Jonathan Bliss, fan, best friend, husband

BIOGRAPHY

Cecilia Fannon is a prize-winning playwright and author who makes her home in Newport Beach, California. In 1994, her play, *Green Icebergs,* won the top prize in the California Playwrights Competition and went on to premiere at South Coast Repertory in Costa Mesa in the fall of that same year. *Green Icebergs* was nominated for the Susan Smith Blackburn Award. In 1993, another of her plays, *To Distraction,* won second prize in the California Playwrights Competition, had a staged reading at South Coast Repertory, and was broadcast on KCRW/National Public Radio in 1994. *To Distraction* also has a staged reading at ShowBiz Expo West at the Los Angeles Convention Center in summer, 1995.

Ms Fannon is the author of nonfiction books for young adults, including *Soviet Union, Women Around the World, Women Leaders,* and *Antarctica.* Her short stories have been published in literary magazines and anthologized in *Flash Fiction.* She has written for the Emmy-award-winning daytime serial, *Guiding Light* and the Emmy-winning, animated series, *Where on Earth is Carmen Sandiego?* She is editor of the Costa Mesa Libraries Newsletter and is currently at work on a seismic comedy, *To a Fault,* about the predicted apocalypse in southern California.

AUTHOR'S NOTE

I grew up in a two-story house in Flushing, New York. Upstairs were my parents, grandmother, brother and sister, and Ike, the parakeet. Downstairs—my aunt, uncle, and four female cousins, who sang and danced like the Lennon Sisters (like my mother and aunt before them, the Andrew Sisters clones). My brother sang in a choir and was once chosen to be Infant of Prague in a church procession; my sister won Latin and French medals. My father performed the ball 'n' the jack after several martinis at family parties. My uncle was a practical joker and teller of tall tales. Ike, naturally, could sing. When I was a freshman in high school, I joined a glee club where I was later asked to mime the words to the Hallelujah Chorus. Thus, my career as observer and chronicler was born.

But it isn't enough to observe and record or just be sore about not being a child cynosure. In teaching playwriting, I talk about the passion to write—not mere urgency, but passion about what I'm writing. Studying Italian and traveling to Italy, I fell head over heels in love with the country, its language, its romance, its people, its argumentativeness, its perpetual, philosophical shrug, which suggests "Don't worry so much." Waiter in my play embodies the Italian passion in me; other passions include baseball, Renaissance painting, fine food, loving, hating, seething, and striking out on one's own.

ORIGINAL PRODUCTION

Green Icebergs was originally produced at the South Coast Repertory, Costa Mesa, California, October 21, 1994. It was directed by David Emmes with the following cast:

Waiter . . . . Hal Landon, Jr.
Beth. . . . . Annie LaRussa
Veronica. . . . . Nike Doukas
Justus . . . . Jeff Allin
Claude . . . . Robb Curtis-Brown

CHARACTERS

All the characters are in their mid-thirties, except for Waiter, approximately 55.

VERONICA

CLAUDE

BETH

JUSTUS

WAITER

SETTING

The setting is an ancient hill town in Tuscany. My thought was of San Gimignano, a sort of Italian Mont St. Michel, which I call Silvia (its original Roman name). Most of the action takes place in a Piazza with an elegant outdoor caffè, adjacent to a hotel. This might be suggested by the use of a table and colorful umbrella, perhaps an archway entrance to the hotel, and a sliver view of countryside. A bed can be used to represent the bedroom scenes in Acts One and Two. The paintings mentioned can by represented by reproduced parts of Lippi's paintings or just the words in the text. No walls or doors.

TIME

The present.

GREEN ICEBERGS

ACT I

Shafts of light to indicate morning. A man in a white shirt and black pants enters. He carries a jacket, cummerbund, and tie. He dons these, deliberately. As he does so, his posture goes from a vague stoop to straight and tall. The light grows stronger. He holds his hands out from his sides, looks out to audience.

WAITER: The raiment of office. Perhaps because here in Toscana our nearness to Milano gives us ideas of fashion, but I believe our clothes suggest who we are. When we take them off, that is when trouble arises. We develop a mild amnesia and are temporarily lost. Have you noticed, in pictures of Adam and Eve leaving Paradise, how lost they look, how sad? They have no clothes. They don't know themselves. *(Pause. He exits.)*
(A woman with dark hair, Veronica, enters, sits, her back to the audience. Beth, also dark-haired, crosses in front of Veronica but doesn't see her. She exits to the hotel next door. Justus enters, reading a book. He approaches Veronica, reading aloud.)
JUSTUS: For a monk, Filippo Lippi wielded a mean paintbrush. *(He sits opposite Veronica, still reading.)* While painting Santa Margherita Convent in 1456…blah, blah, blah…the Fra apparently stole time to sequester his… artistic instrument in Sister Lucrezia.
VERONICA: You're quoting, of course.
JUSTUS: How mortifying. One of life's most embarrassing moments.
VERONICA: My husband has those. He relives July 1989, when he played in a tennis tournament before 600 people with his thing out.
JUSTUS: My. *(In the calling voice of a linesman.)* Out! *(Beat.)* Did he win?
VERONICA: Yes.
JUSTUS: *(Standing.)* At least…he had *that.*
VERONICA: It put him off his game, though.
JUSTUS: Doesn't play anymore?
(She shakes her head 'no'.)
Too bad. Excellent exercise.
VERONICA: Yes. What do you suppose people did before there was exercise.

JUSTUS: There was always exercise. Of a certain genre.

VERONICA: The Lippi genre.

JUSTUS: Precisely. I hope this doesn't come across as any sort of come-on, but from the back, you look like…I thought you were my wife.

VERONICA: If I thought you *were* coming on and using Lippi and his amorous romps as, well, lure, and if I were single and you were single, a night of abandon in Tuscany under the grapevines would sound delirious, especially if you were neatly to return to your job—let me guess—curator of Renaissance paintings at the art museum in Racine, Wisconsin. *(Pause.)* Your wife is beautiful, of course.

JUSTUS: Ha! You're funny.

VERONICA: Is your wife funny?

JUSTUS: Beth? No, I wouldn't say. Sometimes, I guess she can be. In general, I'd say she's…uh, quiet. If I had only one adjective.

VERONICA: Quiet women make good wives.

JUSTUS: Really? I never heard that.

VERONICA: Neither have I. The Quiet Woman. *(Pause.)* Am I right? Curator? Something to do with art?

JUSTUS: I'm flattered, but…no…didn't even study it at Claremont. But I was, however briefly, an editor for a well-regarded publisher in the Bay Area. A project I ushered through, one of the last books before the house closed, was *Gentlemen of the Adriatic,*—I gave it the title—about Venetian painters the Renaissance: Giorgione, Titian, Veronese, Tintoretto—gorgeous color plates. Geniuses, all, who captured the sensuality and physicality of their time—though I'm not familiar with their entire canon—who gave me this fleeting glimpse, this tear in the fabric of time, a truly visceral response that…what. You're smiling.

VERONICA: I'm impressed. Claremont grad, book publisher, art historian…

JUSTUS: No, no. Well, in a dilettantish fashion. And I've long been attracted to the Renaissance. Not just the painters, but the idea: rebirth. Recrudescence. And the paintings. Art changed so profoundly. I mean, one minute, in the Middle Ages, there was paint on wood, then the next… *(Snaps his fingers.)*…the Renaissance. The tongue of art was loosened, and all the paintings suddenly burst forth in garrulous color. If you look at them, you feel they can actually speak.

VERONICA: *(Excited by this; indicates art book.)* May I see?

JUSTUS: The plates are small, but you still get a sense of Lippi.

(He pulls his chair close to hers, lays the book flat. He turns pages. She turns a page back.)

VERONICA: The Annunciation. With…*(Counting silently.)*…*six* people. I thought it was intimate, just Mary and the Angel. Turns out to be a party.

JUSTUS: Brunch for six. These gents off to the side have nothing better to do than hang out…watch.

VERONICA: Fifteenth Century hall monitors.

JUSTUS: I guess. And who do you suppose these two are, scurrying up the side staircase?

VERONICA: Angels?

JUSTUS: Hard to say. It is the moment of revelation where Mary finds herself quite suddenly with child. Maybe they're hurrying off to spread the news.

VERONICA: Or are about to become copycats.

JUSTUS: They do look boy and girl, at that.

(They look at one another a long beat, turn a page together.)

It says Lucrezia was the model for most of the women in his paintings, including the Madonnas.

VERONICA: She must have been extraordinary. A nun, a temptress. Imagine.

JUSTUS: I am. Mary Magdalene in a white habit.

VERONICA: That bountiful, luxurious hair waiting to be unbound.

JUSTUS: Waiting for the right man to do it.

VERONICA: Oh yes, there had to be the right chemistry, the conjunction of the planets, et cetera. Did he marry her, our Fra?

JUSTUS: *(Nodding, sitting down.)* Shotgun, from what I understand. Lucrezia's nun cronies ganged up on him, said he couldn't have the painting assignment unless he did the decent thing. Filippino arrived nine months later.

VERONICA: So. In summary. You're married, I'm married, I resemble Beth but probably laugh more, you and Claude suffer from bouts of embarrassment, only yours are of a more intimate stamp, and we're having a…flirtation in an Italian caffè, based on the wayward urges of a monk dead half a millennium. May I buy you a sweet vermouth?

(He looks away.)

You looked away. I've scared you.

JUSTUS: No! No, you haven't.

VERONICA: I'm not entirely sure I believe that. You can say no.

JUSTUS: Why on earth would I do that and spoil this continental moment.

VERONICA: Good for you. For us.

JUSTUS: *(Laughs. Nervous gesture.)* I mean. It has a sort of subterranean…I don't quite know…

VERONICA: *(Supplying.)*…stimulus.

JUSTUS: Yes. Perhaps more *Medi*terranean.

(They laugh. Pause. He looks at her hair.)

JUSTUS: At first glance, I truly thought...but the more we talk, I realize the resemblance is slight.

VERONICA: She's quiet.

JUSTUS: Is *he* quiet?

VERONICA: Claude? Not particularly. He talks a lot, though sometimes I think of it as silence because I don't listen as attentively as I should. *(Pause.)* I get to review Fermat's last theorem...or stats from Baseball's Hall of Fame: number of RBI leaders whose first name is Frank or who was walked five times intentionally in a single game against Cincinnati.

(He shrugs: Who? She shrugs back: No Idea.)

JUSTUS: Well...he tells you what he's thinking. I look at Beth sometimes while she's illustrating a parchment and wonder what she's thinking. She looks up, catches me looking. She smiles. I smile. We both smile. Lots of smiling makes me uneasy, so I grab a novel and pretend to read. *(Pause.)* I've become confessional...of a sudden.

VERONICA: Italy seems the place.

JUSTUS: Yes.

VERONICA: I chose Italy so we could have a romantic anniversary far away. Last week, in fact. Our ninth.

JUSTUS: You don't say. Beth and I celebrated our ninth last month, September.

VERONICA: And how did you do that?

JUSTUS: How did we do what?

VERONICA: Sorry. I didn't see the chalk line.

JUSTUS: No, that's quite all right. We had chocolate cheesecake and...maybe not all right, just unexpected. *(Pause.)* You take me by surprise.

VERONICA: Maybe that's how Lucrezia felt when the Fra approached—"taken by surprise."

JUSTUS: I'm not accustomed to someone so...to you.

VERONICA: Can you become accustomed to someone in five minutes?

JUSTUS: I guess I'd like to think so. You know, fit them in a pigeonhole. Makes it all safe.

(Waiter enters, talking.)

WAITER: I hope you have not felt abandoned. *(Sees book.)* Ah! Art lovers.

(Veronica and Justus exchange a glance.)

I myself am a great appreciator of Fra Lippi. The Tarquinia Madonna is a particular favorite. A reproduction must be in your book.

(Justus flips through, finds it. Waiter leans over to see.)

There. No halo, you notice. I believe Lippi did that to remind us that the

Madonna was, first and foremost, a human being, with all the hopes, sorrows, and desires that entails. *Allora.* What delicacy may I bring for you?

VERONICA: Two sweet vermouth, please.

(Waiter wrinkles his nose.)

WAITER: If I may say, *Signora...*this is perhaps not the best selection. You would prefer something you can savor, something which evokes pleasant memories of sunny Italy in the future. Something out of the ordinary—*prosecco.* It will, I assure you, be *un'esperienza. (Waiter sighs.)*

(She looks at Justus. He shrugs yes. She nods at Waiter.)

Va bene. Subito. (Waiter exits.)

JUSTUS: I don't know if I can handle this.

VERONICA: *Un'esperienza* with a stranger?

JUSTUS: Any of it. Italy. *Prosecco* at noon. Keeping up with you. You say...the unexpected.

VERONICA: *(Finishing.)* That keep me from fitting in one of your pigeonholes. Maybe it's just you who thinks I say the unexpected. Ordinarily I'm circumspect.

JUSTUS: I have trouble with that.

VERONICA: In college, a professor confided in me he was having an affair with a student. Then he pleaded most desperately I keep it a secret. I did. Years later, I found out everyone knew anyway.

JUSTUS: That was his line—entrusting female students with his secret. *(Pause.)* Did it work?

VERONICA: It was a titillating story, but no. Perhaps if I'd been less cautious...

JUSTUS: Ah, regrets.

VERONICA: Mm. You've had some?

JUSTUS: Oh yes, yes.

(They run out of words for a few moments.)

VERONICA: Did you mention your name?

JUSTUS: Justus Gilmartin.

(She reaches her hand across. He takes it.)

VERONICA: Veronica Padget. I was afraid you wouldn't take my hand.

JUSTUS: *(Still holding it.)* Why wouldn't I?

(They barely notice as Waiter arrives. He carries glasses, a bottle, carafe. With serious showmanship, he opens the bottle, begins to decant.)

WAITER: Most important not to excite the sediment.

(They undo handclasp, cross to watch Waiter.)

Ritual demands delicate care in the preparation of beverage. *(He sieves wine, pours contents into two tall, thin glasses.)* This *prosecco* was bottled last spring when barometric and lunar conditions were just so. Pouring must also be performed under optimum conditions. *Ecco! Salute! (He waits for them to sip.)*

(Simultaneously.)

VERONICA: Delicious, thank you.

JUSTUS: Dry, very dry…excellent.

WAITER: Have you noticed? The sun is already in a different position since I took your order. Time does have wings.

(They nod, ad lib concurrence. Waiter bows, exits.)

VERONICA: What are you feeling right this moment?

JUSTUS: That sounds like a question one woman might ask another.

VERONICA: How charmingly sexist. A gender pigeonhole. Squeeze into it. For me.

JUSTUS: Okay—fine. I feel fine.

VERONICA: Be more specific.

JUSTUS: Uncomfortable. Nothing I can't live through. Does Claude know you're… this way?

VERONICA: I'm not. A unique opportunity has presented itself. One moment I was wondering if I might buy my husband a present; the next I was interrupted by a man who found inspiration in the stirrings of a long-dead monk and was sharing it with his wife—or, rather a reasonable approximation.

JUSTUS: The Fra's tale has a certain impetuosity I thought Beth might appreciate.

VERONICA: And is she impetuous?

JUSTUS: On occasion, certainly. When we first met—in a quiet sort of way— not in the universal sense of impetuous.

VERONICA: My husband's brand of impetuosity is watching a soccer match with a bunch of strange Italian men. *(Pause.)* I, on the other hand, am discussing the Fra's sex life. And mine.

JUSTUS: And mine.

VERONICA: Were we? More *prosecco?*

JUSTUS: I'm afraid to. *(He drinks anyway.)*

VERONICA: Part with a single detail.

JUSTUS: It doesn't seem exactly…right.

VERONICA: It's not. But it will be a secret.

JUSTUS: If you tell me something. A trade.

VERONICA: Fair.

JUSTUS: Okay. Here goes. Don't laugh.

(She shakes her head 'no'.)

We smoke candied cigarettes after. You know, the kind made of corn syrup with dyed red tips? We're reformed smokers.

VERONICA: You smoke them?

JUSTUS: Well, we pretend. You know. I put two in my mouth, pretend to light both, Paul Henreid, hand one to Beth. Then we puff.

VERONICA: Holy smokes.

JUSTUS: You promised not to make fun.

VERONICA: I promised not to laugh. Was it your idea or hers?

JUSTUS: One detail. Those were the rules. It is now your turn.

VERONICA: Claude likes jokes.

JUSTUS: Uh-huh. Before, during, or after?

VERONICA: Well, mostly before…it makes him hard.

> (Justus starts to snicker.)

I haven't said anything funny yet.

JUSTUS: Give me a second to appreciate this. I must ask. Do you have to have a new joke every time? I mean, isn't that awfully demanding?

VERONICA: He doesn't mind repetition, but I do try to collect new material. It seems to have better results.

> (He laughs again.)

Would you like me to tell you a joke?

JUSTUS: (Laughs again, but swallows it.) It's not a universal. Claude's…predilection.

VERONICA: What a relief. I've been meaning to ask but I can't seem to fit it into conversations with my students. "More violets, Henry, and by the way, do you and the Mrs. find foreplay…amusing?"

JUSTUS: What do you teach, gardening?

VERONICA: No. Begins with gar. Gar-*nish*. Swans from carrot strips, pampas grass from celery, roses from tomato skins. I'm the *trompe-l'oeil* maven of Ralph's produce department—give me a daikon radish, I'll carve you a chrysanthemum.

JUSTUS: How unusual.

VERONICA: You mean how stultifying. *I* was certainly stultified. Enough to write a food column for a newspaper to satisfy my literary pretensions. "Scrumptious Meals in Moments for the Stressed Triathlete." Not exactly M.F.K. Fisher. That's why our Fra chat has been a delightful departure. So much better than "Where did you go to college—really?—how fascinating," and the answer is Berkeley, Comp Lit, where I spent a lot of time reading Simone de Beauvoir, Emma Goldman, Angela Davis. When Patty Hearst got out of prison, renounced the Symbionese Liberation Army, then married her bodyguard, my brush with revolution ended. After that, I had a pot-sticker period at a local Mongolian restaurant where I met and married the man farthest from anarchism I could find: a math major.

JUSTUS: I don't know—I might not make the anarchist list, either, though Erik the Red, my ancestor on mother's side, might qualify me. He conquered Iceland pretty thoroughly. I mean, I manage the Portulaca Penthouses in Huntington Beach where I oversee leaf-blowing and painting speed bumps yellow. Have you ever seen a ground-floor penthouse? And the view! A panoramic view of oil derricks, which gives you a fair idea of the state of the portulaca. However. The job manages to keep my wife, a latter day illuminator, in gold leaf and also allows us to come to Italy.

VERONICA: Huntington Beach.

JUSTUS: South of L.A. by about…

VERONICA: I'm from Huntington Beach.

JUSTUS: *(Points to himself.)* I live in Newport Beach. What a coincidence.

VERONICA: Is there such a thing? More wine?

JUSTUS: Please.

(She pours. They both drink.)

VERONICA: You got quiet.

JUSTUS: I am quiet.

VERONICA: Like your wife.

JUSTUS: Yes. We are.

VERONICA: You haven't struck me that way

JUSTUS: Trust me. I am. Beth and I are from the same tree.

VERONICA: Mm. The one with gold leaves. Is that good?

JUSTUS: Yes. Most of the time. Sometimes. Lots of standoffs, actually. The expression "Silence takes up more space than noise" has a lot of currency in our place.

VERONICA: How un-Fra of you. Or do you suppose they were quiet when they slid up the side stairs.

JUSTUS: I imagine…he and Lucrezia were noisier than Beth and I. All that rustling, getting out of cassocks and gowns…

VERONICA: Breathless. The anticipation.

JUSTUS: And no binding bras.

VERONICA: No jockey shorts. Suppose they did it often?

JUSTUS: Frequently and noisily. He painted her over and over. He must have been…

VERONICA: …Obsessed.

JUSTUS: Over and over.

VERONICA: Breathless.

JUSTUS: It makes a person…winded. But exhilarated.

VERONICA: Yes. To the top of the stairs, to the secret chamber.

JUSTUS: Was it locked?

VERONICA: No doubt. But locks have keys.

JUSTUS: They do indeed.

> *(Pause.)*

VERONICA: And locksmiths.

> *(Another pause.)*

JUSTUS: Veronica, you're a very…prepossessing woman, but…we live a town apart. This is not good.

VERONICA: Meaning, if I lived in Chicago, you'd have some interest?

JUSTUS: *(Laughs.)* It's not a matter of…interest.

VERONICA: Good. Things are looking up.

JUSTUS: As I am painfully aware.

VERONICA: Oh my. This is actually happening.

JUSTUS: It is? I mean, it is. So you're suggesting…

VERONICA: …the museum in the Piazza.

JUSTUS: To see Lippi.

VERONICA: Mm. Make sure there are no haloes. Then there's the charming hotel next door.

> *(He laughs.)*

JUSTUS: I'm calling your bluff. What time?

VERONICA: Now.

JUSTUS: You're serious.

VERONICA: Never. More.

> *(Pause. She opens her bag, puts lire on the table. He picks up some lire, hands them back to her, puts some of his own down.)*

JUSTUS: This should be fifty-fifty, don't you agree?

> *(She smiles. They reach their hands out at the same moment.)*

> *(Waiter comes in as they exit. He lights a candle on a table. He exits. Stars begin to twinkle. Claude enters, holding a small package. Waiter glides in, holds the chair for Claude.)*

WAITER: *Signore!* A beautiful evening, no? The sun has taken the magic of the day with him, but we are left with this velvet pallet. *(He gestures to the sky, scatters stars. He sighs.)* You will be dining alone?

CLAUDE: My wife is upstairs dressing.

WAITER: And she will be beautiful.

CLAUDE: *(Pause.)* Italians lost, two to one.

WAITER: Ah, yes. A momentary sadness. It did not, *spero,* spoil your first day in Silvia.

CLAUDE: I took a walk to the next town.

WAITER: But you have not yet seen this one.

CLAUDE: All these towers and narrow streets, I…how do you know? That today's my first day.

WAITER: In a small town, it is not difficult to spot newcomers.

CLAUDE: They come by busloads.

WAITER: With thick-soled shoes, and hardly enough breath to climb to the top of La Rocca. By the city gate, they enter the first curio shop—the proprietor is a very rich man—then return to their bus, in order to leave by four P.M., *in punto.* Also, I saw you walking from the hotel next door.

CLAUDE: Uh-huh. There's a job in the U.S. government for you.

WAITER: That is a kind thought, but I am, as you see, otherwise occupied. May I bring you an *aperitivo* while you wait?

CLAUDE: No, I'll just…

(Waiter disappears. Veronica enters, a little breathless.)

VERONICA: Sorry I'm late.

CLAUDE: *(Still looking after Waiter.)* Our Waiter's a spy.

VERONICA: I'd say charming. We met earlier.

CLAUDE: You've said that about every waiter in Italy.

VERONICA: I guess I've just been lucky.

CLAUDE: And they're not what you'd think. They're all so thin, the men.

VERONICA: You're thin.

CLAUDE: Love handles are sprouting. Thin with love handles—what's more disgusting than that? Men're pissing me off. They scarf down mountains of pasta and all look like the young Vittorio de Sica. *(He moves from side to side, exercising his love handles.)*

VERONICA: What's the matter with the old Vittorio de Sica?

CLAUDE: God almighty. We never should have come to this country—you like everybody. If Luca Brazzi came in, you'd take a shine to him. You *are* shining, you know.

VERONICA: Oil. All that extra virgin.

CLAUDE: I get fat, you radiate. Now I can be jealous of the olives. That sounded pathetic.

VERONICA: You don't like Italy.

CLAUDE: I do. Okay, maybe it's not my favorite spot, but it's, you know, all right. Food's good.

VERONICA: Ten thousand dollars for pasta.

CLAUDE: No no no no. It's better than that. I get to skip vocational rehab at O.C.C., though I do miss my classmates—18-year-olds with acne and IQs below a hundred who seem to actually *understand* computers. *What does this have to do with math?* Why did I have to learn the word "downsizing?" Okay, I'm good now. And Italy's great.

VERONICA: *(Agreeing.)* They like sports.

CLAUDE: Yup. *Europe's* good that way. You see the magazine with Princess Di in a Phillies jacket? This country, it's soccer, wall to wall. Giorgio Canaglia, talk about an Italian superstar, 'course he zoomed out, became a leader for the New York Cosmos back in the eighties—golden years, they loved him, cried when he left. And now they got Baggio, two Baggios, can you imagine? *(Pause.)* You were gone all afternoon.

VERONICA: I wish I had your kind of enthusiasm for sports, Claude, but I just can't seem to…I don't know…incorporate the concept of enjoying tension as it mounts; I prefer to release it.

CLAUDE: I know that. I wish I could like museums more, but all that Etruscan stuff—makes me feel like a nap. Fruit paintings are okay, if I don't have to look at too many of them at once. That's where you were? The museum?

VERONICA: Mm. Lovely one nearby with overpriced gift shop attached—scented rosary beads and the like. I agonized over the perfect postcards to send to friends who hate getting them, that sort of thing.

CLAUDE: You're not pissed I didn't go with you. I mean, it's our anniversary trip—I coulda made the effort.

VERONICA: Why should you do something you dislike? I'm not mad.

CLAUDE: A few more urns wouldn't kill me.

VERONICA: You had your game to watch. Now. I got you something.—*(She takes a small wrapped package from her purse, hands it to him.)*

CLAUDE: God, I didn't get you anything—let's order something to drink, something with lots of body, why not celebrate. Where is that waiter.
(He turns just as Waiter arrives, carrying a tray with wine, ice bucket, glasses, a small cruet.)

WAITER: Usually, I would not think to intrude, but tonight seems to call for a special *aperitivo*. *Spumante* and *grappa*—if you do not like, I will whisk it away, *prestissimo*.

CLAUDE: I think my wife would rather have…

VERONICA: That's okay. This seems…this will be fine.

WAITER: Sometimes it is necessary to be adventurous, no?
(He waits for them to try. They do, reluctantly. Waiter looks up into the sky.)
Considera che questo giorno non verrà mai più.

CLAUDE: Mm.

VERONICA: Very good. What did you just say?

WAITER: "Consider that this day never comes again." Dante was a wise man.

CLAUDE: *(Dismissively.)* Thank you.

(Waiter takes the hint, exits.)

CLAUDE: What's his problem? I mean, choosing our drinks. We could die of alcohol poisoning.

VERONICA: I'm sure. A Dante-spouting waiter who goes up for murder one. You haven't opened your gift.

(Claude does so.)

CLAUDE: A fruit painting! It's great.

VERONICA: Do you really like it? Maybe you'd like something else.

CLAUDE: No, it's perfect. A pear. And a little fly down here. They look...good.

VERONICA: The Italians don't say stilllife, you know. They say *natura morta,* dead nature.

CLAUDE: Italians. What do they know. They lost the game today.

VERONICA: I'm sorry to hear that.

CLAUDE: No, it was all right...I walked to the next town—great, uh, olive groves, grapevines—then back up through the piazza. *(Beat.)* Funny. I thought I saw you there—I called your name, but you didn't answer. You were going into the museum with some guy.

(She laughs nervously.)

I know. You're gone one afternoon in Italy, I'm completely paranoid. It's just that every goddam bricklayer here is a poet, and you seem to be, well, you know, sort of liking it. All these Italians. How can I compete?

VERONICA: There's no competition, that's sports talk. And he wasn't Italian.

CLAUDE: Who wasn't?

VERONICA: Going into the museum. A Newport Beach denizen, on vacation with his wife, Beth, who looks something like me—that's how we got to talking. By accident.

CLAUDE: Oh. Where was *she?* Mrs. Newport.

VERONICA: Exploring for something...gold leaf, I think. She illustrates diplomas, certificates, licenses, that sort of thing, and apparently Italy has better or thinner or golder—I don't know, gold.

CLAUDE: You didn't meet her. Beth.

VERONICA: No. *(Pause.)* I wonder if the *osso buco* is any good. It's really a Milanese specialty.

CLAUDE: Who the hell is Beth and why am I talking about her? Mr. Newport probably made her up anyway. Does he wear pants with little semaphores all over them?

VERONICA: Have you heard of the new disorder, paranoia fatigue? I can't remember who suffers from it—the one who dreams up the stories or the one who listens. What are you going to order, or shall we continue on about Mrs. Gilmartin.

CLAUDE: You know his last name!

VERONICA: You know the last names of every soccer player in the world, and you've never met them.

CLAUDE: That's just it. I don't get personal. Too dangerous—you gotta learn to play it close to the vest, Veronica, not give out information to a stranger. Shit. This guy you met could be head of an international robbery ring, Their Man in Tuscany, and right now he's having one of his henchman ripping off our house back home. Interpol is probably scouring the Italian hillside for him as we speak.

VERONICA: We'll let the Waiter decide. He seems to have our best interests at heart.

CLAUDE: I have to tell you, I'm mildly pissed.

VERONICA: No, I don't think so. You were mildly pissed leaving L.A. airport and have made an upward progression since then to what I'd call vexed. Why not relax? Or pretend to relax. The drink is fabulous.

CLAUDE: I don't like *spumante*.

VERONICA: No. The Waiter brought it. Why don't you call him over and have it out with him, find out who he really is, why he's being so cordial. How can you trust a man like that, especially with your food?
(She joins the banter here; Claude is pleased.)
When you think of it, where does he get off, giving us liquor he picks? Next thing you know, he'll be advising us on wardrobes and decorating our house. I'll bet if you dug a little dirt, he's related to Sacco and Vanzetti.

CLAUDE: Or, or knows who really shot Kennedy or Reagan or the Pope. Or who offed Pope John Paul the First. *(He thinks for a moment.)* Might even know where Jimmy Hoffa is.

VERONICA: Vegas, probably.

CLAUDE: Yeah, parking cars at Luxor. With D.B. Cooper. *Osso buco* sounds good.
(Waiter appears.)

WAITER: May I please recommend the *osso buco*. It is excellent this evening. *(Whisking the glass from Claude.)* This drink is not for everyone. I will bring you chianti, a medium-bodied wine. *(Waiter whisks off.)*

CLAUDE: You have to admit, he's a scary dude. Every word he says comes out a shrug.

VERONICA: Attentive.

CLAUDE: The best face on things. I like that about you. Personally, I think the guy needs subtitles.

VERONICA: You've seen too many Oliver Stone movies.

CLAUDE: You're right. I gotta get less suspicious. *(Pause. He looks over Veronica's shoulder.)*
(Veronica turns her head; Justus and Beth have entered, holding hands.)

VERONICA: Oh my.

CLAUDE: The guy from the museum! What's his name, again? *(He waves.)*

VERONICA: Justus. Why are you waving?

CLAUDE: He's a nice guy, right?, that's what you said. And whaddya know, he *is* married, though she doesn't look anything like you. Definitely needs glasses.
(Justus and Beth stop; Justus says something to Beth. They come over.)

CLAUDE: Hello! Veronica told me about your museum trip this afternoon. I'm Claude... *(Gestures back and forth between himself and Veronica.)*...the husband.
(Beth looks up at Justus.)

JUSTUS: *(To Beth.)* For a moment—this afternoon, that is,—I thought Veronica was you. The hair—something. *(To Veronica.)* My wife, Beth. Veronica.
(They nod at one another. A second of silence.)

CLAUDE: Why don't you join us. Americans in Italy.

JUSTUS: Italy is overrun with Americans.

CLAUDE: But not from Newport Beach. *(To Beth.)* Can you beat it? We're neighbors—Huntington Beach.

BETH: *(To Justus.)* You didn't tell me.

JUSTUS: No. We, uh, should be getting to our table.
(Simultaneously.)

VERONICA: Of course.

CLAUDE: C'mon, stay. Have some chianti, or whatever the Waiter thinks is a good choice. *(Turns, à la Ed McMahon.)* And heeere's Waiter, anticipating your thoughts.
(Waiter flashes over, pulls a table next to Veronica's, with the dexterity and speed of a magician. Justus sits across from her, Beth across from Claude.)

CLAUDE: *(To Waiter.)* Could we have...

WAITER: *Detto, fatto. (He disappears.)*

CLAUDE: *(To Beth.)* Now. How do you feel about him. I mean, doesn't it make you feel, you know, kind of creepy?

BETH: Not really. I tend to trust people.

CLAUDE: What a great way to be. Isn't that a great way to be, Veronica? Of course, you're like that too, in some ways. Maybe Justus is right. Maybe you are a lot like Beth here.

VERONICA: *(Drains her glass.)* I'll switch to chianti now.

JUSTUS: It was a superficial likeness—some fleeting...I really have no basis for comparison.

CLAUDE: But you do! You two spent time in the museum together. Would Beth like the same paintings as Veronica?

BETH: Actually, I don't much like museums.

CLAUDE: Hey, did you hear that! Thank God, I'm not alone on the planet.

BETH: In the Uffizi, they make you climb all those stairs with all those people behind you and you can't stop, or everyone will fall down like dominoes. I felt like I was having a heart attack.

JUSTUS: We had to leave.

VERONICA: You didn't see the Botticellis?

BETH: I didn't see anything. It's okay. When I leave a museum, I'm so grateful to be outside, I just don't remember anything I've seen.

JUSTUS: She's an illuminator. Rhode Island School of Design. Doubleday offered her a lucrative job right out of school.

BETH: I couldn't live in New York. I missed California.

CLAUDE: Mm. Sun, space, lots of lane changes.

BETH: New York's foreign. They speak a private language. I'd understand the words but never knew what they meant. "What could I bring to the job?" the Human Resource woman at Doubleday asked. I didn't understand what she meant.

VERONICA: Italy must be unbearable for you.

(Waiter enters, bearing wine, a basket of breadsticks. He fills the glasses. Then he exits.)

BETH: It's okay, really. Justus likes it. And the food is good.

JUSTUS: Ah. Only among strangers does one hear the unvarnished truth. In other words, she's here on sufferance. Mine.

BETH: No. I didn't mean that. I meant you like Italy more than I do. *(To Veronica and Claude.)* He wanted to come for our honeymoon. "Forty percent of the world's art," he always says with a sigh. *(To Justus.)* You wanted to come so much, that I wanted it *for* you.

JUSTUS: That's sweet. Silly to think two people can derive equal pleasure from the same thing.

CLAUDE: I'm with you, Beth. I like the soccer, I gotta say. But Italy's not—whatever it is for Veronica, or for you, Justus.

(A moment of silence.)

JUSTUS: *(Lifting his glass.)* Well, here's to us all.

(They sip.)

CLAUDE: *(To Beth.)* I hear you were searching for gold paint. Did you find any?

BETH: They were out. In a couple of weeks, they expect a new shipment. They'll send it to me in California.

JUSTUS: You could have ordered the paint from the fax at home is what you're saying, that your entire afternoon was a waste.

BETH: No. I read. It was fine. I worked on a Bat Mitzvah Scroll. I took a nap. *(To Veronica.)* Justus seemed interested in one particular painter.

VERONICA: Oh, yes. Lippi. Inspiring.

JUSTUS: *(To Veronica.)* He was Botticelli's teacher, did I tell you? I've read up.

CLAUDE: Between shopping and reading, you're getting good vacation mileage.

JUSTUS: In a little bookstore around the corner, I found a volume on Lippi—hand-bound—quite beautiful—superior quality linen in the mull—that's the cloth strip pasted up the back of the sewn signatures. I'm a bug on mulls.

VERONICA: *(To Claude.)* Justus used to be an editor at a prestigious publishing house that unfortunately had to close.

CLAUDE: *(To Justus.)* And to think you still like books.

BETH: He loves books and paintings.

CLAUDE: *(To Beth.)* Veronica too. Huh. *(To Veronica and Justus.)* Great you two—bumped into each other.
(Waiter arrives with more wine and a plate of olives and cheese.)

WAITER: Very sad news. The *osso buco* will be delayed so Chef can prepare a proper *gremolada*. It will, I promise, be worth the wait however. Most things are.

CLAUDE: *(To Waiter, who's leaving.)* Thank you. Thank you for that. I appreciate the advice. I do, really.

WAITER: *Prego, signore.*
(Waiter exits. Silence.)

VERONICA: That was a wonderful, condescending, moment.

CLAUDE: What. I said thank you.

VERONICA: Mm. The words were 'thank you.' The tone was disapproving. *(To Justus.)* Claude can't help it; he comes from a long line of disapprovers. His father is one of those people who quizzes waiters as to why the bread pudding is so extortionate, especially since we *give* our wheat to the Russians. This takes place at a Denny's, usually. Then Dad leaves a quarter tip.

CLAUDE: I'm not like my father.

VERONICA: You leave tips, true.
(Claude glares for half a second, turns to Beth, almost as if they were alone.)

CLAUDE: Tell me about yourself. Do you come from a large family?

BETH: I have a sister.

CLAUDE: How nice. Sisters stay close, don't they?

BETH: I don't know about sisters in general. In my case, well, we don't get along.

CLAUDE: Ah.

JUSTUS: *(To Veronica.)* I didn't know you were eating here tonight.

VERONICA: No. Neither did I.

JUSTUS: Well.

CLAUDE: *(To Beth.)* You're the quiet type.

BETH: I'm not good with people. Travel's hard for me.

CLAUDE: I bet. It's not exactly my favorite sport.

BETH: Do you have one?

CLAUDE: Soccer. Then hockey, basketball, baseball, football, and golf. Tennis and car racing not quite as much. Track, pole vaulting, synchronized swimming, and polo, a notch down…luge, discus, and aerobic pairs competition…maybe half a notch down from that, bowling and camel wrestling, bottom rung—not that they don't involve a lot of practice…

BETH: You play any of them?

CLAUDE: Tennis. *(Beat.)* Retired.

(Veronica and Justus react.)

VERONICA: Mull. I love the word. I'd never heard it before. One day you learn something new, next you wonder how you survived so long without it.

JUSTUS: Yes, I know from whence you speak. Did I tell you, I discovered that Fra spirited Lucrezia away from the convent. They didn't actually marry until after Filippino's birth.

VERONICA: The daring! Cohabitation in the Quattrocento.

JUSTUS: All rather romantic, really.

VERONICA: And cloaked in mystery.

JUSTUS: Yes. His end was particularly mysterious. Some suggest he was poisoned by a jilted lover.

VERONICA: No! Poor Fra! Don't you wish we could find out somehow for sure? Examine all the paintings? Go on a tour of museums to pick up the scent.

JUSTUS: I like your enthusiasm.

VERONICA: Thank you.

JUSTUS: We could do it. We could take the train north to Turin or south to Rome, there are three Lippis there. Or the Prato Cathedral for the frescoes. Then on to Berlin. We'll do the continent. We won't stop until we see all of him.

VERONICA: Write a book on his life. What would we call it?

JUSTUS: And with the money from the book, we could buy an original Lippi.

VERONICA: It's an exhilarating love story, isn't it?

(Justus answers with a glance.)

CLAUDE: *(To Beth.)* Are you sports-minded?

BETH: *(Shakes her head.)* I wish. Not very coordinated. Justus once thought we could take fencing. *(She shrugs.)*

CLAUDE: *(Beat.)* I guess we really missed something in that museum today.

BETH: I guess.

CLAUDE: *(To Justus.)* I was just saying. We really missed out this afternoon, Beth and I.

(Simultaneously.)

JUSTUS: Yes.

VERONICA: No.

CLAUDE: Interesting. I can't speak for Beth, but I'm getting that weird, left field kinda feeling. Like maybe a ball might sail my way, but the rest of the team seems to be doing so nicely without me.

VERONICA: You can go to the museum tomorrow to see the Lippis.

JUSTUS: From one until four.

VERONICA: *(To Beth.)* Maybe you could join him.

CLAUDE: It closes at four?

BETH: I'm really not very interested. Justus, I think I don't feel much like dinner.

JUSTUS: But the *osso buco*...

CLAUDE: Four until six-thirty is a long time. Veronica.

VERONICA: Yes.

BETH: I don't care about *osso buco*.

JUSTUS: That's not so. It's your favorite, and I'm sure if our Waiter recommends it, you'll love it.

CLAUDE: *(Beat.)* I'm waiting for that fly ball.

BETH: I have a headache.

JUSTUS: Don't you have aspirin? *(To others.)* She's prone to headaches. Lots of headachy people in her family. *(To Beth.)* Food will make it go away.

CLAUDE: Maybe she wants to go to her room.

VERONICA: *(To Beth.)* This waiter really knows his stuff. Waitering is a true profession in this country, not actors or college students waiting to become something else. We found him to be something of a scholar.

BETH: We?

JUSTUS: He's a treasure chest...filled to the brim with insights. Probably *does* know just the thing for headaches.

BETH: *(Dully.)* I don't think...

CLAUDE: *(To Veronica.)* Will I wait all night, you think?

JUSTUS: *(To Claude and Veronica.)* On the other hand, it has been a long day, and we seem to be tired, and you seem to be...interrupted, so...

(Waiter arrives with covered silver dishes on a trolley, just as Beth pushes her chair back. The trolley traps her. She exchanges a long, locked glance with Waiter.)

WAITER: *Eccoci.* Dinner, as Americans say.

(Beth caves, pulls her chair back to the table.)

Patience is a virtue, and I can see you are abundant in it. It is very European to understand the beauty of waiting. Un-American, at the same time. *(He deftly uses a spoon and fork in one hand to dish up Beth first.)* Food is comfortable. Like a good pillow.

CLAUDE: *(To Waiter.)* Let me ask you, since you seem to know everything, what is so great about this meal?

VERONICA: *(Warning.)* Claude.

(Waiter shrugs, continues dishing.)

CLAUDE: No, I'm serious. Shin bones and rice. Big deal. I could get an Italian cookbook from any library and do this in my own kitchen.

JUSTUS: *(Nervous. To Waiter.)* Smells heavenly.

WAITER: It has to do with tradition, which has to do with waiting, which has to do with art.

VERONICA: Exactly.

CLAUDE: Oh, come on, Veronica, you can't buy into all this. *(To Waiter.)* What're you getting at?

WAITER: Earlier, Chef made a *gremolada.* When he was ready to sprinkle the sauce—the essential sauce—on the cooked veal, his nose wasn't pleased with the redolence. He went backwards, sniffing, each ingredient. He found the culprit in the anchovy, which he abruptly threw out, as well as the sauce. He thereupon checked his supply of anchovies until he found one to his liking, and began the process of the sauce once more.

CLAUDE: Boy, the veil's really lifted for me now.

JUSTUS: Michelangelo sculpted two Pietàs before he found the right piece of marble. Destroyed the other two. *(Tastes.)* Excellent. You see, the art of it is the patience. That's what he's trying to say. This meal wouldn't be the perfection it is if we had an actor as a chef.

CLAUDE: *(To Waiter.)* Is that right, has he got it?

WAITER: It is one possible interpretation.

CLAUDE: Gosh, thanks. Beth, what do you think.

BETH: I don't really know.

CLAUDE: Sure you do.

VERONICA: She has a headache; leave her alone.

JUSTUS: Well put.

BETH: I think…I think, if you're very lucky, there are assigned positions in life. You get to be something. Some people, most people, don't get to be something. Some get to be more than one thing, but not too often, and they're usually confused, anyway. Michelangelo got to be two things. Da Vinci got to be many things. The Chef got to be a Chef. I got to be an illuminator.

WAITER: I believe you all have everything you want right now. *(He disappears fast.)*

CLAUDE: The guy's quicksilver. Beth, you're saying, I think, that you do one thing and that suits you fine, is that it?

JUSTUS: She's always been very contented. She doesn't have a call to do anything but what she's doing, be anywhere but home.

VERONICA: I think that's the way to be.

CLAUDE: Really? You coulda fooled me. You always wanna be somewhere else. *(To Justus.)* She cried over a painting of Venice at the Getty Museum.

VERONICA: It was a Canaletto—the wedding ring ceremony where the Doge goes out on a huge boat, throws a gold ring into the Adriatic, marrying himself to the sea. So beautiful.

CLAUDE: Yeah, I know that's how *you* see it. You know what I see? The painting he didn't paint—about a split second after the old Doge-eroo turned his back. Two hundred and fifty wild-eyed Italians diving into that giant cesspool to get back the stupid ring. You get swept away by these things that mean zip. *(To Justus.)* You thought Veronica was Beth? They're nothing alike. Nothing.

JUSTUS: Maybe you're right.

CLAUDE: Or maybe you didn't think she was Beth. Maybe you just walked up to her and started talking.

JUSTUS: It was by accident.

CLAUDE: It's one possible interpretation.

VERONICA: You can ask the Waiter.

CLAUDE: I'm sure I can. I can also ask him for a sliver of the True Cross which I'm sure he'll produce along with a Certificate of Authenticity. Tell me Beth, do you peg our Waiter as an honest guy, one, say, you'd trust to babysit your newborn?

JUSTUS: We don't have a newborn.

CLAUDE: This is a "what if" question, Justus, and I was talking to your wife.

JUSTUS: I'm terribly sorry to have answered out of turn. *(To Veronica.)* Is he always like this?

VERONICA: I could say no, but…I won't.

BETH: I don't know the Waiter well enough to say. And…*(Drops eyes.)*…we don't have children.

VERONICA: Not everyone has to. That's the way it's presented to us, you know, through the media, like you're unnatural if you don't. Every once in a while, I admit, I wish I had one. A window into the future. *(She sighs.)*

JUSTUS: Beth doesn't want them. She's happy the way things are.

CLAUDE: And you're not.

VERONICA: He didn't say that. Why don't you eat, Claude.

CLAUDE: Yes he did. He implied.

VERONICA: I feel like all I do in Italy is eat and drink. I wonder what a great Tuscan dessert is.

JUSTUS: I would say Claude's is a good guess. What I like about Beth is she's rooted. Her mother died when she was two, and she's been the apple of Dad's eye since. My parents were so busy throwing dishes across the room at each other, they never noticed me. I've often wondered what it would be like to have parents who actually like you. Or even see you. *(To Beth.)* You're really lucky, you know.

CLAUDE: So you're jealous of Beth and her family.

VERONICA: *(Sotto.)* Supposition. And rude.

JUSTUS: I hope I didn't come across as jealous. Did I, Beth?

BETH: You compare a lot. I mean where there's no comparison.

JUSTUS: "Happy families are all alike; every unhappy family is unhappy in its own way."

(Veronica and Beth's lines run together.)

VERONICA: *Anna Karenina!* I love that novel too.

BETH: I'm saying it wrong.

CLAUDE: Guess nobody here read *The Boys of Summer* 'bout the Brooklyn Dodgers. *That* was a happy family.

JUSTUS: In point of fact, I was quoting the opening line—I can't say I loved the book. I wanted my family to be an "alike happy" family.

CLAUDE: Dodgers '55.

JUSTUS: Beth's, more exactly.

BETH: My father praises what I do. Everything. From ashtrays made at camp to opening a can of soup. It's nice to hear. But sometimes it gets hard. I mean. If I make mistakes, how will I know? What's the difference between succeeding and failing? How often have I disappointed him and not known? *(She bends her head—big speech for her. Pause.)*

JUSTUS: Really a high level of complaint, though. To be smothered in love versus being ignored.

VERONICA: We're upsetting Beth—she isn't touching her food.

JUSTUS: She has a small appetite.

CLAUDE: Beth's right here at the table—she can actually speak for herself.

BETH: It's okay.

JUSTUS: She's shy.

VERONICA: Yes. Very.

(Claude turns his head; contemplates.)

CLAUDE: Why do I keep thinking the Waiter should arrive about now and give us the meal-in-review.

(Waiter floats into view, napkin on arm.)

You're about one-tenth of a second late.

WAITER: How were your dinners? I see a dog box for the *Signora?*

(He nods in Beth's direction who shakes her head no.)

And now…for dessert. We have tonight *cenci*—fried lovers' knots.

CLAUDE: Nuts? Jesus. These people are as bad as the French—they use every part of the body.

VERONICA: They sound lovely. *Cappuccino,* please.

WAITER: *Un Cappuccino.* And, *forse,* compliments of the house, pink *grappa*—save *la signora* with the headache. Can I get you something special?

JUSTUS: She's tired.

VERONICA: She doesn't eat much.

BETH: I'll have a coke.

CLAUDE: Good!

(Waiter is about to disappear.)

Excuse me? Sir? *Signore?*

(Waiter moves in close.)

I've been wondering…

WAITER: *Signore?*

CLAUDE: Since you seem to know about patience and food and other things, I was hoping you could fill us in here…

WAITER: If I am able.

CLAUDE: Why do I think you are. Anyway, we've been having a little talk about a painter, 'scuse me, artist…

VERONICA: Fra Filippo Lippi.

CLAUDE: Right.

WAITER: A great master. Much underrated.

CLAUDE: You think we…*(Indicates Beth.)*…should check this guy out? My wife and her husband can't say enough about him.

WAITER: They are in possession of fine taste, then. The Frate holds an allure, both in his painting and in his life. As to your pilgrimage to the museum…It is up to you and *signora.*

CLAUDE: You think the story's true? He took up with a nun?

WAITER: These are simply myths, much embroidered over time. Who knows the truth?

BETH: A few hours ago, I never heard of Lippi.

CLAUDE: Bingo. All of a sudden, we're sitting here, talking about some freelance monk who slept with some nun, who interrupts my dinner, who I feel dumb not knowing.

BETH: I *miss* not knowing him.

JUSTUS: Beth, that's easily remedied.

VERONICA: Yes, I agree with Justus...

BETH: Like my mother. I don't have a true memory of her—just bits and pieces my father's told me. I don't miss her. I miss my father's version of her.

VERONICA: The museum opens at...

BETH: If I went, I wouldn't see the painter as you do. You both do.

JUSTUS: This is absurd. One marches oneself over to the museum and gleans what one will from Lippi.

WAITER: Or other artists. There are, in fact, many many others.

CLAUDE: It's like there's this hearing problem. *She doesn't want to.* Her mother died. The monk's dead, the nun's dead—it makes her feel...How does it make you feel?

BETH: Betrayed. Mixed up. Like one of those glass paperweights you shake and the snow swirls every which way...

CLAUDE: *(Indicating his stomach.)*...only it's trapped inside you; couldn't have said it better myself.

VERONICA: You could take antacid, then go see the paintings.

WAITER: *(Overlapping Veronica's line; to Claude.)* Perhaps *un'acqua minerale frizzante* for signore? Or something else? I have a very large pantry.

CLAUDE: I don't think you stock peace on your shelves, do you? 'Cause that's what I want. People want to live near the beach. Not me. Ocean's churning all the time, makes me tense. I want to watch guys on TV play games that last a certain amount of time, and I want it to be snowing, and the fire to be going, and maybe I'm thinking about getting a dog, calling him Rex, a big one with good digestion, so I don't have to worry about the vet or listen to Rex's stomach grumble. Since you mentioned this monk, *my* stomach's been at it. Even his name, Lippi, sounds like trouble. I don't want to see any of his damn paintings—I'm already tight in the gut. The monk dude was real comfortable losing control. That's not me. Not me. You go see your paintings, Veronica, see all you want. Just don't make me have to see them. Okay? *(He turns to Waiter.)* So hold the mineral water. And thanks. Thanks a lot. *(He takes lire from his wallet, hands it, folded, to Waiter.)* All of you.

(Waiter accepts the money. Claude pushes his chair back, leaves. Veronica waits a beat, then follows after him. Beth, Justus, and Waiter watch them a few beats.)

WAITER: I believe a cat would be best for him. Not noisy or demanding. *(Reconsidering.)* Eppur si muove.

JUSTUS: Beg pardon?

WAITER: What Galileo said to his Inquisitors when forced to swear the earth stood still: "Nevertheless, it *does* move."

JUSTUS: *(Struck by this.)* Yes it does, it surely does.

BETH: If you'll excuse me…

(She stands. Justus does, too.)

WAITER: I have not attended to your order.

JUSTUS: But you have. *(He takes out a wad of lire, hands it to Waiter. Then he sticks out his hand, pumps Waiter's arm.)* It does move. Nevertheless. Yes.

(A light comes up on a double bed. Claude moves closer to the weak reading lamp. Veronica enters, wearing a peignoir. She moves to the bed, stopping about a foot away.)

VERONICA: You look like a model. White sheets, starched PJs. As if *Life* Magazine were coming to take your picture. *(Pause. Broaching the subject.)* About dinner…

CLAUDE: *(Ignoring.)* I can rumple them. I can rip the sleeves off in a single motion—the Incredible Hulk.

VERONICA: No. I meant…it was a compliment.

(He considers this, nods, goes back to his book. She moves a little closer.)

I can always count on you to look this way, very…nice. Neat. And clean. *(Pause.)* My remark about the antacid was uncalled for.

(Claude puts his book down, fiddles with the lamp.)

CLAUDE: Italians mustn't read in bed—I can't see a thing.

VERONICA: *(Sitting on the edge of the bed.)* For all the talk, I think the *osso buco* was unexceptional, really. If we bought the right pots, you and I could probably do it just as well. Together. Could be a lot of fun.

CLAUDE: Italians get A in Sheets, nice 'n' white, like when I was a kid. *(Launching into conspiracy theory.)* Yeah, maybe around the time Kennedy got shot. Sheets went to blue, then, then floral. God. Now they're www dot ugly.

VERONICA: We should've had dinner by ourselves. Claude.

CLAUDE: I've seen sheets with these big black and green and purple things, paisleys, giant one-celled animals come to crush the life outta you when you're asleep.

VERONICA: *(Deflated; she takes a step back.)* Sheets. *(She goes to the window.)*

CLAUDE: Just my own theory. What's your feeling about sheets?

VERONICA: Fra Lippi escaped from prison by cutting up sheets and making them into a ladder.

CLAUDE: I'll bet they were white.

VERONICA: But wasn't it…bold? Romantic? He did it to be near Lucrezia.

CLAUDE: Very impressive. A little nutso. He was probably restless, like you. Me, it's natural to be in bed. Ridiculous. People have heart attacks and strokes in their sleep—this hotel could collapse or go up in flames tonight—anything could happen…are we close to Vesuvius?…but I feel safe. You don't feel that way. When I watch you sleep, I get the feeling you'd like to be up, moving around.

VERONICA: I sleep. I'm not sentimental about it.

CLAUDE: What I want is to give you the sense I have of it. Settled. Nice.

VERONICA: Maybe I'll wash my hair.

CLAUDE: Shampoo used to smell better. Now it reminds me of cough medicine from when I had croup.

VERONICA: Wonderful. Mine's supposed to be aroma therapy.

CLAUDE: God, that depresses me. It used to come in yellow and green, and after you washed, you'd smell it all day long. Probably had lead glaze and cyclamates, but you knew it did the trick, and you didn't get crazy going to the drug store. Now we have aisles of glop and aisles of after-glop that I'm convinced cause baldness. Or leprosy. Maybe both.

VERONICA: You seem to have made a study of shampoos. And sheets.

CLAUDE: I could go on. Shaving cream, for example. We could be having fun, reviewing *The Baseball Encyclopedia,* but instead, we stand under ugly fluorescent bulbs in mile-long aisles, reading, searching for answers in tiny print on plastic tubes. Doesn't it make you feel…weirded out?

VERONICA: I don't like to think much about things like that. I just kind of reach for one and don't let it get to me.

CLAUDE: *(Taking the covers off.)* That's the way to do it. Wanna take a walk? We could cut up the sheets and drop down to the courtyard.

VERONICA: You're making fun of Fra.

CLAUDE: No. Okay, a little. You seem so caught up, like you have a crush on him. I admit—that was major league paranoid.

VERONICA: Maybe not. *(Beat.)* Know why lobsters come in different sizes?

CLAUDE: I'm sure there's a tie-in here.

VERONICA: They can't grow bigger and remain in their shells. So they slither out, go into deeper water. If they live through the experience, they grow new shells.

CLAUDE: Uh-huh. Gee. Interesting.

VERONICA: Lippi did that.

CLAUDE: Turned into a lobster.

VERONICA: *(Annoyed.)* Took a chance. Removed his habit. *(Small voice.)* Must've been scary.

CLAUDE: Guy who steals a nun doesn't strike me as Caspar Milquetoast.

VERONICA: But a man obsessed is not in complete control. Can you imagine a passion so great, that one day you just…act on it? Violate your vows, put everything at risk?

CLAUDE: No.

VERONICA: Never?

CLAUDE: What's the question again?

VERONICA: Never mind.

CLAUDE: Are you asking about me or him. Lippi.

VERONICA: I was asking about…passion. If you ever feel that passionate about something, you just have to act on it?

CLAUDE: Definitely.

VERONICA: You do?

CLAUDE: All the time.

VERONICA: *(She comes forward again, hopeful.)* About?

CLAUDE: Well. Let me think. Huh. This isn't easy. I'm on the spot. Like reading all day in bed and only having to get up to eat.

VERONICA: That's lassitude.

CLAUDE: …Or here. Going on for Gretzky and scoring. That's a big one.

VERONICA: Fantasy.

CLAUDE: I mean, I have others. Uh…flying a plane in a dangerous situation. The Doug McClure movie where the flight crew and all the passengers get botulism from the chicken and he has to land the plane safely even though he's flashing back to napalm bombings over Nam—I loved that movie. Guy things, I guess, not things you'd probably like to do.

VERONICA: Very heroic things. *(She gets up, moves away.)*

CLAUDE: I'm sure I can come up with less heroic stuff. Tomorrow probably, when it's too late, and you're off somewhere, it'll pop into my head.

VERONICA: Not important.

CLAUDE: I got it, I got it. Passion. Okay, I had a dream last night—probably all the churches and crypts and crumpled bodies of saints—how can you stand that stuff? But anyway, we're in this church, and a bunch of people are staring down at us. I wanna ask you who the hell *are* they, but I realize I can't say shit—we're cement or marble, and we're on our backs on tombs. All of a sudden, I don't care I can't talk. It's restful. We can just lie there and be quiet together, and I'm suddenly so…*happy.*

VERONICA: How awful.

CLAUDE: No, you see, I knew you'd say that. But it was great, really great. Great place to be.

VERONICA: Dead.

CLAUDE: No. At peace with everything. And together. Not awful at all.

VERONICA: *Natura morta.*

(She moves towards the door. He moves down closer, almost reaching for her.)

CLAUDE: Where are you going?

VERONICA: Downstairs. For a breath.

CLAUDE: Okay. Not too long.

VERONICA: No.

CLAUDE: Maybe I'll come up with a really good passion by morning.

VERONICA: *(Opening door.)* Maybe.

(Click as door closes.)

(The sky darkens. A moon rises to bathe the caffè table in light. Veronica enters, goes to the view area, looking at the twinkling lights of a distant town. Her back is to the audience. In the shadow of the restaurant, Waiter watches, Claude's stilllife held behind his back.)

WAITER: The air is still. It will not be so tomorrow.

VERONICA: No? What will it be.

WAITER: *(Breathes in.)* Only the promise of change can I predict, not the conditions.

VERONICA: Neither can I.

WAITER: You are preoccupied.

VERONICA: How can you tell?

WAITER: You are in your night dress.

VERONICA: *(Realizing; clutching her robe shut.)* Oh yes.

WAITER: And you have forgotten something besides clothes. *(He produces the stilllife.)*

VERONICA: The painting. Thank you.

WAITER: May I take a look?

(She unwraps it, hands it to him. He looks at it, then her, then it. He frowns.)
It is very…unlike you.

VERONICA: How do you mean.

WAITER: Not like Frate's paintings, all flesh and blood and human life. I cannot see you in a pear and a fly. You lack, pardon me for saying, simplicity.

VERONICA: Thank you. I chose it for my husband.

WAITER: Not that *he* is simple.

VERONICA: Of course you didn't mean that.

WAITER: The fullness of Lippi's paintings, the rich subjects, the embracing of a life larger than a pear and a fly—that would be more you. And there exists some physical resemblance to Lucrezia.

VERONICA: No. Really?

WAITER: Lippi saw in her such diverse and ecstatic women as the Mother of God and Salome.

VERONICA: I'm not like them. I mean…so extreme.

WAITER: Not at all. But Lippi perceived in Lucrezia these many sides, these complexities. What a remarkable woman to have left the safety of the convent for the real world, no?

VERONICA: I don't know. I picture life in the convent for her as gray. Walls and floors, even her soul. She needed to leave, to sit in a bright meadow, to grind colors for Fra, to love him, bear his children.

WAITER: Ah! Then the palette became a full rainbow. Did it remain that way, outside? Or did her freedom eventually lose its rosy color, too.

VERONICA: I feel foolish, guessing things about Lucrezia. But if the images are true, she appears serene. It might've been a harder life, an earthier life, but I think a better one for her.

WAITER: I think it is a good guess. And I believe for Lippi, too, his life was more colorful, more rounded. Perhaps he would have been an insignificant painter, another drudge from the Middle Ages, had she not come into his life.

VERONICA: Maybe the Renaissance would've been delayed.

WAITER: True. Lucrezia was his breath of air. *(Quoting:)*
"Saints and saints and saints again.
I could not paint all night—
Ouf! I leaned out of window for fresh air."

VERONICA: He said that?

WAITER: The poet Browning said it. Like you, he was much moved by Lippi. In his poem, he imagined himself to be the artist inside his cubicle, bound in monastic robe, gasping for air.

VERONICA: Fra made a ladder. From sheets. Escaped out the window.

WAITER: For a time. So goes the story. By good fortune, we now have elevators…though not as dramatic an exit as bedsheets.

(Veronica shivers; holds her elbows.)

You are shivering. Do not allow me to detain you.

(She begins to walk off.)

Signora!

(She stops.)

WAITER: You have left behind the painting.

VERONICA: I keep forgetting. Good night.

WAITER: *Buona notte.*

(Veronica runs to the hotel next door. The caffè area goes dark.)

(Sun comes up behind the caffè area. As in Scene I, a woman sits with her back to the audience. Claude streaks in.)

CLAUDE: Veronica?

(Beth turns.)

BETH: There is a resemblance then. I'm flattered. Veronica's pretty.

(Claude runs his hand through his hair.)

CLAUDE: I don't know how to say this to you.

BETH: You don't have to. They're gone.

CLAUDE: Where? Wait. I bet Our Waiter, Mr. Shell Answer Man, knows. Hell, he probably set 'em up, took 'em on a tour: *(Imitate Waiter's Italian accent.)* See Sister Lucrezia's Convent. See where Frate, horny bastard, is buried. See the haystack where the couple rutted.

BETH: You're upset. Maybe you should sit.

(She stands, pushes a chair towards him. He reluctantly sits.)

CLAUDE: How did you know? For me, it was the undented pillow, the cold sheets. The still life. Shit. What the hell is happening here.

BETH: *(Squinting into the sun; a pause.)* I can't say. I have only his words to go by. *(Holds up a paper with filigreed border.)*

CLAUDE: What manners. Such beautiful paper to tell you good-bye.

BETH: It's mine. I mean, I illuminated it.

CLAUDE: Nice touch. Theft.

BETH: *(Reciting.)* "I've not been alive for some time. I've been in hibernation, waiting for my own personal Renaissance."

CLAUDE: *(Overlapping.)* Guy's certifiable.

BETH: *(Continues reading.)* "When you said in the caffè how you were homesick for California, it occurred to me that I'm not. Our life together there is easy, and, to be honest, I'm exhausted from it."

CLAUDE: He leaves 'cause he's *not* homesick? I'm getting a semiautomatic. I mean, don't you want to drill him or at least maim him in some meaningful area?

BETH: *(Ignoring Claude.)* I heard the door close—I knew Justus was leaving. I couldn't move. I couldn't breathe.

CLAUDE: *(Exploding.)* What do they expect us to do?

BETH: Nothing. We're spectators. They're in the movie, and we're in the audience, eating popcorn.

CLAUDE: I'm filing a missing persons. No, I'm calling the American Embassy, then I'm gonna have that museum closed down. I'm *not* gonna *sit* here and *take* it.

BETH: The travel agency opens in two hours. I'm changing my plane tickets. *(Corrects herself.)* Ticket.

(Silence. Waiter enters, stops as he sees them.)

WAITER: *(To himself / partly to audience.)* Si assomigliano come due gocce d'acqua.

CLAUDE: *(Sarcastically, to Beth.)* Oh this helps. Poetry.

WAITER: I observe that you are as two drops of water.

CLAUDE: Uh-huh. Swell.

WAITER: *(Trying again.)* Peas in the shell. *(Seeing they are too distraught to hear.)* I merely wanted to suggest that indoors would offer a shelter during breakfast…*(Still no response; he sniffs the air.)* Can you not smell the storm? *Allora.*

(He exits. Claude and Beth look lost. Black.)

(END OF ACT ONE.)

ACT II

A year and a half later. Caffè area. Waiter enters, carrying a vase with flowers. He places it just so on the table. He examines a leaf—plucks off an inchworm, puts it in a handkerchief.

WAITER: *(To worm.)* You could have been found by an artist who might paint you, a Janus who might worship you…or a poet who might write you an ode. *Peccato!* You have been found by a fussy waiter. *(Squeezes it. Sighs.)* My patrons will eat without seeing you. Have I done them a service? Or have

I altered the course of history by getting rid of you? No act has a single motive.

(Voices from off.)

WAITER: Or single consequence.

(He exits momentarily. Beth enters, fiddles absently with her handbag. She sits, tentatively at a table. Waiter reappears. Beth jumps up.)

Signora, so nice to see you again. Please sit. Will *Signore* be joining you?

BETH: Yes.

WAITER: Excellent. Shall I bring you, compliments of the house, our *benvenuto* cocktail?

BETH: No, I don't think we're going to stay. For lunch. It's too late for lunch, isn't it. For anything. Okay. Maybe just water.

WAITER: Water. *Subito.* Relax a moment, it is a glorious Spring day, no?

BETH: Yes. I hadn't really noticed.

WAITER: You have come from Milano?

BETH: Yes, this morning. Do I look jetlagged?

WAITER: Not at all. This is the time of day the train arrives from Milano. Some passengers have traveled a short distance. Others a very long distance, such as yourself, yet they all bear in their faces the strain of the city, even the airport.

BETH: *(She tries her Italian.)* I'll try the ben…the cocktail.

WAITER: Excellent.

(He exits. Beth takes out a lip gloss and a mirror, swipes her lips. She does not see Claude arrive and sit across from her.)

CLAUDE: Hi.

(Beth jumps, lets out a yipe.)

Sorry. We're all checked in, everything's set. Are you sure you're okay?

(She nods, smiles.)

We have good weather, that's good. A good omen. Or not. Should we have gone to a dude ranch in Montana and not come back to the scene of the crime?

BETH: My counselor says I need closure. It's prettier than I remember here. I'm fine.

CLAUDE: Yeah, well, closure looks like it's giving you a headache—did you see Our Waiter? He must know you have a headache and is already getting aspirin.

BETH: I saw him. He said I look strained and is bringing me a cocktail.

CLAUDE: This guy should be reported to Mothers Against Drunk Drivers, I mean, John Belushi woulda loved this guy, loved him. I wonder what I feel like having. Maybe he'll know.

BETH: He doesn't know, you know…you're you. I mean, who you're not. Justus.

CLAUDE: I hope you haven't placed big dollars on this, because Our Guy knows.

BETH: He had nothing to do with it—with them.

CLAUDE: Yeah. And Iago was really an altar boy having a bad moment when he dropped the handkerchief. Don't think Galileo didn't have a few jollies over this whole thing.

BETH: You sound bitter.

CLAUDE: No. I'm not, really. I wouldn't have met you. You know that. And I'm peaceful, very peaceful and at ease, like I never was before…When I think of it, I think we should've mailed them a thank-you note.

BETH: I couldn't keep up with their address changes.

CLAUDE: Uh-huh. Their artistic quest. What a lot of pompous bullshit, chasing around Europe to look at some dead fart's frescoes. Could you puke? Is that a reasonable thing for adults to do? Or ditching his job and sticking you with the gas and electric? Christ.

BETH: He knew I could manage. Why would he go back to that job or to California? He'd already turned the page in his life.

CLAUDE: You sound like you like him.

BETH: *(Blinking.)* Maybe I do. I have to think there was something about him I liked, otherwise my temples throb and I'll start thinking everything was my fault. Claude, I keep hoping Justus…all that…is behind me. Us.

CLAUDE: *(He takes her hand.)* I can't imagine anyone leaving you like that. When I think of it, it pisses me off. Royally.

BETH: I wish you would stop feeling that way. It doesn't do any good.

CLAUDE: Right again. You're so good at forgiveness.

BETH: I mean, if I feel angry, I'm the one who's angry, not you.

CLAUDE: Are you saying, wait a second, are you saying that you forgive Justus and Veronica and what happened—even though, deep down, you're pissed.

BETH: Angry.

CLAUDE: Crap. It took a trip to Italy for you to admit it.

BETH: I wouldn't be human.

CLAUDE: *(Impulsively shakes her shoulders.)* No, you wouldn't. You know what? I'm proud of you. I know it's hard for you to say what you just said.

BETH: I didn't say very much.

CLAUDE: That's just it. You don't have to say a lot, but what you do say makes me so fucking happy, I can't tell you.

BETH: *(Hesitant.)* What makes you happy.

CLAUDE: Rage, fury, blood, guts—it's so normal. I was wondering where you'd put it all. Don't get me wrong, I liked your calmness, the way you handled everything, including the American Express bills from their hotel in Prato and Munich and Florence and Spoleto, but it wasn't *right*, not saying what you felt. I kept thinking, when we were dating, you'd stand up one night, in the middle of Souplantation, and start screaming you'd like to tear his balls off and bronze them, mail them to his mother.

BETH: *(Smiling.)* It never occurred to me to be that mad at him.

CLAUDE: You don't think it was all Veronica's idea.

BETH: No.

CLAUDE: Veronica and Justus are twin hurricanes. All they leave behind is wreckage. FEMA should send us money.

BETH: I wish you'd told me this before we came all the way over here. I thought this was going to put an end to it, to smooth things over.

CLAUDE: Smooth things over! What are we, unruly cowlicks? We're settling scores. We're here to face 'em, look 'em in the eye, like they never did to us, tell 'em they stink on dry ice. Boy it's a good thing Veronica doesn't want kids, can you imagine what the two of them would produce? Judas Iscariot. Marge Schott. Artie Shaw—eight times he got married. I don't get it. Most married people don't cheat. I read that in Ann Landers or some-where. And the ones who do have the good grace to shut up about it and not shoot their mouths off to their spouses *on the very day they do it.*

BETH: You mean, you would prefer them to lie after they cheat?

CLAUDE: Put that way, I guess I'd have to say yes.

BETH: C'mon.

CLAUDE: No, really. We married total amoral sociopaths.

BETH: We're not married to them anymore.

CLAUDE: *(Sarcastic.)* We got lucky, what can I say.

BETH: I feel lucky. *(Pause.)* Do you?

CLAUDE: Where the hell is Our Waiter.

BETH: Claude?

CLAUDE: You know how I feel about you. *(He pats her hands.)* Holy shit. Here he comes, and he's got a humongous glass of pinkness.

WAITER: Ah! *Benvenuto.* It is my pleasure to greet you again. I took the liberty. *(He places an exotic drink before Claude, too.)*

CLAUDE: Thanks. So. Anything new in old Italy?

WAITER: We have had two harsh winters, during which time I indulged myself in reading many books. Might I offer my congratulations on your nuptials?

CLAUDE: I suppose somebody's already told you you're observant.

WAITER: *(Overlapping.)* Mille grazie.

CLAUDE: So. Huh. Many books. What was the most interesting thing you read.

WAITER: A difficult question—so many to recall.

CLAUDE: That's fine. We got a minute.

WAITER: Perhaps a magazine article regarding icebergs.

CLAUDE: Two miserable winters'll do it.

WAITER: But have you ever heard of *green* icebergs?

BETH: Are they real?

WAITER: The point, *precisamente*. In years past, people have reported seeing them in Antarctic waters. Scientists thought it a visual hallucination. Of course, now we find out there are, indeed, green icebergs. They soak up all the little green things in the water.

CLAUDE: Ah. Good to know.

WAITER: But it is only the bottoms that are green. The icebergs must become so rich with life, they are tipped over on their heads. Then their true colors are revealed. *(Pause.)* Shall I expect you for dinner?

CLAUDE: Expect away.

(Waiter exits.)

I wanna like the guy, I do.

BETH: I'd like to see a green iceberg, green and glistening against a blue sky— peaceful.

CLAUDE: Exposed.

BETH: We don't have to see them, you know. We can…send regrets. I'll illuminate the note. Or we can just slip away now.

CLAUDE: No way. We're seeing 'em. They invite us, we're here. C'mon, Beth, in your heart of hearts, don't you want to? And wouldn't it be good if they were slightly unhappy? Wouldn't it be nice if Justus still had a little thing for you and you could look at him and tell him you're happily married, that he blew the best thing that ever happened to him? Don't you feel that?

BETH: *(Low.)* No.

CLAUDE: Why?

BETH: Because it would never happen. I think he did what he had to. I'm feeling this drink.

CLAUDE: You're supposed to.

BETH: Well, okay. Maybe I'll finish it and order another.

CLAUDE: Okay. Don't you ever wonder, you know—in the middle of the night, driving down the freeway, or or or…smelling the red peppers at Ralph's— if he really, I mean *really* loved you?

BETH: When I was little, my father told me every day he loved me. He told me my mother loved me. I believed him. I went to school and teachers loved me. I believed them, too. I came to expect love.

(Pause.) I don't want to know that any of those people ever lied. It's better not knowing.

CLAUDE: I guess you're right. I'd like you to hate him, is all.

(She shakes her head.)

Yeah. Fantasy. It's okay. You can wish what you wish. *(Beat.)* Listen, I gotta walk, I gotta do something, I, uh, I don't know what, but I've gotta, you know…you wanna come?

BETH: *(Nodding.)* You go. I'll be…

CLAUDE: Okay. Long as you're…well, okay. *(He exits.)*

(Beth stands, crosses to view area, her back to audience. Justus enters.)

JUSTUS: You should always be framed thus.

(Beth turns.)

BETH: Hello.

JUSTUS: Ah! I could have watched you fondly without your ever knowing, but I broke the spell.

BETH: When did you get to town?

JUSTUS: Within the hour…we're barely settled in our room. *(He goes to her, brushes her cheek with a kiss.)* I understand congratulations are in order. Honestly, I'm not surprised. From what Veronica describes of Claude, you and he will make an excellent partnership…you have much in common. *(Pause.)* Actually, I was hoping to see you first. I want this to be as pleasant an evening as possible. Veronica seems to think Claude might get his back up about this or that, but I assured her that would not be the case with you. *(He takes an envelope from his pocket.)* The money we owe you. And then some.

(She doesn't take it.)

Beth, please. Take it. You deserve it.

BETH: It would be better if you gave it to both of us.

JUSTUS: Oh. All right. That's fine. *(Tucks it back in his jacket.)* I was merely trying to avoid any discomfort.

BETH: It's just that…

JUSTUS: *(Holding up his hand.)* No explanations necessary.

BETH: …we do things as a couple.

JUSTUS: Yes. That's very…is that a barbed comment? I don't seem to remember that was your style.

BETH: It's a fact.

JUSTUS: Yes, but it was delivered in such a way...The "we" had a certain ring to it. As if *we,* you and I, didn't. Or perhaps you mean Veronica and I don't do things properly as a couple like yourselves.

(She looks at him, turns back to the sunset.)

That was uncalled for. Excuse me. I suppose there was a smidgeon of jealousy involved. Consider it a compliment. I stand here next to you, and it all comes flooding back. I feel perfectly natural being your husband, and the fact that Claude is your husband doesn't seem right at all, yet there it is. Marriage is odd, isn't it? I mean, couples? Where did anyone get the notion we should pair off. Why not threes or fours. Or trades. But then we've done that, haven't we.

BETH: No, we didn't.

JUSTUS: In a manner of speaking. You needn't be so literal.

BETH: Don't criticize me.

JUSTUS: I was attempting to point out...never mind. Is Claude, how do I phrase this, working out?

BETH: *(Smiles.)* You make him sound like a charley horse.

JUSTUS: And you've picked up his snappy comebacks.

BETH: Then my counseling's paid off.

JUSTUS: Ah, so it's not an altogether paradisic relationship.

BETH: I talk to my counselor about being deserted. *(Beat.)* Claude is working out fine.

JUSTUS: Good. I'm glad you've adjusted. His sports don't bother you? Veronica said he was absent while present for hours at a stretch—a television junkie.

BETH: We're taking fencing lessons together.

JUSTUS: We had a chance to do that years ago. You refused. *(He regains composure, puts his hand on his heart.)* One to the old heart, eh?

BETH: I hadn't thought of it that way.

JUSTUS: No. Well. What a wonderful way to let loose your aggressions. I behaved so poorly last year. When I give in to those moments of worrying about you, Veronica says what tough moral fiber you're made of—that I should worry more about myself. You're looking at me like I'm a stranger.

BETH: You have some gray hairs.

JUSTUS: Thank you for noticing. I had taken to plucking them out, can you imagine the vanity, but Veronica said I was leaving them all over the sink, so I desisted.

BETH: Distinguished. Like your father.

JUSTUS: That bastard. How can you wish someone who's dead would die?

BETH: He had nice hair.

JUSTUS: Now I recognize the old Beth. Always remembering the good about people. Do you ever have evil thoughts, really ugly thoughts, wishing misfortune on friends and loved ones?

(She turns away.)

C'mon. You can tell me. I won't breathe a word.

BETH: It's one of those trick questions. I feel like I've flunked the test before I answer.

JUSTUS: I'm sorry. I guess most of us are not satisfied with truly "good" people.

(He reaches out, touches her arm. She shrinks.)

You're shivering.

BETH: There's a little breeze…

(He puts his hands on her shoulders, turns her.)

Justus…

JUSTUS: I never said a proper good-bye.

(He goes to kiss her, but she turns her head and slips from his embrace.)

BETH: You still haven't.

('Herod's Banquet,' by Lippi, is lowered, a bench slides in. A light shines from a window. Veronica enters, sits in a shaft of light, admiring the painting. Claude enters, observes her from a distance. Veronica stands, goes to the painting, touches it.)

CLAUDE: Is that the one? That started the whole thing?

VERONICA: Somehow, I just knew you'd come looking for me.

CLAUDE: Just a curious kinda guy. *Is* he the one?

VERONICA: It's an oil copy of a fresco Lippi painted in Prato Cathedral. And no.

CLAUDE: So only originals cause you to fall from grace.

VERONICA: You came to fight. I can understand that.

CLAUDE: No. I came to wish you a fond hello after our year and a half apart, and also to see if I'd dreamed you up. Ya know, nine years of marriage, sushi on Tuesday nights, weekly trips to Fluff'N'Fold, listening to our song occasionally. Or was it mine. Next, our dream trip to Italy. Where, as it turns out, you met the direct descendant of Erik the Red. How do you like your seal meat these days, scared or stunned?

VERONICA: *(Laughs.)* You were funniest when you were angry.

CLAUDE: I'm not angry.

VERONICA: No? You seem angry.

CLAUDE: Honest. I'm not. I'm happily remarried, as you know, still in my McJob, dusting other people's mother boards and disk drives for the last remaining moments before optical filaments the size of nose hairs replace them and I go back to community college to learn the fine points of vacuum-tweezing. No, I'm not angry. I'm vengeful.

VERONICA: Claude. I'm sorry. I truly am.

CLAUDE: *(Looking at painting.)* You look like her, you know.

VERONICA: You think?

CLAUDE: Absolutely. The face of serenity. But look at her. It's kind of a "What can I say? shit happens" look as she watches the chopped off head of St. John the Baptist being passed around like a canapé. Oops, your former profession, pardon me. But now you're a famous author and cutting radishes is far behind you.

VERONICA: How did you know it was John the Baptist.

CLAUDE: Thank you. His head's on a platter.

VERONICA: That was stupid. Of course you knew.

CLAUDE: My aren't we condescending.

VERONICA: *(Sighs.)* I think I'll go back to the hotel now to get ready for dinner, which I anticipate being...dinner. Do you have a nice room?

CLAUDE: Perfect. Looking out on olive trees. You talk like him.

VERONICA: I believe we have reservations for eight. We know you both like to go to bed early. *(She brushes past.)*

CLAUDE: Excuse me?

(She turns.)

Were we having a conversation?

VERONICA: Actually not. You were spying on me.

CLAUDE: I came to see if I'd missed something. About three months after you left, I woke up one morning and thought that people aren't knowable just because you live with them and love them.

VERONICA: I guess that's true.

CLAUDE: Would it have made a difference if I'd been a Lippi fan, if I'd used a lot of big words and Erik the Red was my great great great great great great whatever, if I'd watched less sports on T.V....I mean, would we be sniping at each other now?

VERONICA: How would Beth feel if she knew you were here.

CLAUDE: *(Moving close to her, shaking his finger.)* Don't, don't don't don't...do that. I'm asking. I think you should answer these questions, and I'm not doing it over some bullshit dinner where everyone's acting like everything is perfectly normal, and we're all good friends.

VERONICA: Stop pointing. I'll answer your questions. But I might not have the answers.

CLAUDE: Try. Tell me if you knew you were going to ditch me ahead of time.

VERONICA: I didn't and I did.

CLAUDE: Jesus, Veronica.

VERONICA: I didn't plan it. It wasn't specifically in my head to do anything except visit Italy.

CLAUDE: Enter the Viking. So it was pure lust.

VERONICA: No. Justus was a catalyst.

CLAUDE: Don't tell me you were channeling for Lucrezia.

VERONICA: A catalyst for my feelings, which I have had as long as I can remember. I've always loved fairy tales because the people in them keep being swept away. Circumstances beyond their control sweep them into another place. I'd like to ride in a race car, or sail through the air on the back of a great winged bird.

CLAUDE: So Justus mistook you for Beth, and you were half-packed, ready to take off with the first guy who…swooped low enough.

VERONICA: Your words, but something to that effect.

CLAUDE: It's so…shallow.

VERONICA: Which is, of course, why I wasn't able to tell you my feelings. You begin hurling accusations.

CLAUDE: You're right. You were always right, your most annoying habit, by the way.

VERONICA: Thank you.

CLAUDE: *(Smiles.)* So. Is the Nordic prince everything you imagined? *(Holds his arms out to the side, flying.)* Big enough wing span?

VERONICA: *(Smiles back.)* Adequate. He flies high and low.

CLAUDE: Uh-oh. I feel a baseball analogy coming on.

VERONICA: I'm rather nostalgic for them. Go right ahead.

CLAUDE: Does he have a fastball, a curve, *and* a changeup?

VERONICA: Is Beth better at sports than I am?

CLAUDE: Unh-uh. You answer first.

VERONICA: The first two. *(Beat.)* Your turn.

CLAUDE: Some sports.

VERONICA: Such as?

CLAUDE: Fencing.

(She laughs, disbelieving.)

Okay me again. Why didn't we ever find you a good shrink?

VERONICA: Nice. I'm baring my soul and you're suggesting I'm nuts.

CLAUDE: Listen, most people who want to fly off on the back of a big bird—I mean what bird is big enough to carry you, Veronica—it's not exactly normal. They have drugs to take care of all kinds of things.

VERONICA: Happiness? I'm fine the way I am.

CLAUDE: No you're not. You need something. I read that oxytocin, which causes birth contractions, is also good for monogamy. You can get shots.

VERONICA: *(Laughs.)* Claude! You're kidding, right?

CLAUDE: Yeah.

(He's half-serious. She laughs, leans her hand on his shoulder.)

No I'm not. It is absolutely true. The FDA has literature on it.

(He smiles. She hits his wrist.)

VERONICA: You really had me going. Shots.

CLAUDE: Yeah. Divorce lawyers would never let it be marketed. Can you imagine what it would do to business?

(Veronica puts her hand up, cups his cheek.)

VERONICA: Was the divorce hard, Claude?

CLAUDE: No, no. I had Beth. She was going through the same thing.

VERONICA: I'm glad. I mean, not glad, just...you know.

CLAUDE: Kind of like a low mark on a report card. A "D." Take this course again.

VERONICA: Aww. You were a good husband.

CLAUDE: Really? Wasn't I a pain in the ass? All that television?

VERONICA: It wasn't that bad. Well, it was. *(She laughs. Pause.)* Really. It wasn't *you.*

CLAUDE: I watch less now. I wear headphones when a really important game is on.

VERONICA: I'm glad you've worked something out.

CLAUDE: She does really beautiful work. Illumination. She's like one of those medieval monks. Not... *(Nods to painting.)*...him.

VERONICA: No, of course.

CLAUDE: She likes her quiet. I like it too.

VERONICA: So. She's been good for you. Good.

CLAUDE: No Sergio Franchi at top volume.

VERONICA: No, huh?

CLAUDE: Is Justus a Franchi fan?

VERONICA: We've been moving around so much, we don't really play music.

CLAUDE: So. A whole new place for you. Swept away.

VERONICA: Yes.

CLAUDE: You think you'll stay that way? Together?

VERONICA: Without drugs?

CLAUDE: Kinda restricting for you. Too many rules. *(Turns to painting.)* He didn't follow rules so good. Two bambinos.

VERONICA: You've been reading up.

CLAUDE: With the nun-wife.

VERONICA: He abhorred convention.

CLAUDE: Well, I'm a conventional guy. I just wish…If I were to do something, like wheel out a Ferrari or give you a ride on a rocket ship right now, would that excite you?

VERONICA: Yes. Would it excite you?

CLAUDE: Would you come back? I mean not necessarily to our old life, but to me?

VERONICA: I don't know. You asked me what excited me. It doesn't necessarily take a Ferrari.

CLAUDE: Or a medieval painting.

VERONICA: Or that.

CLAUDE: Or mistaken identity.

VERONICA: *(Moving closer to him.)* Or that either.

CLAUDE: *(Moving closer to her.)* What, then?

VERONICA: Ideas. *(Closer still.)* You.

CLAUDE: Beg pardon? I didn't get that…

VERONICA: But you did. Let me repeat. *(She moves close to his ear.)* You.

CLAUDE: Oh, Veronica. *(She kisses his neck, face. He doesn't stop her.)* I've missed this. Us.

VERONICA: I know. *(She walks around him in a tight circle, faces him.)* I read it on your face. I smell it on your skin.

CLAUDE: *(Breathes in.)* Smell what? I smell your perfume.

VERONICA: I don't wear perfume. You smell me. I smell you. *(Kisses his mouth lightly.)* Pheromones.
(He kisses back, then stops.)

CLAUDE: We're in a public place.

VERONICA: We can make it less public.

CLAUDE: *(Coming out of his haze.)* What're you saying? We'll go off somewhere, like you and Justus last year?
(She pulls away. Beat.)

VERONICA: Why did you come here today?

CLAUDE: No. I came to find out…

VERONICA: …if I deserted you on the most basic level, if I had lost my attraction to you. Well, rest easy. *(Pause.)* You're *very* desirable, Claude. And you're a hypocrite. You're shocked I make a pass at you, when that's exactly what you had in mind. Maybe if I'd let you make the first move, we could be enjoying ourselves.

CLAUDE: What about Justus? Wouldn't he know?

VERONICA: And wouldn't you just love *that*.

CLAUDE: No, I wouldn't.
(Veronica laughs.)

CLAUDE: I loved you. I—still do. I came to find out how come I can love two women at the same time. Something I'll just have to live with, I guess.

VERONICA: Only three percent of mammals are monogamous.

CLAUDE: Fine. Good to know ninety-seven percent live in torment like me.

VERONICA: *(Sad.)* I mean…it's perfectly natural to love two people at the same time.

CLAUDE: Or three. Or a dozen. Why put a limit on it. I can love the whole world if I fucking want to.

VERONICA: Yes you can.

CLAUDE: What do you mean?

VERONICA: I mean you can. Don't be strict with yourself.

CLAUDE: Somebody's got to.

(She shakes her head no. She exits, her shoes echoing down the hallway.)

(The light slightly shifts. Beth enters museum, sits on the bench. She looks at the painting for a long moment. She opens her purse, takes out a paper bag and puts it over her head. Waiter glides soundlessly in. He watches her a moment. He clears his throat. A startled Beth shouts inside the bag.)

WAITER: A thousand pardons, *Signora*. This is something I wished to have avoided. *(He takes her elbow, leads her to the bench. She continues to wear the bag. He looks at the painting.)* Is it the severed head?

BETH: No.

(Waiter gently pulls bag off.)

It's that no one seems to care. *(Points to painting.)* Look. That woman is dancing.

WAITER: She is Salome. It is her nature to dance.

BETH: It is?

WAITER: So legend has it. But you are quite right. It is a banquet in which no one seems to be paying close attention to anyone else. They have all come with separate and different agendas. How like life, no?

BETH: I shouldn't be here. I don't like museums. The people in the paintings seem to look at me. *(Shivers.)*

WAITER: What an interesting thought. The figures look at you. You see things with the pure eyes of a child.

BETH: I feel like a child. When I was three, my father took me to a department store. He had to use the restroom, told me to sit in a chair and wait. I waited. A half hour passed. I would've waited for him…forever. Some time later, he told me he'd forgotten where he'd told me to sit, and how frantic he was.

WAITER: As a child, *quindi,* you had no way of knowing if he'd return for you. *(She nods.)*

BETH: I still feel like that child, in that chair.

WAITER: You are grown.

BETH: Yes, only now it's worse. *(She turns directly to him.)* Claude still loves Veronica.

WAITER: Yes, I see. Love is complicated. Much like this painting, a later work of Frate. He deliberately juxtaposed the characters in it so they would form different relationships. Yet the piece is harmonious, do you agree?

BETH: I'm afraid.

WAITER: But you have nothing to fear.

BETH: It might happen, all over again.

WAITER: We might have a tornado or an earthquake. Anything might happen.

BETH: That's what I'm afraid of.

WAITER: *(Trying another tack.)* Your illumination, Frate's work, are fraught with intricacies and ambiguities. Love is no different. Its unexpectedness, its complications are the very qualities which endear us to it.

BETH: I thought I knew what love meant. My father loved me because I was his daughter. Justus loved me because I was satisfied with life. *(Choked.)* I don't know if Claude loves me. *(Points to painting.)* That man, with his head chopped off, was loved. He grew up, people loved him, or so he thought. Then one day. *(She makes a guillotine chop; she starts breathing heavily.)* How can that happen?

WAITER: This will not happen to you. I assure you.

BETH: It might. You said anything can happen.

WAITER: It's too Biblical, for one thing.

BETH: But it's how I feel…beheaded, unable to speak. People talk over and around me and somehow I'm not there at all. I don't matter.

WAITER: You're right, you know, you shouldn't go to museums. *(Pause. Calming.)* You have allowed yourself to love again. This is what counts.

BETH: I'd like very much to believe you.

WAITER: *Bene.* Perhaps you have heard the tale of the tortoise who meets a stranded scorpion. The tortoise gives the scorpion a ride on his back across a stream. The scorpion stings the tortoise. "How can you be so cruel and ungrateful to sting me?" asks the tortoise. Replies the scorpion "It is my nature to sting, your nature to trust. Why do you make me a villain and yourself valiant?"

BETH: I'm afraid I don't get it.

WAITER: It is your nature to trust. Some people, your husband, for example, will come to love you for this singular trait. *(He indicates paintings.)* Do not place so much emphasis on Biblical renderings. Paint on canvas, nothing more. *(He stands.)* Let us take a *cappuccino* break and you can describe to me your latest illumination project…*(He neatly folds her paper bag.)*…for which you will not need a breathing sack.

BETH: *(Standing.)* I don't mean to be valiant.

WAITER: Of course not. But you are.

(She takes one more gander at the painting, then walks toward the exit. Waiter stops, looks at Salome with a raised eyebrow. He follows Beth off.)

(Veronica and Justus enter, walk to view area near the caffè.)

JUSTUS: She was…the same. She looked the same. Quiet. Something nice about her lack of change.

VERONICA: What an odd thing to say.

JUSTUS: No, You can just rely on her to be Beth.

VERONICA: But why would you? It's the reason you left her.

JUSTUS: Is it? I don't think so. I was searching for something. Intensity. Your intensity.

VERONICA: I don't miss the past, any of it. You do. The routine you had with Beth. Even with your parents.

JUSTUS: I suppose. In some odd, abstruse way. Let's not make this into something.

VERONICA: I'm merely wondering why you harken back to those times I've heard you characterize as "numbing."

JUSTUS: I would characterize them that way still. But there's a kind of nostalgia in remembering them, like looking in a photo album.

VERONICA: You'd have it back?

JUSTUS: I would *not.* Observation of my past does not signify wanting it back. *(He closes in on her, takes her hand, kisses it.)* Do you remember the last line from *Anna Karenina*?

VERONICA: I saw you'd been reading that again.

JUSTUS: It goes: "My life now…every minute of it is no longer meaningless, as it was before, but it has an unquestionable meaning of the goodness which I have the power to put into it." It's as if the words were written by me.

VERONICA: You would've edited it.

JUSTUS: My. That *is* a compliment.

VERONICA: And true. You should reconsider Viking's offer—I'm sure the job is still there.

JUSTUS: *(Sweeps his arm.)* And give all this up? Seriously. I wouldn't dream of not being with you on this book tour.

(He grabs her hand, kisses it. She looks at him somberly, then over his shoulder.)

VERONICA: Our latecomers.

(Claude and Beth enter. The men shake hands. The women embrace, awkwardly. The men hold out chairs for the women.)

BETH: We're late. Sorry.

VERONICA: *(Animated.)* There are no clocks in Italy. I was just telling Justus about my phone call to New York—Helene, my agent—to whom I said 'no,' my book is not particularly filmic, why should I meet with a producer because he's Italian. I reminded Helene how special tonight's dinner is; no stranger could take precedence. That color suits you, Beth, doesn't it, Justus?

BETH: Thank you.

JUSTUS: *(Absently.)* Yes. *(To Veronica.)* Film rights could be very lucrative.

VERONICA: *(Smiling.)* That's not what my book's about, not what I'm about. And it won't be what the next book's about. Certainly you knew that, Justus. Claude, is that a new sports jacket?

CLAUDE: Yes. Ten years old.

JUSTUS: I could meet the producer. It's not right to snub people your agent recommends. And it might make her more willing to get a larger advance for your next project.

VERONICA: I said no. Categorically. I'm here to drink and breathe Italy in, to be reinspired, not listen to broken English from the producer of one of those incomprehensible movies about men on mopeds in downtown Milan. I'm starving, are you? I haven't seen Our Waiter yet. Does anyone actually know his name? Sometimes I think he's someone the four of us imagined, that he doesn't really exist. He's so mysterious.

BETH: He exists. I saw him.

CLAUDE: Yeah, we did. Gotta be Galileo. Or Dante.

JUSTUS: Whatever it is, he's not here. I think we should be getting this dinner under way. *(To Veronica.)* This is a career move. We have to be careful to think in the long-term.

VERONICA: Really, Justus, you're obsessing, it's not like you.

JUSTUS: *(To Beth.)* You see, if Hollywood wants to do it as a film, we'll all be on easy street.

CLAUDE: Film. I hate people who say 'film.' What's wrong with 'movie?' Why can't you talk like a guy from Newport Beach instead of Siskel and Ebert.

VERONICA: That's silly, Claude. There are 'film' festivals all over the world. 'Film' is a perfectly acceptable word.

JUSTUS: I'll say 'movie' then. I have nothing against the word 'movie.' *(To Beth.)* Where did you meet Our Waiter?

BETH: At the museum.

VERONICA: I thought you didn't like museums.

BETH: I don't. But I went, and he was there.

CLAUDE: And? Did you talk?

JUSTUS: It's most unlikely Beth would initiate a conversation. She's painfully shy.

CLAUDE: I also hate it when you do that.

VERONICA: Oh, but we all speak for Beth. It makes us nervous because she's so quiet.

JUSTUS: It's just that I know her so well.

CLAUDE: Not anymore.

JUSTUS: That might be, I grant you. Fencing—what a shock! And going to museums on her own, surely not something I picture her doing.

BETH: I went to see Lippi.

VERONICA: Now this is interesting. I'm surprised we didn't see you there.

JUSTUS: We?

VERONICA: Claude and I. We, too, bumped into one another.

JUSTUS: What a coincidence.

VERONICA: Yes it was.

CLAUDE: I wanted to know what the big noise was all about—what you two thought was so great about this guy you wrote a book on him.

VERONICA: Just doing his research. Very good, Claude.

CLAUDE: Could you please stop being breezy?

JUSTUS: She was being pleasant.

CLAUDE: I love how you two interpret each other. Do you ever have a normal conversation?

BETH: I didn't like the painting.

VERONICA: You're being tiresome, Claude. We were going to have a lovely dinner.

JUSTUS: By the looks of it, however, Our Waiter has forgotten our reservations. Did anyone check to see if the caffe's open? We should have chosen a better spot. Veronica, I simply don't want you to misstep. Aggravating your agent's a misstep. *(To others.)* Helene arranged a fairly extravagant promotional tour—we'd like to talk to you about it.

VERONICA: *(To Beth.)* You know, I'm interested in virtue. I've been reading about a saint, a woman, who was martyred in the 4th Century: Saint Ursula. Have you heard of her?

BETH: No, I can't say I know much about saints.

VERONICA: You strike me as…saintly.

CLAUDE: *(To Veronica.)* There's no reason to pick on Beth.

JUSTUS: *(Not listening, but to Claude.)* I think it's a misstep.

VERONICA: I'm being sincere. At first I thought it was her shyness, but I realize it's more…commitment. Ursula was that way, too, I think.

(Claude rolls his eyes; Veronica redirects to Beth.)

Ursula and her betrothed made a pilgrimage to Rome to get the Pope's blessing on their upcoming marriage. All went well until they stopped in Cologne on the voyage home. Ursula and her retinue of 11,000 maidens encountered The Hun. The leader requested her virtue. Ursula declined. They were all slaughtered.

CLAUDE: That's virtue for you. She took all her friends with her.

BETH: There's something very sad but pure about it. Do you think the story's true?

VERONICA: Could be. I'm thinking of writing a book.

CLAUDE: How big was the boat?

JUSTUS: *(Testy, to Claude.)* This is a *fascinating* topic.

CLAUDE: Oh, okay, I wasn't sure.

BETH: *(Looks at Claude.)* It would be something I might read.

VERONICA: Thank you. Thank you, Beth. *(Silence a moment.)* Justus, why don't you give them…you know. The check.

JUSTUS: *(He does an embarrassing drum roll on the table. He reaches inside his jacket pocket, slips the envelope across the table halfway.)* For you. *(To Veronica.)*

VERONICA: A belated wedding present.

JUSTUS: Yes. We wish both of you every happiness. And we thank you for being so gracious…to make *us*…*(He looks at Veronica.)*…possible.

(Claude shakes his head a little.)

We've got a few interviews—all low-key, PEN in New York, then one on the West Coast, followed by Michael Silverblatt on Book Worm—you're invited to all. Someone from the show will call you with the details. You can get time off from work, can't you, Claude?

CLAUDE: No. *(To Beth.)* We haven't talked about this. Is it okay? You'd tell me if you really wanted to do it, right?

JUSTUS: *(Irritated.)* We're talking highly regarded media people here. Silverblatt's call is the equivalent of literary knighthood—you are tapped but once. Did I tell you *A Renaissance Affair* got a quarter of a million printing in hard cover—that's not even beginning to approach what it'll be in paper and for, well, for a figure almost unprecedented in this economy. I know. I was offered a job by a publisher.

CLAUDE: Viking? Just a guess.

JUSTUS: *(Nods.)* Of course I turned it down. I couldn't possibly throw myself into that madness with your career just taking wing.

(Claude does a Big Bird swoop for Veronica.)

(To others.) You see, Veronica's book is very special in that it's both literary *and* commercial. She's riding a big wave, and I believe, I *know* we should all support her. *(Changes tactic.)* With you two on the publicity tour, I know our project will be a smash.

VERONICA: What he means is you two are an important part of this. In fact, you two actually tied the knot, so, in essence, you are the bigger part of the love story—the whole reason for the book.

JUSTUS: Bigger part? Unfortunate comparative, Veronica.

CLAUDE: No.

VERONICA: Look. We know there's still some animosity about the way we handled things last year. But look at you two. You're a beautiful couple, a matched set. The outcome, in a sense, warranted our actions. Let's celebrate together. The four of us.

JUSTUS: Which is pretty damned generous since she wrote the book...

VERONICA: *(Interrupting his hostility.)*...You were an inspired editor. *(To Claude.)* I understand your anger, but here's a chance to set things right again.

(Claude smolders; to Beth.)

Call it recompense. Call it what you deserve. It's money you should have.

BETH: The book's about us?

VERONICA: About lovers. Passion. *(To Claude.)* Didn't you read Kirkus? Justus sent the review.

BETH: No. It's about us?

VERONICA: Yes, yes, of course it's about us. The whole account: How Justus and I met, our affair with Lippi then with each other, then eventually, how you two fell under the spell. The embers of 90s sexuality is fanned by a story of a wayward monk. It's really damn good reading. *(Shrugs; to Justus.)* It's not necessary they be interviewed. We'll respect their privacy. That's what they want. *(To Claude, dripping with acid.)* And only getting up to have meals. How's that working out?

JUSTUS: *(To Beth and Claude.)* Wait a minute. Are you saying no? Just like that? We work and you reap the rewards including a gratis trip to Italy?

CLAUDE: *(Leaning over the table.)* I'm saying if you don't stop using words like 'gratis' I'm gonna pound your nose into veal scaloppini.

JUSTUS: I'm sorry for you, Beth, though it was your decision and your decision alone to take up with him. God knows, if you'd asked me, I would have warned you off. The stories Veronica's told me...

BETH: *(Interrupting.)* I didn't ask you.

(Veronica laughs.)

VERONICA: The purpose of this reunion isn't short-temperedness.

BETH: No; it's closure.

JUSTUS: Oh, God spare us your psychobabble.

CLAUDE: Don't talk to my wife that way, you two-timing, stuffed-shirt...*janitor.* You have no more morals than she does.

(Indicates Veronica. Justus jumps up.)

VERONICA: Sit down, Justus.

JUSTUS: That's enough!

VERONICA: *(To Claude.)* My morals seemed to suit you for nine years.

(Waiter cruises in, bearing an exotic drink, decorated with an Italian or Papal flag. He's speaking.)

WAITER: I hope I have given you enough time to reacquaint yourselves.

(He hands Justus a drink at about the same moment Justus looks like he'd like to punch Claude's lights out. Instead, he takes the drink, quaffs it. Waiter watches with surprise. Then he dispenses other drinks.)

I have christened it the Fra Filippo. If Fra Angelico has a *liquore,* why not another for Frate?

CLAUDE: *(To himself.)* Oh boy. First we return to Lippi-land, then we get Mr. Boston and his familiar quotations.

JUSTUS: *(Somewhat calmed.)* Excellent. You're quite the inventor.

WAITER: I'm glad you approve. *(To Beth.)* Signora is better this evening?

BETH: I'm...better. Thank you for our talk. *(She smiles at Waiter.)*

(Claude and Waiter's following lines are spoken simultaneously.)

CLAUDE: The Italian Dr. Joyce Brothers, passing out advice in museums.

WAITER: *Parlato col placido sorriso dell'amor.*

CLAUDE: Huh boy.

JUSTUS: How euphonious. What did you say?

WAITER: *(To Beth.)* I look on her face and I think of a phrase from *Traviata*— "the calm smile of love."

(Waiter places a drink before Claude, holds one for himself.)

I wish to propose a toast. *(Pause.)* To fond desire.

CLAUDE: That's it.

(He bounds up, pops Waiter. Low giggle from Veronica.)

That felt good. *(He takes the check from the table, wads it up, stuffs it into Justus's pocket.)* See ya in the 'films,' Veronica.

(He reaches his hand out to Beth. She stands, takes his hand. They exit.)
JUSTUS: The man is a Neanderthal.
(Veronica helps Waiter to his feet. He smoothes his hair, drinks his drink.)
VERONICA: Really? I always thought he had a rustic polish.
WAITER: *Dulcis est desipere in loco.*
VERONICA: I understood the "sweet." What's the rest?
WAITER: I said, or rather, Horace said, "It is sweet to unbend on occasion."
VERONICA: Sweet to unbend. I'll commit that to memory.
JUSTUS: They don't come more generous than you, Sir.
(Waiter, rubbing his jaw, graciously nods.)

(A bed slides in. Beth climbs between the sheets. Claude enters from bathroom in his Brooks Brothers PJs holding an ice bag on his knuckles. He approaches, sits on the edge.)
CLAUDE: I need a lot of reassurance.
BETH: Okay.
CLAUDE: You need less.
BETH: I do?
CLAUDE: Don't you?
BETH: I think now, maybe less.
CLAUDE: Now?
BETH: Yes. As opposed to last week.
CLAUDE: You came on my account.
BETH: I came for me, too. I just didn't know it.
CLAUDE: So it's okay now. You're okay. I mean, even though I clocked Galileo.
BETH: There was something about it I enjoyed.
CLAUDE: Yeah? Huh.
BETH: Technically, I don't think you clocked him. You'd have to K.O. him, right?
CLAUDE: Right. You been watching fights? Wow. That's great, really, really...you know, I haven't got any idea why I did it. Fact is, I...kinda sorta like him. Anyway, I'm gonna apologize first thing. Some day you'll tell me what you talked about in the museum. Maybe. If you want. Never mind. It hadda be good.
(Pause. She twists her hair; he notices her neck.)
CLAUDE: Did I ever tell you...you have an honest, beautiful neck?
BETH: Thank you. Can necks be honest?
CLAUDE: Yours.

BETH: We talked about the future.

CLAUDE: Galileo has a crystal ball?

BETH: Sort of.

CLAUDE: So. What's the future like.

BETH: He said comfortable.

CLAUDE: Comfortable?

BETH: That's what he said.

CLAUDE: I love it. Don't have a clue what it means, do you?

BETH: I think he means without boulders. Our path.

CLAUDE: I'd like to make it that way for you.

BETH: You have.

CLAUDE: Thanks. Veronica got something right—you're saintly.

BETH: I'm not a saint. See? No halo.

CLAUDE: Sometimes, in the right light..

> *(She leans forward, kisses him.)*

BETH: What's wrong?

CLAUDE: *(Pause.)* I deliberately followed Veronica inside the museum.

BETH: Yes.

CLAUDE: I wanted…I don't know what I wanted. To see her.

BETH: Okay.

CLAUDE: I don't have to tell you, do I.

BETH: You can if you want.

CLAUDE: I mean…where was I when the marriage went south? It wasn't Justus. It coulda been anybody—woulda been somebody. I thought in terms of a duet kinda deal. Only the left hand was…a little off. *(This isn't direct enough. He elucidates.)* I…I…Listen. I loved her. *(Correcting himself.)* Love her. You wanna kill me? *(Beat.)* Veronica said only three percent of mammals are monogamous.

BETH: Egg-layers do better. Swans and eagles mate for life.

CLAUDE: So. We just learn to sprout feathers.

> *(Beth looks away.)*
>
> Sorry. Stupid. Stupid.

BETH: No. It's just—some of them must be so lonely. The mate dies. They have no second chance.

CLAUDE: Yeah. Boy, that's really…we do. We have that chance.

BETH: We do. I don't think we quite knew it when we took it. But it's worked out. Maybe fate.

CLAUDE: Maybe like Lippi and Lucrezia. Maybe we should read her stupid book.

BETH: I don't think we need to.

CLAUDE: Thanks. I really didn't feel like it. I'd like to be just like you.

BETH: You wouldn't be you. And I'd have no fencing partner.

CLAUDE: Good point. Beth.

BETH: Yes?

CLAUDE: You believe Galileo? It'll be the comfort thing for us?

BETH: I do.

CLAUDE: Me too. Even if egg-layers do better.

BETH: Oh. There's that, too, in the crystal ball.

CLAUDE: What, an egg?

BETH: So he says.

CLAUDE: Wow. I'm starting to appreciate this guy. Did he say when?

(She shakes her head 'no'.)

Huh. I guess it's up to us.

BETH: I guess.

(He reaches out a hand, she takes it. He kisses her knuckles. They look at each other a long beat, the possibility dawning. Bed pulls offstage.)

(Caffè. The sun moves into A.M. position. Waiter enters with fluted napkins, sets them on the table. He looks into the sky.)

WAITER: One wonders which arrives first, weather or circumstance. Does barometric pressure signal a change of heart, or the heart which has an effect on weather? Meteorology has long been a hobby of mine. Unpredictable, ungovernable. Like a precocious but adorable child.

(Justus rushes in. He and Waiter lock glances.)

JUSTUS: What have you to say?

WAITER: I do not entirely understand the question.

JUSTUS: You do. Tell me. Reach into that wellspring of Italian clichés. I am in need.

WAITER: *(Spreading his hands.)* Amor legge senza legge. Love rules without rules.

JUSTUS: *(Stamping; impatient.)* More specific. Tell me something.

WAITER: What might I possibly tell you that you don't know?

JUSTUS: Who I am, for one.

WAITER: You are you. You are a man in love.

JUSTUS: Yes. Like him. Like Lippi.

WAITER: Perhaps.

JUSTUS: *(Angry.)* I've grown to despise him. His simple robe and simple-minded desire, his overwhelming fixation on one person, his lack of constancy to his craft, his religious calling. He was self aggrandizing, you know. *(He laughs bitterly.)* Sounds like me.

WAITER: In one important respect, you are quite different. *(Pause.)* You are alive.

(Justus laughs, then the thought makes sense to him.)

JUSTUS: I'll look in the museum. I've got to find her.

(He runs off. Beth enters, from another direction, in a dress. She holds her elbows as if cold. Waiter approaches her.)

WAITER: I will help Signore who is struggling with luggage, no doubt.

(Waiter exits. Beth goes to the view area, feels the air for rain, turns her back to the audience. Justus reenters. He sees her, stops dead.)

JUSTUS: There you are. I've been looking uphill down dale—frantic, if you want to know.

(Beth turns. He reacts: The wind's gone out of him.)

JUSTUS: Beth.

BETH: I'm sorry.

JUSTUS: No, no, don't be sorry, please don't be sorry. She's not in the room. I went for a *Herald Tribune* and pastry, and by the time I came back…My God. Don't tell me Claude's gone.

BETH: *(Interrupting.)* Packing. Upstairs.

JUSTUS: You're sure.

BETH: I'm sure.

JUSTUS: Yes, I suppose so. He's not that adventurous, sorry to say. But he did the smart thing marrying you. He had the guts for that.

BETH: You and Veronica never married.

JUSTUS: *(Shakes his head.)* We agreed it would subtract from the thrill. How ludicrous. What thrill am I experiencing right this moment. *(Shifts.)* Oh Beth, I can't bear this. I can't lose her. Where has she gone.

BETH: I don't know.

JUSTUS: *(Desperate.)* You've got to help me. I have to find her. How come you're immune to this and I'm not? Why can't she be…why isn't she more like you? Why couldn't you be her?

BETH: Because I can't. I'm a wife. Veronica's a quest.

JUSTUS: I hate you for that. I truly do. You, you…with your fixed place in the universe. Nothing reaches you or touches you. You can't be her because you don't have the passion.

BETH: Maybe not.

JUSTUS: There, see? A perfect example of what I mean. *(Angrier.)* You haven't time for a quest.

BETH: I don't think you're allowed to guess anymore what I have time for.

JUSTUS: There it is. The Claude vocabulary. In no time at all, you two'll be twins, happy as clams.

BETH: The 'happy family' you used to want. You don't anymore?

JUSTUS: *(Anguished.)* Yes, of course. I have no concept what it is but I still want it. I didn't mean what I said before.

BETH: You're right in a way; I'm happy in my small universe. Veronica's keeps expanding.

JUSTUS: You know, don't you. Tell me where she is.

BETH: Why would I know.

JUSTUS: You know more than you say. You hide behind that great wall of shyness and quiet. Can't you see I'm in pain? Tell me where she is.

BETH: I don't know.

JUSTUS: You do! You're lying. She probably told Claude and he told you. Tell me. *(He grabs her wrist.)*

BETH: Justus!

JUSTUS: Help me.

> *(Pause.)*

BETH: She said...something about a new project, St. Ursula. Look in the library. Or bookstore.

JUSTUS: *(Dully.)* She could be anywhere.

BETH: Yes, she could.

JUSTUS: *(Covering his eyes.)* She's all I want.

BETH: Then go look for her.

JUSTUS: *(He nods.)* But if I can't find her?

BETH: You will.

JUSTUS: Yes. I will.

> *(He hesitates, exits. Beth remains. Waiter enters with Claude and suitcases on wheels.)*

CLAUDE: I can't believe you're helping me.

WAITER: Why should I not?

CLAUDE: Well...I slugged you.

WAITER: *È vero.* But I think better me than another. *(Pause.)* Your face is full with the happy anticipation of home.

CLAUDE: Really? What else is it full of?

WAITER: The future is as uncharted as the heavens.

CLAUDE: In the true spirit of Galileo.

BETH: We'd better say our *arrivedercis* now.

WAITER: *Arrivederci* is perhaps not the right word. The other couple will no doubt return to these hills, so for them, it is the correct closing word. But for you two, I see you contentedly in Hunting Beach, California, not here again.

CLAUDE: You must be right. You always are.

WAITER: Not always. That is a blessing. Life without surprise would be tiresome.

BETH: Would you be surprised if they got back together?

WAITER: Not at all. Actions tend to reproduce themselves.

CLAUDE: You're a pretty smart guy. *(Pause. He thinks.)* I've got one more question. *(Waiter shrugs "of course.")* About those icebergs, the green jobs. *(Beth loops her arm through Claude's.)*

WAITER: Ah yes. They are rare. Only a few are able to divulge their unique color.

CLAUDE: But we are. That's what you were saying.

WAITER: Your lives, like green icebergs, were turned upside down, and your true selves, your goodness is evident in your faces.

CLAUDE: Boy. That's a relief. I was worried I hadn't sucked up enough algae.

BETH: Claude. We'd better be going. *(Claude extends his hand. Waiter shakes it heartily. Waiter then kisses Beth's hand.)* 'Bye. Thank you.

CLAUDE: *(Overlapping Beth's good-bye.)* Yeah, thanks, for everything. 'Bye.

WAITER: *Buon viaggio.*

(Beth and Claude exit. Waiter watches them go.)

(The light dims; Waiter in suffused light looks after them. The process of removing his jacket, tie, cummerbund takes the same time as his final words.)

They look so nice, so well-dressed for the return voyage. The costume of pilgrims: a dress, a scarf, a bag carried on one shoulder, a coat for protection from the elements. But they dress not just for practicality. They dress because they are ready—ready to conceal their secrets and to understand their own significance. *(His stature diminishes.)* For the brief journey. *(Light slowly dies as he exits. Black.)*

END OF PLAY

Sacrilege

Diane Shaffer

Dedicated to Jack Shaffer

ℬIOGRAPHY

Sacrilege marks Diane Shaffer's Broadway debut. As an actress, she has acted and sung in industrials, regional theatre, and off-off Broadway. She joined a group of street singers called "The Steinettes." The Steinettes appeared in the Robert Altman films *Popeye* and *Health* as well as commercials, television, radio, and nightclubs. She received a BFA from NYU School of the Arts and is a former member of the Actor's Studio Playwrights/Directors Unit. Alexander Cohen, producer of *Sacrilege* has optioned Diane's next play which explores the media's commercialization of suffering. She is eternally grateful to "The Holy One."

AUTHOR'S NOTE

In *Sacrilege,* the character of Sister Grace recounts an incident from the Gnostic Gospels: "The disciples asked Christ, 'What is the way? What is the place which we shall go?' Jesus answered, 'The place you can reach. Stand there.' I wrote this play as a direct challenge to those men of the Vatican who would dare presume to limit a woman's reach.

I chose my first holy communion picture for the cover of this book because it captures my "age of innocence," when I believed with a full heart, mind, and soul that the Church was unquestionably perfect.

ORIGINAL PRODUCTION:

Sacrilege was first produced at the Stamford Center for the Arts before moving to the Belasco Theatre in N.Y. It was directed by Don Scardino with the following cast:

Sister Grace	Ellen Burstyn
Crackerjack	Brian Tarantina
Ramon	Giancarlo Esposito
Sister Joseph	Jane Cecil
Father Jerome	Damian Young
Cardinal King	Herb Foster
Sister Virgilia	Augusta Dabney
Bishop Foley	Reno Roop
Monsignor Frigerio	Frank Raiter

CHARACTERS

SISTER GRACE: Sister of Charity Catholic nun. Founder and Director of th Houston Street Crisis Center. Mid-fifties. Cropped silver hair dusted with remnants of obstinate blonde. Her indomitable determination bestows blessings and trials on whoever or whatever she encounters. The reach of her heart, mind, and soul is immeasurable.

RAMON: Thirty-ish. Hispanic. Small and wiry. Underneath his macho exterior is a gentle, sensitive man empowered by his victory over heartbreak and homelessness.

CARDINAL KING: Head of the Sacred College of Cardinals which places him second only to the Pope in the hierarchy of the Catholic Church. Late sixties. Radiant with the glow of the good life. Handles people and events with the relentless diplomacy of a politician.

CRACKERJACK: Thirty-ish. Amiable Washington Square Park drug pusher. Self-destructed in Frisco years ago. Fled to New York City to make good and return in glory.

SISTER VIRGILIA: Sister of Charity Catholic nun. Seventy-five. Nosy. Cantankerous. God's policewoman.

SISTER JOSEPH: Carmelite nun. Late seventies to eighty. An unsung heroine. A true "foot soldier of God."

FATHER JEROME: Public relations liaison for the Vatican Embassy. Mid to late thirties. Ambitious. Ingratiating.

BISHOP FOLEY: Works for Vatican Embassy disseminating Vatican pronouncements to American clergy. Canon lawyer. Austere. Nervous. Direct. Precise. Fifty-ish.

MONSIGNOR FRIGERIO: Canon lawyer. Sixty. Bemused.

SETTING

The action of the play takes place over the last six years in and around New York City and Washington, D.C.

SACRILEGE

ACT I
Scene I

New York City, six years ago. Washington Square Park. Stage right are chess boards, benches. Early spring morning. A turbulent sky. We hear "Glory to God in the Highest" from Handel's Messiah loudly playing. Sister Grace, in scarlet sweat suit, is immersed in her daily T'ai Chi practice. A simple wooden cross on a black cord hangs around her neck. A worn knapsack is on the ground beside her. Grace is unaware that Crackerjack and Ramon have just entered.

CRACKERJACK: *(To offstage passerby.)* Smoke, smoke, my friend. Smoke. Best cess in the park. Check it out...herb...fine herb...babe...
   (Crackerjack and Ramon spot Grace. Jolted, Ramon stops.)
CRACKERJACK: Eh my man...you look like you 'bout ready to jump track. What's up?
RAMON: That's a nun.
CRACKERJACK: There goes the neighborhood.
RAMON: She's out here every fuckin' day.
CRACKERJACK: I swear...damn parks ain't even safe no more. Gotta get back to Frisco, man. Frisco's where it's at. *(To offstage passerby.)* Excuse me, sir, can I sell you some rocket fuel this morning? Good for heart trouble. Yo captain...I gotta go build my empire, you understand? Lose the nun. She's tripping.
   (Ramon stealthily approaches behind Sister Grace. She senses his close proximity, but calmly continues her T'ai Chi. Ramon reaches for the knapsack but is sidetracked by the books.)
CRACKERJACK: What the fuck you doing!
   (Ramon rustles through books. Ransacks the knapsack pulling from it a sandwich, prayer book, etc.)
RAMON: Something I been wanting to do for a long time.
CRACKERJACK: Aw c'mon man. This ain't your thing.
RAMON: Where the hell's your money!
GRACE: Change purse. Side pocket. Just unsnap it.

CRACKERJACK: You'll have to excuse my friend here.

(Grace takes headphones off. Music stops.)

CRACKERJACK: He seems to have mistaken you for a nun. (Takes the sandwich) Really tripped his trigger. Sorry about that. Have a nice day. (To Ramon.) We're out of here.

GRACE: I am a nun.

CRACKERJACK: Shit. (Tosses sandwich back.) This here's a real nun, brother! You don't fuck with them!

RAMON: Well, they fucked with me.

CRACKERJACK: Of course they fucked with you! They fucked with everybody! That's their job! Nothing to be scared of, Sister. He's really a very nice person.

GRACE: I know.

CRACKERJACK: I never seen him do anything like this before. (Looking over Ramon's shoulder at contents of change purse.) You best give it up, Homes. You picked the wrong person to score some cash flow.

RAMON: (Taking what little money is there.) I know who I picked. Have a nice, long walk home, Sister. And don't come back. Comprende? I'd hate to see you get hurt.

GRACE: You're the one who gets hurt.

RAMON: Say what?

GRACE: That's why I'm giving you the money. So you don't hurt yourself.

(Crackerjack thinks this is hysterical.)

RAMON: Run that by me again.

GRACE: I'm giving you the money.

RAMON: You ain't giving me shit! I'm taking it!

GRACE: Sorry. I can't let you do that.

RAMON: Who's gonna stop me?

GRACE: I am.

RAMON: You are.

GRACE: Yeah.

CRACKERJACK: I like that. That's cute.

GRACE: Thank you.

RAMON: How you gonna stop me?

GRACE: Can't steal a gift, can you?

RAMON: Knock it off with that shit, already! You got a serious attitude problem, you know that? See this? See it? I just stole it!

GRACE: You're welcome.

CRACKERJACK: "You're welcome"…that's a classic…

RAMON: I ripped you the fuck off! You understand English? I don't thank you and you don't welcome me!

GRACE: *De nada.*

RAMON: You're crazy!

GRACE: So I'm told. But then I know a lot of crazy people. I consider myself very fortunate.

RAMON: Well, we know a lot of crazy people, too. Only we do more than just pray for them.

GRACE: We have something in common. So nice to finally meet you gentlemen. What are your names?

CRACKERJACK: My name is Crackerjack. That's Cracker-jack.

RAMON: You're steppin' in some really dangerous shit.

GRACE: I run the Houston Street Crisis Center. Why don't you guys come over?

CRACKERJACK: Crisis Center! Well, I sure hope it's a helluva *big* crisis center cuz this whole fuckin' town is in a crisis! You hear what I'm sayin' to ya? This whole world, man, is in a fuckin' crisis! Even *I* can figure that story out!

RAMON: Give it up, Cracker. She's a wolf in sheep's clothing.

(Ramon crosses to stage right, Crackerjack following. Lights up on chess boards, benches, railing. Grace watches Ramon set up board and begin a game with himself.)

CRACKERJACK: *(To a passerby.)* Twenty bucks the first game! What do you say, sir? Ten. O.K. Five. We'll go easy on you. You know, you look like a very busy entrepreneur. I can sympathize with that. Purple tops. Keep you going all day. Ground floor to the store.

(Man hurries away. Crackerjack scans sky.)

CRACKERJACK: Shit's gonna blow. Nobody's gonna stop.

GRACE: *(Crosses to chess board.)* We play for the umbrella.

RAMON: Aw man...

CRACKERJACK: This is a girl's umbrella.

GRACE: I know. C'mon. You like flowers, don't you?

RAMON: He'll sell it.

GRACE: If you win.

RAMON: If I win...

(Grace makes a compelling move. Ramon is intrigued. They play. Grace gives Crackerjack sandwich from knapsack. He offers Ramon half. Ramon refuses.)

GRACE: Why don't you stop by the Center tonight for a hot meal and a warm bed? *(Offers card to Ramon.)* This is my number and the address.

(Ramon doesn't acknowledge card. Amused, Crackerjack takes it. Ramon and Grace continue playing. She holds books from her knapsack out to him.)

GRACE: Here, take these. Please.

RAMON: You're distracting me!

GRACE: What's your name?

CRACKERJACK: His name is Ramon.

RAMON: Fuck you, man.

CRACKERJACK: I'm just bustin' your balls!

GRACE: Well, Ramon, whatever the Catholic Church took from you, I doubt you found it in my knapsack.

RAMON: You don't know what faith I am. Or was.

GRACE: Oh I can spot a lapsed Catholic a mile away. Just like you spotted me.

CRACKERJACK: ...ooooooooooohhhhhhh...

RAMON: You should mind you own fucking business.

GRACE: As soon as you start minding yours. You think I haven't noticed you watching me? Checkmate.

CRACKERJACK: *Whoa!*

(*Grace holds umbrella out to Ramon. Crackerjack takes it. Ramon puts Grace's money on the table.*)

RAMON: Take your money back.

GRACE: It was a gift.

RAMON: But you won.

GRACE: I wasn't playing for the money.

RAMON: You gonna take it back or do I make you take it back?

GRACE: That supposed to scare me?

CRACKERJACK: Yeah, you ain't too good at this gangsta shit, Ray.

GRACE: I'm here every morning. I'd appreciate it if you'd come a little earlier tomorrow as I can't be late for my hospital rounds. I'll leave the books right there. I didn't give them to you, O.K.? We'll just pretend you stole them. *Via con Dios.*

RAMON: Hey! Who the hell are you, anyway?

GRACE: Aaahhh...the soul stirs. Sister Grace. But if the "Sister" makes you uncomfortable, just call me "Grace." Ramon. Thank you.

(*When neither Grace or Ramon take the money, Crackerjack pockets it. Grace puts headphones back on. "Glory to God in the Highest" resumes. Begins her exit. She looks to the darkened sky. Ramon picks up the books. Quickly becomes absorbed in them. Crackerjack follows Grace offstage where last bit of dialogue is heard.*)

CRACKERJACK: You know what you need, Sister? A chess agent. We go 50/50. You wouldn't be gamblin' cuz you'd give your money to the church, right? We'll do lunch! (*Crackerjack re-enters.*) What do you think, Homes? We cut her in. I could get ten fucking games goin' at once, man! We could capitalize on the nun aspect. I mean...that's different! Eh! Eh, my man! Is that not fucking brilliant or what! Hunh? O.K...like somethin's goin' down and you ain't talkin'.

N: Nuthin' to talk about.

KERJACK: You're the man. C'mon. Let's go check out this Crisis Center thing. Score some chow. Probably a shithole. Eh! Let's go!

MON: No.

CRACKERJACK: I'm starving!

RAMON: You just had a sandwich!

CRACKERJACK: That was an appetizer.

RAMON: Nah, you go ahead.

CRACKERJACK: She's got your number, man. I think you should talk to her.

RAMON: *About what!*

CRACKERJACK: Forget it. I'll bring you something back. *(Tosses umbrella to Ramon.)* I don't want this fuckin' thing. *(Exits.)*

(Ramon knocks chess pieces off table with umbrella.)

(Transition.)

ACT I
Scene II

One week later. Meeting room at the Vatican Embassy in Washington D.C. Antique chair stands on an expensive Persian rug center stage. A graceful antique end table is beside chair. Father Jerome is seated. Enter Sister Joseph followed by Sister Grace who carries a stuffed manila folder.

SISTER JOSEPH: Sister Grace, I'd like you to meet Father Jerome, our public relations liaison. Father Jerome, this is Sister Grace.

FATHER: Good morning, Sister Grace! Welcome to the Embassy!

GRACE: Thank you, Father. I'm delighted to be here.

FATHER: My pleasure. I've heard so much about you. Seems every time I turn around your name is in the papers.

(Cardinal King enters.)

FATHER: I believe you're already acquainted with his Eminence Cardinal King from the Vatican?

GRACE: Yes, well acquainted. So nice to see you again, Cardinal King.

KING: Nice to see you too, Sister. Sorry we kept you waiting so long.

GRACE: Patience is a virtue at which I'm forced to excel.

KING: Please have a seat.

GRACE: Thank you.

KING: May we get you a cup of tea?

GRACE: I'd love a cup.

FATHER: Sister Joseph?

(Sister Joseph exits.)

GRACE: Are you in Washington for this dialogue?

KING: Actually, I'm here on diplomatic assignments. His Holiness asked me to sit in on your discussion with Father Jerome.

GRACE: Well, that's hopeful.

FATHER: Cardinal King, you have a meeting at two.

KING: Oh yes…is it the Northern Ireland Ecumenical something or other?

FATHER: It's your golf game, sir.

KING: Oh. Well, we'd better cancel that. Let us pray: Holy Father in Heaven, we ask you to bestow your blessings upon us. Open our hearts and minds in the true spirit of reconciliation. Let us leave this gathering today with only one prayer on our lips: that we may serve You with a stronger and more fervent resolve. In the name of the Father and of the Son and of the Holy Spirit. Amen.

ALL: Amen.

KING: Sister, do you have a copy of the *Village Voice* with you?

GRACE: I don't see why I would need one.

KING: Father Jerome…

FATHER: Page forty-two.

GRACE: Pardon me, Cardinal, pardon me. I thought my Sisters from the Boston parishes were joining us. This was to be a dialogue about women in the Church. I don't understand.

FATHER: That was before your interview appeared in the *Village Voice*. We have every intention of rescheduling the Sisters of Boston at a later date. Cardinal King?

(Sister Joseph enters. Serves Grace tea. Touches Grace's hand. They exchange a smile.)

KING: This interview caused quite a stir in Rome. You still enjoy shaking things up, don't you?

GRACE: Excuse me, gentlemen, just one moment. Thank you, Sister Joseph. Thank you. I'm sorry. You were saying?

KING: His Holiness is deeply disturbed by this interview.

GRACE: The Pope actually read my interview?

KING: Yes. You'd be amazed at how many bishops and cardinals sent him copies.

GRACE: Then I'll bet he was disturbed.

FATHER: Excuse me. That will be all, Sister Joseph.

SISTER JOSEPH: Father, I was wondering if I might…em…if I may stay and listen to the…to the dialogue.

FATHER: Certainly not.

SISTER JOSEPH: Perhaps you'd like me to take notes…

FATHER: No, Sister, this is an informal meeting. You are excused.

SISTER JOSEPH: Thank you, Father Jerome. *(Sister Joseph exits.)*

KING: It's been brought to my attention that in the last five years, you've been called to meetings with your Provincial Superior, your Diocesan Chancellor and the Vicar for the Religious. At every one of these meetings, you've been formally reprimanded for expressing personal opinions in direct opposition to the Church. I have here in my hand a very recent, very controversial newspaper interview. I hope you have an explanation.

GRACE: The *Voice* has supported me ever since my initial association with Father Daniel Berrigan on the Viet Nam War protests. Remember?

KING: Like it was yesterday.

GRACE: They also covered our nuclear disarmament rally.

KING: We know.

GRACE: They asked Father Dan and me for interviews regarding the crisis in the American Catholic Church. We were both delighted to accept. I was told Father Berrigan would be here today.

FATHER: Father Berrigan was summoned to Rome.

GRACE: Just for the record, I'm hip to what's happening here. Okay. Go ahead.

FATHER: What do you mean?

GRACE: Isolate us so you can pick us off one by one.

FATHER: Let's not start off on the wrong foot, Sister Grace.

GRACE: Yes, let's not. What would you gentlemen like to ask me?

KING: Who gave you permission to do this interview on the problems of the American Catholic Church?

GRACE: The *crisis* in the American Catholic Church

KING: I stand corrected.

GRACE: I'm well aware that you've already had a lengthy phone conversation with Mother Superior about me. She told you I did ask her permission. She spent two days in solitude before concluding it was a matter my own conscience must decide. And may I add that she has not regretted granting me that freedom.

KING: Sister, would you agree that unity strengthens the Church and dissent weakens it?

GRACE: You're comparing me with Martin Luther. "Insubordination is the breakdown of the Church."

FATHER: Just answer the question, Sister.

GRACE: I'd like to ask you a question.

FATHER: As your host today, I must ask you to please cooperate.

GRACE: I've been cooperating for a lifetime.

KING: Please, feel free to ask anything you like.

GRACE: Thank you. I have spent an inordinate portion of my adult life studying official doctrine of the Church. I know my Bible inside and out. I spent countless hours in the library of Notre Dame University researching the Church's official stand on every issue conceivable. The only thing I could find in all those years of searching that God demands of me is that I love the Lord my God with my whole heart, my whole soul and with all my mind and that I love my neighbor as myself. All other commandments were created by man. Not woman. Man. You. I chose long ago to imitate Jesus Christ and live not according to the laws of men but according to the laws of God. I speak for many, granted not all my sisters, when I petition the Church for the entrance of women to the priesthood. I request an audience with His Holiness Pope John Paul II to present our grievances and beg his consideration. I've attempted to contact him many times but have always failed. So my question is, would you please give this message and petition to our most Holy Pope?

KING: Oh, the Pope has received your message. *(Reading from* Village Voice.) I quote you: "The men of the Vatican whose decisions rule our spiritual lives live isolated existences of privilege and power and are out of touch with the problems unique to American Catholic women." Then…you launch into a litany of Church sins: the Inquisition…the hoarding of enormous Church wealth…here we have Galileo…a little shadowy anti-Semitism… birth control…and let's not forget…the barring of women from the priesthood.

GRACE: Excuse me, but the rest of the article…you have to read the…

FATHER: We've read it.

GRACE: But you think I'm fighting against the Church. I'm…I'm not! I'm fighting within it. I love the Church. That's why I'm…

FATHER: Sister Grace, the Pope oversees one billion parishioners. It's not every day he sends an emissary to deliver a message to one of them.

KING: Our Holy Father has asked me to tell you that what you profess in your prayers is between you and God. What you profess in public is a matter to be taken into consideration by the Church as long as you are a member of that Church. You are creating dissent.

GRACE: I am not creating dissent! I am merely giving it a voice!

FATHER: And a rather loud one.

GRACE: Who will hear me if I whisper, Father?

FATHER: God.

GRACE: It's not God who isn't listening!

FATHER: Why don't we get you more tea?

GRACE: I don't need more tea!

KING: We have instructed your Mother Superior to discourage you from staging any more public rebellions, delivering commencement addresses to theology graduates and agitating your fellows nuns.

GRACE: Am I discouraged or forbidden?

KING: Discouraged.

FATHER: You took a vow of obedience.

GRACE: The vow of obedience can be and has been used as a convenient device to subjugate the people of the Church. But the fear of excommunication has held us hostage since the birth of organized religion. You've got us by the throat. Any challenge to your authority only tightens the grip.

FATHER: Even you will agree, Sister Grace, that in ruling any large body of people, a certain degree of authority is necessary to prevent anarchy. That is not intrinsically a bad thing. On the contrary, it is a very good thing.

GRACE: So is arsenic, in small doses.

FATHER: The sheep rely on their shepherd for guidance and sanctuary.

GRACE: Guidance and sanctuary can also be provided by a shepherdess.

FATHER: Jesus Christ was not a shepherdess.

GRACE: I believe the nature of God transcends the duality of sex, therefore Jesus Christ, being the perfect embodiment of God on earth, would also be transcendent of sex.

FATHER: Nevertheless, he was a man.

GRACE: A man who preached a spirituality characterized by what are traditionally considered feminine virtues: humility, patience, nonviolence, compassion for the poor.

FATHER: I think it would be far more productive to focus on the Church since that's what you seem to have a problem with. Cardinal King…would you like to…jump in here?

KING: No, no. You're doing just fine.

FATHER: Our masculine clergy represent Christ as father and bridegroom. The feminine is represented by the congregation as mother and bride. Polarities exist, Sister Grace. It's called nature. Why are we even talking about this?

GRACE: This is what I thought I was called here for.

KING: In any religion…in any spiritual discipline…there are certain mysteries that are indigenous to that particular belief system. Why did Christ resurrect Himself in three days instead of four? Why was He born in Israel instead of China or Egypt? These are fundamental mysteries that we'll never comprehend during our lives on earth.

GRACE: Are you insinuating that the reason you can be a priest and I can't is a fundamental mystery?

FATHER: Sister Grace, you're becoming tiresome.

GRACE: No, sir. What's tiresome is women being made to feel like intruders in their own home.

KING: Please excuse Father Jerome. He didn't mean to sound patronizing, did you, Father Jerome?

FATHER: Of course not. I'm so sorry, Sister Grace.

KING: Your tenacity is to be admired, as always.

GRACE: It has been a long time, hasn't it, Cardinal King? How much longer?

KING: The Church stands firm in its ruling to admit only men to the priesthood. We understand your position and deeply regret any suffering this may cause you. However, we feel it is against the will of God to rule otherwise.

GRACE: There is no formally declared doctrine stating that women can't be priests! Where is it? Show it to me.

FATHER: The Pope has decreed this subject closed to discussion.

GRACE: But how can we heal if we don't expose the wound?

FATHER: You'd heal if you stopped scratching it.

KING: Sister Grace, I'm sure the next time we meet will be under more agreeable circumstances.

FATHER: *(Indicating petition.)* You can leave that on the table.

GRACE: No. I think I'll...uhm...I prefer to...

KING: I will personally deliver your petition to His Holiness. In private.

GRACE: Thank you.

KING: *(Perusing petition.)* Very impressive.

GRACE: You'll notice there are a lot of men's names in there.

KING: I see.

GRACE: About seventy percent of all Catholics think women should be priests.

KING: I am aware of that. May I suggest you keep a low profile for awhile.

(Enter Sister Joseph.)

SISTER JOSEPH: Excuse me, just pretend I'm not even here.

(As Sister Joseph clears tea, lights fade to black on King, Father and Sister Joseph. After clearing tea, Sister Joseph exits. Father and King remain onstage. She both prays and remembers dialogue with clergy.)

GRACE: Was I clear? Was I kind?

FATHER: The Episcopalians now have a woman bishop. Perhaps you should consider your possibilities with the Episcopalians.

GRACE: If you want to put your house in order, you don't move next door.

FATHER: Are you sure we can't bring you more tea, Sister Grace?

GRACE: I failed. Again and again and again I failed.

FATHER: When we celebrate communion, we're recreating the Lord's Last Supper. I fail to see how using women to perform this sacrament would support its authenticity as women were not present at the Last Supper.

GRACE: No, they only served it.

KING: You are attempting to undermine the most fundamental principle that Peter built this Church upon 2,000 years ago: that the Catholic church is not affected by social, cultural or political trends. We are immune to time. As it was in the beginning, is now and ever shall be.

GRACE: Jesus, take my hand and lead me through this darkness.

KING: If we grant you ordination, what next? Abortion? Divorce?

FATHER: For thousands of years, there were no women priests.

GRACE: New archeological evidence has been discovered that proves beyond a shadow of a doubt that women served as priests in the early centuries of the Church.

FATHER: Conjecture.

KING: We're not here to make you happy. We're here to safeguard your soul.

GRACE: Why have you allowed this desire to grow in me if not for Your glory?

KING: Sister, may I give you a word of advice? Off the record?

GRACE: He advised me to re-direct my abundant energies to my daily vocation as a nun. And then he complimented me.

KING: Congratulations on your fine work at the Houston Street Crisis Center. I'm a little uncomfortable in admitting that you're an inspiration to me. You always have been.

GRACE: I inspire him. Off the record.

KING: Oh Sister…if there ever is a time…I hope you'll be the first.

GRACE: Beloved,

Forgive me my inadequacies

I know what's being asked of me.

And I don't have the words or thoughts or activities to drown out your voice any longer.

I accept.

Come my Lord…for I am ready.

(Transition.)

Act I

Scene III

One month later. The Houston Street Crisis Center. Sister Grace's office. Just before noon. Sister Grace's desk at one end of the room, statue of Mary at other end. In between is a beat-up end table with lamp and chess set on it. Elaborate phone system, but outdated PA system. Sister Grace is seated behind her desk. Sister Virgilia sits across from her.

VIRGILIA: I still don't see why I have to learn a computer! My 3x5 cards have worked just fine for years!

GRACE: Sister Virgilia, we now have over three thousand contributors.

VIRGILIA: So get bigger file cabinets! All this money we're throwing away on computers should go for new catechism books!

VOICE OVER PA SYSTEM: Security to the reception room, security to reception.

(Grace's phone rings. She pushes a button.)

GRACE: Yes?

VOICE ON PHONE SPEAKER: Sister Grace, Crackerjack's been in an accident. He and a friend are on their way to your office. I'm sorry, I couldn't keep them in reception.

GRACE: That's fine, Sister. No need for security. *(Pushes speaker phone off.)* What am I going to do with him?

VIRGILIA: Crackerjack's been trying to sell drugs in the food line again.

GRACE: I know. I'll handle it.

VIRGILIA: Good day, Sister Grace.

GRACE: Good day, Sister Virgilia.

(Virgilia exits. Offstage, we hear the following dialogue tumbling over itself.)

RAMON: *(Offstage.)* Where's her office?

VIRGILIA: *(Offstage.)* Young man, if you ever try to sell drugs in this soup kitchen again…

RAMON: *(Offstage.)* Get out of the way!

(Enter Ramon, distraught. He half carries, half drags a doped-up Crackerjack. Crackerjack has a blood soaked T-shirt tied around his head. Sister Virgilia peers in after them.)

CRACKERJACK: I'm workin' undercover, Sister.

VIRGILIA: What trouble have you gotten yourself into this time!

GRACE: *(Rushes to help Crackerjack to a chair.)* Oh my God, what happened!

CRACKERJACK: All I did was tell this great Spic joke.

GRACE: Yeah, who'd you tell it to!

CRACKERJACK: Spics. *(To Ramon.)* You ain't a Spic. You'se a brother.

RAMON: You just sit tight, my man…

CRACKERJACK: *(To Grace.)* You'se a brother, too, Sister.

GRACE: Gee, thanks. *(Putting surgical gloves on. Gingerly unwraps T-shirt from around Crackerjack's head.)* All right now, Crackerjack, I'm just going to take a look at your head, O.K.? I'll be very careful…

CRACKERJACK: Everything's copasetic.

RAMON: He said they hit him with some kind of pipe.

GRACE: When was the last time you had a tetanus shot?

RAMON: Look at the fuckin' guy, man! He never had a tetanus shot in his life! What the fuck is wrong with you!

GRACE: Take it easy!

RAMON: Well, hurry up!

GRACE: Will you please calm down?

RAMON: He's hurtin', man!

CRACKERJACK: I don't feel a fuckin' thing.

> *(Virgilia dashes out.)*

GRACE: *(Taking his pulse.)* What did you take, Crackerjack? Some reds? Did you take some reds today?

RAMON: What difference does it make!

GRACE: It might make a very big difference. First, we've gotta stop the bleeding. Here, put these on.

RAMON: He doesn't mainline, O.K.?

GRACE: Look, don't give me a hard time.

RAMON: We gonna help this guy or waste time with this bullshit!

CRACKERJACK: Put them on!

> *(Ramon puts on gloves.)*

GRACE: Two deep gashes, but…he looks O.K. to me. You got a hard head, Crackerjack! Hold this. Right here. No, you have to press. Good. *(Grace works other head wound.)*

RAMON: So what do you think?

GRACE: I think he's going to be O.K. but he still needs X-rays.

RAMON: I'll take him.

GRACE: How do you feel?

CRACKERJACK: Huh?

GRACE: You dizzy?

CRACKERJACK: Yeah…your picture's comin' in a little fuzzy.

GRACE: All right, Ramon, hold these just like this…no, press…*press.* You won't hurt him. I'll be right back.

RAMON: Hurry up.

(Grace exits. Crackerjack chuckles to himself.)

VOICE OVER PA: Attention please: Volunteers are needed for the clothing drive. Anyone with access to a car, *legitimate* access to a car, please contact Sister Seraphita by Friday. We need all the help we can get. Thank you.

RAMON: This place is a fuckin' zoo.

CRACKERJACK: I told you I'd get you in here, didn't I? One way or another.

RAMON: Hey, if I knew you wanted me to come that bad...

CRACKERJACK: I just figured you might get off on their tuna surprise.

RAMON: If you say so.

CRACKERJACK: I fucked up again.

RAMON: Don't worry about it.

CRACKERJACK: Yeah, but this shit's gettin' chronic, man. Gotta get back to Frisco. Best three days of my life. I don't remember any of it.

RAMON: We'll get you there.

CRACKERJACK: Hey thanks, man. Really. I'm not just yankin' your chain or anything. *Gracias.*

RAMON: *De nada.*

(Grace bustles in with bandages. Starts work on Crackerjack.)

GRACE: How we doing?

RAMON: Bleeding hasn't stopped.

GRACE: Crackerjack, if you're gonna keep screwin' around like this, you're going to need more protection.

CRACKERJACK: I got me some protection.

GRACE: When was the last time you called your guardian angel?

CRACKERJACK: *Ruben!* Damn! I ain't seen him since I was a kid!

GRACE: Ruben?

CRACKERJACK: He'd come see me late at night. He had this great big fuckin' halo, man. And he'd raise his wings and shake his head so all these millions of lights would go scrambling all over the wall. Cracked me up.

GRACE: Maybe it's time you two got together again.

CRACKERJACK: Ah yeah. Ruben.

GRACE: You know, Christ has a pretty good track record.

CRACKERJACK: Not with me.

GRACE: Is that right?

CRACKERJACK: Why didn't He come help me out of this one?

GRACE: He did.

CRACKERJACK: That shit is stagnant water, man.

GRACE: C'mon. Let's go to the dispensary. Get you stitched up and give you some painkillers.

CRACKERJACK: I got a lifetime supply of those.

GRACE: Not in here, you don't. C'mon. Up. That's it. Whoa...steady...you going to make it? *(To Ramon.)* Why don't you stay here. I'll be right back. *(Ramon moves to help her.)*

GRACE: I got him. He's fine.

(As they exit.)

RAMON: Take it easy, Cracker!

CRACKERJACK: My man!

(Grace exits with Crackerjack. Actor playing Ramon should take plenty of time to absorb where he is and why. He discovers statue of Mary. Twelve chimes ring over PA system. Enter Grace. Nuns recite the Angelus over loudspeaker. Ramon turns and sees Grace, who quickly grasps what he's experiencing. Acknowledges the prayer. Ramon falters, trying to remember the words.)

GRACE: Sit down. Can I get you some juice...

RAMON: Oh. You mean...you mean like in fruit juice?

GRACE: Yeah.

RAMON: No, thanks.

GRACE: He's going to be all right, you know.

RAMON: No, he's not. And there's not a fuckin' thing I can do about it. Excuse me.

GRACE: Looks to me like you've been doing a hell of a lot.

RAMON: It's not enough. But he won't listen to me. About anything. I wanted to take him to the hospital. No. We had to come here. It's ten, fifteen blocks further away, but he had to come here. Asshole. And you know, I've been thinking, you shouldn't be doing your T'ai Chi so early in the park like that. It's dangerous.

GRACE: Yeah, someone like you could come along and try to rip off my knapsack.

RAMON: Hey, I'm sorry about that. *(Empties out pockets. Counts money.)* Seven dollars and fifty-eight cents. Are we done with this head game now?

GRACE: No. Give it to the old guy with the tattoos. At least once a week you two play chess. You could beat him with your eyes closed. But you sit down and pretend it's a battle to the death. He wins and walks away with twenty, thirty bucks. I saw you give him a fifty once. And he's not the only one either.

RAMON: Better watch yourself.

GRACE: You trying to scare me again?

RAMON: You should be scared.

GRACE: Why, just because you are?

(Phone rings. Grace pushes button.)

GRACE: Yes?

PHONE VOICE: Cardinal King's office on line two.

GRACE: I'll call him back. Hold my calls, please.

PHONE VOICE: Okay.

GRACE: Sorry.

RAMON: No problem.

(Phone rings again. Grace pushes button.)

GRACE: What is it?

PHONE VOICE: They want to hold.

GRACE: Tell them I'll call back. *(Grace pushes button.)*

RAMON: You seem pretty busy...

GRACE: No, no...please. We won't be interrupted again.

RAMON: Pray for Crackerjack.

GRACE: Why don't we pray right now? Ruben? Crackerjack needs your protection. Carry him lightly and sing to him sweetly. Remind him of his innocence.

RAMON: And please make him shut his big mouth for once. Please make his head stop hurting. And please...if you could just look in on me once in awhile.

GRACE AND RAMON: Amen.

GRACE: You don't ask for much for yourself.

RAMON: Don't want to be disappointed.

GRACE: You disappointed a lot?

RAMON: Yeah.

GRACE: By who? Talk to me, Ramon. Who disappointed you?

(Ramon grows increasingly uncomfortable.)

GRACE: This thing is burning a hole in your heart. I bet you haven't talked about it in years. So why don't you tell me. Why'd you leave the Church?

RAMON: It's over, man. History.

GRACE: It's not over! You act it out everyday! You don't get a handle on it, you're going to live and die in that park!

RAMON: There are worse places.

GRACE: Hurt you that bad...

RAMON: Where do you get off!

GRACE: C'mon, Ramon! Why the self-imposed exile?

RAMON: Just stop!

GRACE: No, you stop! Ducking it! Hiding from it!

RAMON: Oh and I guess there's nothing in your life you never ran away from!

GRACE: We're talking about you!

RAMON: Well, I want to talk about you! What's your story, Grace? You're more restless than half the fuckin' nuts in this place! Think it doesn't show? You're fuckin' out there day in, day out, draggin' people to the Center, ya got a hand in this, ya got a hand in that, volunteering at the hospital...

you're running. Giving out food, clothes…running. What's buggin' you, Grace? What are you running from?

GRACE: It's not what I'm running from. It's what I'm running to.

RAMON: I'm pullin' a blank.

GRACE: The priesthood. I want to be a priest.

RAMON: You're spinning your wheels, man! You're not going to be a Priest. It's a guy thing, O.K.? It's tradition.

GRACE: Tradition. I love that. In some parts of India, it's still a tradition for a widow to throw herself on her husband's funeral pyre. Whether she wants to or not. Tradition doesn't make anything right. Christ said, "Behold! I make all things new!"

RAMON: You're really getting off on this. It's a power trip.

GRACE: Ramon, I have a Master's degree in Theology. Class for class, I took the exact same curriculum as men studying for the priesthood. The only difference between them and me is that upon graduation, they became priests and I became a nun.

RAMON: So?

GRACE: So, how would you feel graduating from medical school having all the qualifications of a doctor only to be told you could only be a nurse?

RAMON: Being a nurse is O.K.

GRACE: Being a nurse is wonderful if that's what you want to be! Being a nun is wonderful if that's what you want to be!

RAMON: Can't you be some other kind of priest?

GRACE: No. Catholicism is my native language. It's in my bones. All of our symbols, rituals and prayers are like windows through which I see God. A really good priest can illuminate those windows. The disciples asked Christ, "What is the way? What is the place which we shall go?" Jesus answered, "The place you can reach. Stand there." The priesthood is where I can reach. I stand there. Where is the place you can reach?

RAMON: I found it once.

(Short, loud rap on door. Enter Virgilia with pink message slip in hand.)

VIRGILIA: Do you know you have a message from the Vatican in your box?

GRACE: Yes, I know, Sister Virgilia. Thank you.

VIRGILIA: It says "urgent!"

GRACE: So is this. I'll call them back as soon as I can. Thank you, Sister Virgilia.

(Virgilia puts message on Grace's desk. Nods to Ramon. Exits.)

GRACE: I'm sorry. You were saying?

RAMON: Yeah, uh…See, my father…the guy was a waste of air space, O.K.? So I grew up on the streets. A lot of static. But my mother always dragged me to church. She sets up this meeting with our priest cuz she sees I'm growin' up pretty pissed off. So I'm waiting in the church for this priest to show up and I hear somethin' really beautiful. Something I never heard before. Silence. Not out there. In here.

GRACE: But you're still on the street.

RAMON: I wasn't always. I was an altar boy for five years. I loved that priest, man. I did. I loved the Church. I even thought about bein' a priest once. Can you believe that?

GRACE: Yes, I can.

RAMON: Pretty fucked up. Anyway, our priest heard about a couple of universities giving scholarships to gifted Hispanics. I applied. I got lucky. I should say they got lucky.

GRACE: Ramon.

RAMON: Didn't know I was "gifted," did you?

GRACE: Well, I just...

RAMON: I was studying religion and philosophy at NYU.

GRACE: You were a religion and philosophy student?

RAMON: Look at your face. What's the big deal? I know architects that are now sleepin' with a bottle over on the Bowery. So? Shit happens.

GRACE: Ramon, how did you...

RAMON: How did I get like this? I found a church, O.K.? Started hanging out with this priest. We got pretty tight. He asked me to help him with this youth group thing. Really, it was just a glorified soup kitchen for runaways, but I said yeah, what the hell. In walks this kid with attitude for days. Now, in case you haven't noticed, I got a little attitude myself. So I sit next to him. No way is the God/church/religion rap going down with this kid. Seemed like no matter what I said or did, I just couldn't connect. But the kid is quick, right? Chess. He let me teach him how to play chess. Instant connection. Great. We start hangin' out, I take him to a couple of Knicks games, give him a couple of books...and it's happenin'. I thought...I really thought he had a grip, you know? I get this call one night. The kid was all over the place. Messed up. Deep. He was sniffin' glue and paint thinner...you name it. So he's on the phone and he's like...in a total panic. Terrorized by...I don't know, demons. I run over to this shithole walk-up. I race up the stairs. I knew. I could smell it in the hallway. I kicked the door down. The kid blew his brains out.

GRACE: Oh, Ramon...I'm so sorry...

RAMON: I freaked. I'm banging on all the neighbors doors, screamin'...nobody would open up. Nobody heard anything. I'm alone with this kid whose brains are like jelly in my hands...so I say...I say...I hold this kid in my arms and say...the Lord is my shepherd and yea, though I walk through the valley of the shadow of death, I will fear no evil." That's all I can remember! So I'm rockin' him back and forth, back and forth, whispering, "I will fear no evil"..."The Lord is my Shepherd." I didn't know the rest of the fuckin' thing, man! I couldn't even think of the right prayers! My mind...it just twisted up!

GRACE: Your prayers were perfect.

RAMON: The priest wouldn't give him a funeral. I couldn't believe it. I said, "What the fuck is your problem, man! He was thirteen years old! That wasn't him pulling the trigger, it was his addict mother, his abusive father!"

GRACE: The priest was an idiot! Why didn't you just go to another Catholic Church! That wouldn't happen today.

RAMON: That's not the point, Grace! He came to *this* church! My church! It was the closest thing to a home he ever had. It should have been us! I said at least let me take up a collection at Mass so I can give him a decent burial. "No can do. Suicide is murder. You commit suicide and you're out of the club." I said "Screw you and your Church."

GRACE: How long ago was that?

RAMON: Three years. I'm dying out here, man. I got nothing.

GRACE: That can be a wonderful place to start.

RAMON: Start what?

GRACE: A new relationship with God.

RAMON: What are you, deaf or something?

GRACE: I've heard every word you've said and I don't think you're angry with the Church. I think you're angry with yourself for not being able to save that kid. Nobody could've saved him, Ramon.

RAMON: I see his face!

GRACE: I know you do. But you can't spend the rest of your life roaming the streets looking for suicides to save. It's not going to bring him back. Love thy neighbor as thyself doesn't mean instead of thyself. Ramon, you were created in the image of God and God is love. Remember that silence in here? It's love. And you must be a very strong person to withstand so much of it. I hate to break it to you pal, but I recognized you a long time ago, just as someone recognized me.

RAMON: Who?

GRACE: Doesn't matter.

RAMON: Un-hunh. Put your cards on the table.

GRACE: A priest from a nearby parish came to mass one Sunday when I was a young girl. He'd just returned from some Appalachian churches and was giving a talk about the poor conditions there. He was so charismatic, so dedicated, that prayers I'd prayed, catechism I had studied, the mass itself just lit up inside me and I understood. I fell to my knees and thanked God for this man. *This* was a priest. And I wanted to be just like him. I waited for him after Mass. I barely introduced myself when I blurted out how much I wanted to be an altar girl but our priest wouldn't allow it, and could he please help me? Do you know that this young priest, fresh out of seminary, allowed me to serve at his Mass? In those days, that was strictly forbidden. Of course, the bishop heard about it and we were both reprimanded. But it was too late. I had already entered a whole new dimension of love from which I've never retreated. You see, it just took one person to look at me and say "yes." And that one "yes" has made all the difference in the world. I look at you. And I say to you, Ramon, "yes."

RAMON: I want some peace.

GRACE: Then don't give your life to God.

RAMON: Who said anything about giving my life to God!

GRACE: What do you think it is when you give your chess money to the poor? When you read your Bible to the old guy with the tattoos…when you see to it that Crackerjack has something to eat every night? You're witnessing. *(Ramon stands. Paces.)*

GRACE: You've been hanging on pretty tight to those books about the saints. Whatcha got in your back pocket?

RAMON: You gave it to me. Saint Francis.

GRACE: Ahh.

RAMON: Hey, I happen to like Saint Francis! Is that all right with you?

GRACE: Why Saint Francis?

RAMON: Because he walked away from the bullshit!

GRACE: And then what?

RAMON: I didn't get that far.

GRACE: He built a church! And he gave his life to God and the poor!

RAMON: I'm afraid. O.K.? You happy? I can't get hurt like that again. I won't make it.

GRACE: You're afraid of the church but you're not afraid to live in the gutter?

RAMON: Ah *Dios mio*…

GRACE: Ramon, we are in the same boat of longing and unfulfillment. I see my suffering in your eyes. Maybe you see yours in mine.

RAMON: I don't want to see it.

GRACE: Then you might as well kiss that silence good-bye. Because God is also truth.

RAMON: Let me go, Grace.

GRACE: Why? So you can roll over and play dead? Huh-unh.

RAMON: *Vete para carajo!* Why me!

GRACE: Because I tend to get real attached to people I share a lifeboat with.

RAMON: I jumped and you stayed. What's it gotten you?

GRACE: Self-respect.

RAMON: Like I don't have any?

GRACE: You tell me.

RAMON: I respect a man who walks away from something he thinks is wrong!

GRACE: You didn't walk away, you ran away! You inflicted far more pain on yourself than if you'd stayed.

RAMON: You're killin' me, Grace.

GRACE: It's like you won't walk through the gates of paradise because you don't like the gatekeeper!

RAMON: I don't want to hear this!

GRACE: You're wasting yourself!

RAMON: That's enough!

GRACE: It's a slap in the face of God!

RAMON: *Cono nome jodas!*

GRACE: I'm sorry, Ramon.

RAMON: Man!

GRACE: I look at you and I see a priest. Tell me I'm wrong.

RAMON: A priest wouldn't do half the stuff I've done.

GRACE: But he would do a lot of the things you have.

RAMON: I don't even think I know the words to Mass anymore.

GRACE: It'll come back to you.

RAMON: I don't know.

GRACE: Ramon, Crackerjack's not going anywhere for a couple days. Why don't I take you up to the men's floor? It's run by the Franciscans. You can have the keys to my office if you want to be alone or you can go to the chapel. We've got some extra Walkmans and tapes in the donation room. You'll find some pajamas there. Take whatever you want. The food's good. No strings attached. You want to leave? Leave. You want to stay? Stay.

RAMON: I don't know. Maybe just tonight.

GRACE: Welcome to the Houston Street Crisis Center.

(Lights fade. No blackout. Ramon exits. Grace lights a candle. Takes off shoes. Puts on tape of Gregorian chant. Sings, sways, dances. Chimes ring three times. Soft knock on door. Ramon opens door a crack.)

GRACE: Hi. Come on in.

RAMON: I heard the music.

GRACE: Can't sleep.

RAMON: Me either. You got some serious fuckin' snore machines up there.

GRACE: Want some tea?

RAMON: No, thanks. What are you doing?

GRACE: Giving thanks.

RAMON: Oh.

GRACE: Do you have a rosary?

RAMON: Yeah. Hey, can we not talk about this stuff anymore? I'm like saturated.

GRACE: Sure. How 'bout a game of chess?

RAMON: You're on. What are we playing for?

GRACE: Extra bingo cards.

RAMON: Big time! All right!

GRACE: You be white.

RAMON: No. You be white, I be black.

(They set up board. Virgilia enters. She's got a whistle around her neck, a flash-light, and keys.)

VIRGILIA: Sister Grace? Oh! Excuse me!

GRACE: Come in, Sister! I want you to meet a friend of mine. This is Ramon. He'll be staying with us a few days.

VIRGILIA: We met earlier today.

RAMON: Hey. How's it goin'?

VIRGILIA: It's going just fine, thank you.

GRACE: Sister Virgilia is our hall monitor this week.

VIRGILIA: When I heard the voices, I thought I'd ask you about the call from the Vatican. But I see you're busy. Are you counseling?

GRACE: No. Just playing chess.

RAMON: You play?

VIRGILIA: No. Do you have any idea what time it is?

GRACE: I know. But this is his first night with us and he couldn't sleep. I'll fill him in on the house rules tomorrow.

(Virgilia glares at Ramon.)

RAMON: I don't sell drugs!

VIRGILIA: Speaking of which, your friend Crackerjack already left. Too many pictures of the Prince of Peace in the dispensary. He said it was, quote, "bugging him out."

RAMON: (To Grace.) See what I'm up against?

GRACE: Did he say where he was going?

VIRGILIA: No.

RAMON: I'll find 'im…soon as I kick your ass. *(Ramon makes a chess move. Then to Virgilia.)* I'm really sorry I said that.

VIRGILIA: Nothing I haven't heard before…sad to say.

RAMON: Thanks for checkin' on him.

VIRGILIA: Did you speak with the Vatican?

GRACE: Yes.

VIRGILIA: Problems?

GRACE: No, everything's fine, Sister Virgilia.

VIRGILIA: I hope you enjoy your stay with us. *(Virgilia's eyes sweep the room suspiciously. She switches on the lamp. Exits.)*

RAMON: Did I just get you in trouble?

GRACE: No, *I* just got me in trouble.

(They resume playing chess.)

RAMON: What's up with the Vatican?

GRACE: I'm organizing a rally in the park about sex education in parochial schools. How they always find out what I'm doing is beyond me.

RAMON: Anything I can do to help?

GRACE: You already did.

(Ramon makes a particularly savvy move.)

GRACE: Ooooooooohhh…

RAMON: *Yes!*

GRACE: Ooooooooohhh…

RAMON: You're slippin', Grace.

(Transition.)

ACT I
Scene IV

Up Gregorian chanting. Just after dawn in the park. Enter Grace. Ramon runs to her.

RAMON: They got Crackerjack! They set him up! They…

GRACE: *(Headphones off. Faint bleedthrough of Gregorian chant.)* Slow down, slow down! Who got Crackerjack?

RAMON: They must have given him some bad drugs. C'mon!

(Ramon and Grace run to opposite side of stage where Crackerjack is dying of a drug overdose. He slips in and out of consciousness. Grace checks his vital signs.)

RAMON: You got to stay awake, Crackerjack!

GRACE: He's in bad shape. Did you call an ambulance?

RAMON: Yes!

GRACE: When?

RAMON: Just now!

GRACE: Go get a cop.

RAMON: They're not there!

GRACE: What do you mean! They're always there! Go get Tommy! Tell him I need him!

RAMON: Forget it, man! Shit like this happens, those guys take a coffee break! One less junkie pusher to hassle with!

GRACE: Get a hold of yourself! I'm telling you he's there!

RAMON: What do you think, I'm fuckin' out of my mind! I looked, man, I looked!

GRACE: All right, easy now, Crackerjack. We're right here beside you. We're going to take real good care of you, all right? Everything's going to be O.K. You just hang on...

CRACKERJACK: I'm burnin' up...

GRACE: The ambulance is on its way. You called St. Vincent's right?

RAMON: Yeah...no...I dialed 911.

GRACE: Ramon, they know me at St. Vincent's!

RAMON: That wasn't the first thing on my mind, O.K.! Jesus Christ! My fuckin' friend is layin' here in the dirt...

GRACE: What did you tell them?

RAMON: There's an O.D. in the park!

GRACE: Wonderful.

RAMON: What!

CRACKERJACK: I'm scared, man. I'm checkin' out.

GRACE: I'm right here, Crackerjack.

CRACKERJACK: I fucked up my whole life.

GRACE: Can you hear me? I need you to concentrate on the sound of my voice. No, you can't fall asleep!

CRACKERJACK: The lights are scrambling...

GRACE: Stay with me, Crackerjack!

RAMON: Where the hell are they?

GRACE: Ramon, get over here.

RAMON: Oh my God...please...I'll do anything.

(Grace checks his pulse, fingertips, pupils. Lays him down.)

RAMON: I will fear no evil...I will fear no evil.

GRACE: Ramon, I need you. Put your jacket under his head.

RAMON: But we have to walk him around!

GRACE: No. We should pray for him now.

RAMON: But the ambulance...

GRACE: Ramon, he's not going to make it.

RAMON: What do you mean he's not going to make it? He's gonna make it!

GRACE: Ramon, it's time.

RAMON: Oh God...no.

GRACE: Let him go home.

RAMON: He's got some heavy shit to answer for. You gotta help him with that.

GRACE: I can help him as a friend but I can't...

RAMON: My man...Sister Grace is going to hear your confession, O.K.? You want me to say it

GRACE: No, Ramon. I don't have the authority to absolve him of his sins.

RAMON: The guy didn't have a moment's peace his whole life. You give him Last Rites now! Do you know the prayers?

GRACE: Of course I do.

RAMON: *Then do it!*

GRACE: These are not just words, Ramon. This is a holy sacrament.

CRACKERJACK: Sister...please...

RAMON: Don't worry, my man. We're gonna get you through this.

CRACKERJACK: Frisco...

RAMON: He deserves Last Rites.

GRACE: You have no grasp of the consequences for me!

RAMON: I know. I fuckin' know that all this crap about God is love and loving thy neighbor as thyself is a crock of shit! Your friend is dying in your arms and you're worried what your bosses at the church will say? I think that makes you just about the biggest hypocrite I ever met. When we gonna stop the bullshit! Face it! It's bullshit! I don't want to hear anymore jive 'bout you being a priest, cuz you ain't got the guts for the job. *(Ramon gathers Crackerjack in his arms.)* The Lord is my Shepherd, I shall not want...I will fear no evil. The Lord is my Shepherd...

GRACE: Alright. Get the thermos out of my knapsack and fill it with water from the fountain.

(Ramon grabs thermos. Exits.)

GRACE: The Lord is my Shepherd. I shall not want. He maketh me to lie down in green pastures; He leadeth me beside the still waters. He restoreth my soul; He leadeth me in the paths of righteousness for His name's sake. Yea, though I walk through the valley of the shadow of death, I will fear no evil: for thou art with me; thy rod and thy staff they comfort me.

(Ramon returns with thermos.)

GRACE: Thou preparest a table before me in the presence of mine enemies: thou anointest my head with oil: my cup runneth over.

GRACE AND RAMON: Surely goodness and mercy shall follow me all the days of my life: and I will dwell in the House of the Lord forever.

GRACE: Pour the water over my hands. Lord, wash away my iniquities. Cleanse me of my sins. *(She stops.)*

RAMON: What's the matter?

GRACE: I'm afraid. Damn it! I'm afraid!

RAMON: What do you think he is!

GRACE: Oh my perfect friend, lift the falsehood of limitation from my shoulders. Strengthen me to withstand the power of channeling thy grace. Use me to liberate this child from his earthly mistakes and free me from the burden of my fear. Amen. What's your name, Crackerjack?

RAMON: Can you remember your name, buddy?

CRACKERJACK: John.

(Faintly, in the distance, the sound of a siren.)

GRACE: Do you believe in God, the Almighty, Creator of Heaven and Earth?

RAMON: He does.

GRACE: Are you truly sorry for your sins and have you begged God's forgiveness? Answer me, John. Are you sorry?

CRACKERJACK: Yes.

(Sound of siren closer.)

GRACE: For these sins and any you may have forgotten, you are forgiven in the name of God. Ramon, say an Act of Contrition for him.

(Ramon whispers prayer while Grace anoints Crackerjack's forehead, eyes, lips, hands and feet with holy water. Ramon leans close to Crackerjack's ear.)

GRACE: Through the mysteries of redemption, may Almighty God release you from all punishments in this life and in the life to come.

RAMON: *Gracias,* John.

GRACE: May He open to you the gates of paradise and welcome you to everlasting joy. By the Authority which the Apostolic See has given me...

(Grace falters. Ramon takes her hand.)

GRACE: Oh my Creator...help me...guide me...
By the Authority God has given me,
I grant you a full pardon and the remission

of all your sins
In the name of the Father and of the Son
and of the Holy Spirit.
Let us pray.
All powerful and merciful God, we commend
to You John, your servant.
In Your mercy and love, blot out the sins
he has committed through human weakness.
In this world he has died;
Let him live with you forever.
We ask this through Christ our Lord.

GRACE AND RAMON: Amen.

(Screaming siren. Flashing red lights. Blackout.)

(END OF ACT I)

ACT II
Scene I

Four years later. We hear Sister Grace being interviewed by Phil Donahue. [Or substitute local newscaster.]

PHIL: And we are back…with Sister Grace from the Houston Street Crisis Center. Sister…c'mon…don't you think if Jesus lived today, the church would make him sick? I mean, most of 'em are rotten from the bottom to the top!

GRACE: Well it's true. A lot of people have left the church, but I've got a joke for you. Guy gets hit by a car. He's lying in the street, dying. He looks up and says, "I'm an ex-Catholic. Get me an ex-priest."

PHIL: *(Laugh.)* I walked right into that one!

GRACE: As far as what Jesus would think of the Church, well, I don't know, but Jesus loved people and the Church is people…so…

PHIL: …so…what you're saying is "Lighten up. Phil!" O.K. Sister Grace. In the trenches…leading the battle for women in the priesthood. Good luck. Sister.

GRACE: Thanks.

PHIL: Tomorrow we'll be talking to Mayor Rudy Guiliani about his Quality of Life Campaign. As if we ever had any in the first place.

(Lights down. Up on stage left classroom. A podium with a small crucifix and a Christmas tree sit on a table in front of room. Ramon is anxiously pacing, looking over his notes, checking his watch. Grace breathlessly flies into the room, throwing off her coat.)

RAMON: Thanks a lot.

GRACE: I'm sorry.

RAMON: That's what you said the last time.

GRACE: I know. I'm...

RAMON: What the hell happened? Too many autograph seekers outside the television studio? Couldn't get through the crowd?

GRACE: People don't ask nuns for autographs.

RAMON: You watch.

GRACE: You're the one who insisted I do this in the first place!

RAMON: And you're the one who insisted I do this!

GRACE: So do it! Let's go!

RAMON: If I flunk this class...

GRACE: Three years of excellent grades. How are you going to flunk?

RAMON: Those grades were in theology and philosophy. Get me in front of a room full of people and ask me to talk about God and I suck!

GRACE: Well, we're going to change that right now. What time's your class?

RAMON: I got an hour and a half.

GRACE: Plenty of time.

RAMON: It's uptown!

GRACE: Right now! I want you to put everything you're feeling into that homily! Don't think! Feel! Go baby go!

RAMON: *(Smoldering.)* Good morning one and all. Welcome to St. Francis Church on the happiest day of the year.

GRACE: O.K., that won't work. What I want you to do is breath into your heart and preach to me from there.

RAMON: Good morning, one and all.

GRACE: Don't give me the "priest's voice," Ramon.

RAMON: Good morning, one and all! I'd like to welcome you to St. Francis Church!

GRACE: Get out from behind that thing. You're using it as a shield.

RAMON: *(Steps out from behind podium.)* St. Francis is the oldest church in New Jersey.

GRACE: Don't care.

RAMON: I trust you had a pleasant morning. It's my very great privilege to discuss with you...

GRACE: Stop! You sound like you're welcoming shareholders to an AT&T convention!

RAMON: You're a pain in the ass, you know that!

GRACE: *SHHHHH!* Priests don't say "ass."

RAMON: Ass, ass, ass!

GRACE: Look at your shoulders. They're up to your ears. Relax! This is supposed to be fun!

RAMON: Yeah, real fun.

GRACE: Bend from the waist and shake it out. Now give me a sound.

RAMON: What kind of sound?

GRACE: Aaaaaahhhhh...

RAMON: Aaaaaahhhhh...

GRACE: *Aaaaaaaaaaahhhhhhhhhhh!!!!!!!*

RAMON: *Aaaaaaaaaaahhhhhhhhhhh!!!!!!!*

GRACE: Good! Now who we talkin' about!

RAMON: God.

GRACE: Who?

RAMON: God!

GRACE: *Goooooodddddd!!!* Let me feel the power of the Almighty surging right up through your toes and out of your mouth!

RAMON: *Ggggoooooooooooddddd!!!!!*

GRACE: Yes! How do you feel about Christmas, Ramon!

RAMON: I love it!

GRACE: Let me hear it!

RAMON: O.K.!

GRACE: Let's go!

RAMON: Good morning everyone! Welcome to St. Francis Church! We have gathered together today to celebrate what is truly the single most joyous day of our liturgical year! This is a day for merrymaking and rejoicing and...

GRACE: Don't act, Ramon! There's nothing worse than a frustrated actor for a priest!

RAMON: Forget it. Just forget it.

GRACE: You can do this!

RAMON: You won't even let me finish the first paragraph!

GRACE: Why should I listen to you impersonate a priest!

RAMON: You're starting to piss me off.

GRACE: Good! At least that's real!

RAMON: Can we just get through this?

GRACE: You have the high honor of preaching God's word and you just want to get through this? Why are you here?

RAMON: To deliver God's message.

GRACE: Well, Ramon, there's no finer message in the world, but you lose me when I see someone who not only isn't connecting with me, but isn't connecting with himself. And therefore he sure isn't connecting with God. And everybody in your congregation is going to know it and they are going to tune you out.

RAMON: What should I do to...

GRACE: You've got to set my soul on fire!

RAMON: Well, yeah, but how?

GRACE: You tell me!

RAMON: I don't know!

GRACE: You're not focusing! Get present, Ramon!

RAMON: You're freakin' me out.

GRACE: Good!

RAMON: I feel very inadequate.

GRACE: What do you tell your parishioners when they come to you and say I feel inadequate?

RAMON: Grace, my assignment is Christmas.

GRACE: The hell with Christmas! Everybody understands Christmas! He was born. We're happy. We're saved. Hallelujah. What we don't understand is suffering. A parishioner comes to you and says my son or daughter has AIDS. Or my husband left me after twenty-five years of marriage. Or my kid has nightmares about race riots and nuclear holocaust. What do you say, Ramon?

RAMON: Pray.

GRACE: Not good enough!

RAMON: Pray a lot.

GRACE: Thank you for sharing! Ding! Next!

RAMON: Well, I guess I'd say...uhm...I'd say...to...

GRACE: Have you ever suffered?

RAMON: A lot.

GRACE: That makes you an expert and I need an expert.

RAMON: I don't really think I know how to...

GRACE: You see, Father, I befriended this runaway kid. And we got really tight, see, and then he killed himself.

RAMON: Aw man, you are somethin' else.

GRACE: And just when I was getting over it, my best buddy died in my arms of an overdose. What kind of God is that? I lost my faith and I can't get it back!

RAMON: This sucks.

GRACE: You're damn right! Don't walk away from me! Hey! Look in my eyes, Ramon! Right here! Why did God take my friends! Help me, Father!

RAMON: I don't know!

GRACE: You *do* know or you'd be dead by now!

RAMON: It's because...because...

GRACE: Because what? What gives you the right to comfort me?

RAMON: Cuz I been there. I know the landscape.

GRACE: What's it look like?

RAMON: An inferno.

GRACE: How'd you get out?

RAMON: I was lifted.

GRACE: By who?

RAMON: Don't laugh.

GRACE: I won't.

RAMON: I was listening to Carlos Santana one night.
   (Background Santana music.)

RAMON: I started thinking...if Christ were alive today, He'd get off on Santana. yeah. I pictured Christ wearin' my boots, my jeans. I put my medal around His neck. I gave Him my voice, my attitude. He was lookin' nasty. And just when I could see Him...and hear Him...I sat Him down. I looked the guy right in the eye and I said, "Don't give me any of that parable hidden meaning stuff cuz I ain't got the time. Let's cut to the chase: What would You do if You were me?" "First," He said, "Santana raises your frequencies. Listen." So I did.
   (Blast of Santana music rocks theatre. Music out.)

RAMON: Then Christ said, "Disappear for a coupla days. Go within." When I went within, I saw...a nest of fuckin' vipers, man...sin, shame, regrets. They were slithering and coiling around me...trying to suffocate the last shred of goodness I had left. Right then and there, in the pitch black, I laid myself across the chopping block. I cried, "Deliver me from this bondage, Lord, or strike me dead." Jesus whispered, "I am the breath of life. Come back to me and all the treasure houses of Solomon will pale next to your goodness." I said, "Brother...it's a done deal."

   Things changed after that. I could sleep at night. But when I woke up, kids were still bleedin' on the sidewalk...mothers still cryin'...so what's the point? This time *He* sits *me* down. *He* looks *me* right in the eye and He says…He says, "It's all you, Ramon. It's the worst in you and I am the best in you. Go back, but this time take Me with you." We've been together so long, it's not a head trip anymore. My Christ is the same as that Christ. *(Indicating crucifix on podium.)* I look at things from His perspective now. Same picture, different angle. And it's breathtaking, man! After you get that, there's only flying!

GRACE: You just graduated.

RAMON: Get out of here.

GRACE: You're going to be a wonderful priest. Just clean up the language a little.

RAMON: Yeah, I'm workin' on that. Hey what time is it! We've got to practice my Christmas…

GRACE: Some things you can't practice.

RAMON: We're done?

GRACE: Yes.

RAMON: Thanks.

GRACE: Beat it. You don't want to be late for class.

RAMON: *Via con dios.*

GRACE: Thank you.

> *(Ramon exits. Lights fade on Grace.)*

> *(Transition.)*

ACT II
Scene II
> *Vatican Embassy meeting room. Enter Sister Joseph followed by Sister Grace.*

SISTER JOSEPH: I saw you on TV! It was like you were speaking directly to me!

GRACE: Thank you.

SISTER JOSEPH: I wish I could see you at Town Hall next week. I was trying to organize a bus trip from the convent, but Mother Superior forbade it. I guess it wouldn't look good. You know.

GRACE: Some other time.

SISTER JOSEPH: I'll get Cardinal King. Keep up the good work!

GRACE: You too, Sister.

> *(Sister Joseph exits. Enter Cardinal King.)*

GRACE: Hi!

KING: Hello, Grace. Thanks for coming to Washington.

GRACE: What's the matter? You look like someone died.

KING: I haven't been sleeping.

GRACE: Why?

KING: Sit down.

GRACE: I'm in trouble, aren't I?

KING: I have to talk to you. As a friend.

GRACE: That bad.

KING: I didn't want you finding out through a summons in the mail.

GRACE: What is it this time? Are they going to banish me to a remote mission in El Salvador and hope for the best? Why don't they just burn me at the stake and get it over with.

KING: We've started proceedings to expel you from the Sisters of Charity.

GRACE: Expulsion!

KING: You will be spared excommunication due to your fine work at the Crisis Center. I'm sorry, Grace.

GRACE: Ex...I don't believe them!

KING: I begged you to ease up but you wouldn't listen!

GRACE: I've transgressed no laws of the Church!

KING: But you have! And you continue to! I forbade you to hold that candlelight vigil in Washington Square Park! Didn't I?

GRACE: But I didn't have it in Washington Square Park!

KING: No! You had it in Central Park with twice as many protesters and twice the amount of press! You were told not to promote sex education in parochial schools, yet there you were! In front of thousands of people waving condoms around extolling the virtues of the cheaper brands, because they have more latex so they're stronger!

GRACE: You think the expensive brands are stronger?

KING: This isn't a joke!

GRACE: You used to appreciate my sense of humor, Cardinal King.

KING: How can I laugh while you're committing suicide? There are witnesses who say you've performed the sacraments. You've been accused of breaking your vow of chastity. You're always shooting your mouth off about reincarnation and...chakras...and I don't know what all! The Church provides automatic excommunication through apostasy, heresy, schism...

GRACE: This is ridiculous! I've been accused of those things for years! What makes this time any different?

KING: I don't know too many nuns who make the cover of *MS Magazine* or go on the Phil Donahue Show.

GRACE: I was invited to talk about women in the priesthood! How could I resist!

KING: This is turning into a media circus!

GRACE: Wait a minute. Bishop Mince and Father Zamora were on the show, too. I don't see them here being scolded. They're off somewhere getting pats on the back for defending the faith, but I'm making a spectacle of myself.

KING: Sister Grace, Catholic women are demonstrating in Philadelphia and Chicago. They're marching on their churches in Atlanta, Boston, and Dallas. The Vatican is being flooded with letters.

GRACE: Praise God!

KING: Sister Grace...

GRACE: Praise God! They're writing!

KING: I don't think you understand what's happening here. You've made yourself into the perfect sacrificial lamb. There will be a hearing. They're going to make an example out of you.

GRACE: What does it tell you when the Vatican, which has survived centuries of scandal, can be provoked by a humble nun speaking her mind on the talk show circuit?

KING: A humble nun? More like a politician.

GRACE: Don't give me that, Michael! What do you think you are! You're an advisor to the Pope! You think I don't know what it takes to get there!

KING: Keep your voice down! What's the matter with you! Your personal attraction to the priesthood has turned you into the worst kind of strident feminist with an ax to grind! You want to preach? Go preach! You can preach at the Center, on the bus, in the park! You can preach till you're blue in the face, you just can't preach in the Church!

GRACE: Wow. And to think you were the reason I wanted to be a priest.

KING: I cannot allow that to cloud my judgment!

GRACE: You said you could hear the angels sing when I was your altar girl.

KING: I never should've encouraged you.

GRACE: Oh, I didn't need much encouragement. I heard them, too.

KING: That doesn't give you license to tear the very fabric of our faith!

GRACE: My first experience of justice was on your altar.

KING: Dammit, Grace! Don't you ever know when to stop! I've been your confessor! Your teacher!

GRACE: My friend.

KING: I demand to be treated with respect!

GRACE: You demand, Michael?

KING: That's right, I demand! I am sick to death of being labeled some patriarchal, macho homophobic! I am sick to death of politically correct pressure groups eyeing me suspiciously every time I pat a child on the head! You know, all hell breaks loose if somebody tells a racist joke, or an anti-Semitic or anti-gay joke. But suddenly, it's very fashionable to be anti-Catholic! But it is the Catholic Church who plants Herself on the front line of the tough issues: capital punishment, abortion, euthanasia, human rights. We maintain the largest nongovernmental relief agencies, hospitals and schools in the world! *Us!* You never mention that on the talk shows, do you? You never mention the Jesuit martyrs of El Salvador! Or that we were crucial to the overthrow of Marcos in the Philippines! The success of Solidarity in Poland!

We are an ancient repository of the richest art, architecture and philosophy in the world! We do not covet democracy's approval! We do not tremble because a group of disgruntled American women decide to mutiny! You know what makes me tremble, Grace? The bombed out churches of Bosnia. You been there lately? I have. Have you been to Russia and seen the tears of joy when old people are allowed to pray in their churches for the first time in eighty years? So you'll forgive me if I do not grovel at your feet because you feel your rights have been violated! Look at me. I'm shaking.

GRACE: I haven't seen you like this since the Vietnam War protests.

KING: Like what?

GRACE: Alive.

KING: It's a different time, Grace.

GRACE: For you maybe.

KING: What do you mean?

GRACE: All the marches, the jail terms, hunger strikes; you never flinched. The civil rights riots? Remember? You stared 'em down, Michael. We've seen bloodshed, devastation; your hands were always steady. But now, every time you face one of these tragedies, you know deep in your heart you're only there as a visiting big shot. You can't stay and help those people. And it's killing you. That's why you tremble.

KING: But I am helping people. I am trying to use my influence to challenge some of the more repressive Church doctrine. I belong in the Vatican. And whether you agree or not I'm there to serve *you.*

GRACE: If you want to change the system, you don't join it. We learned that thirty years ago. Or did you forget?

KING: Why do I let you talk to me like this?

GRACE: I learned it from the Master.

KING: I taught you disrespect?

GRACE: No, Michael. You taught me integrity.

KING: Which is why we're in this mess.

GRACE: We?

KING: You're putting me in a very difficult position. How would it look if they knew I met with you before the proceedings?

GRACE: Why are you meeting with me?

KING: To beg you to return to the teachings of the Church and we'll forget the whole thing.

GRACE: I can't do that.

KING: Did it ever occur to you that for once in your life you might be wrong?

GRACE: Oh, I'm wrong all the time. Not about this.

KING: Pride goeth before a fall.

GRACE: Is that for my benefit or yours?

KING: Yours. I'm trying to help you!

GRACE: No. You're trying to help yourself. Because when you judge me, you judge every prayer you ever taught me. Don't look so stricken, Michael. Didn't you always know it would come to this?

KING: Grace, you're risking your vocation to prove a point that can't be proven. Please! For the love of God! Give it up!

GRACE: How! I'm a priest! I was born a priest! I will always be a priest! I thought you recognized me?

KING: Until the laws are changed, it's my sacred duty to uphold them. You can't win.

GRACE: They might as well kill me.

KING: My hands are tied.

GRACE: Michael, you know the Church is wrong on this, you know that, don't you? Just between you and me. You know that.

KING: God bless you, Grace.

GRACE: See you in the lion's den, my friend. (She exits.)

(Transition.)

ACT II
Scene III

> Same classroom as Act II, Scene II, devoid of Christmas decorations. offstage the sound of a party in progress. Enter Sister Grace, leading Ramon by the arm. He's dressed in priest's robe and collar. He holds a piece of cake on a paper plate with a plastic fork. She closes door and hugs him. He awkwardly puts down cake and hugs her back.

GRACE: Congratulations, Father.

RAMON: Thanks. I wouldn't be here if it weren't for you.

GRACE: Bull. Somehow, some way, you would eventually have gotten here. I just gave you a little push.

RAMON: Yeah, just a little. Thank you.

GRACE: It was a privilege.

RAMON: This should be you.

GRACE: Soon.

RAMON: I'm sorry if…it upsets you…

GRACE: No, no. This is one of the happiest days of my life.

RAMON: Then stop crying! You're as bad as my mother! Oh! Did you see her?

GRACE: Yes. She's lovely. And I'm keeping you from her.

RAMON: No, wait. I want to tell you something. I, ah…during the ordination ceremony, I prayed that I would never disappoint God and I'd never disappoint you. And that someday we'd be assigned the same parish…

GRACE: Sweet.

RAMON: …as priests.

GRACE: During the ordination ceremony, I prayed that you would make straight the way of the Lord. And that you would lead souls to the light. And then I prayed for courage. *(Breaks down.)* I'm sorry.

RAMON: It's O.K.

GRACE: *(Pulling herself together.)* So. I guess the next time I see you will be at the hearing. Are you nervous?

RAMON: Big time.

GRACE: Just tell the truth. *(Takes medal from beneath her blouse and puts it on Ramon.)* St. Michael the Archangel. Defender in battle.

RAMON: You'll need this!

GRACE: He's here.

RAMON: Thanks.

GRACE: Thank *you* for everything you taught me.

RAMON: What!

GRACE: Oh yes. I'll miss you.

RAMON: Grace, my parish is forty-five minutes outside of Manhattan. We'll see each other.

GRACE: I know.

RAMON: We will!

GRACE: Don't get me started again!

(Ramon embraces Grace.)

GRACE: I'm so proud.

RAMON: Blessings.

GRACE: Back at you, Father.

RAMON: Have some cake.

GRACE: I will.

(Ramon exits.)

GRACE: Father Ramon...Father Ramon..."Mother Grace"?

(Transition.)

ACT II
Scene IV

The next day. Mid-morning. St. Paul's Cathedral, Washington D.C. Sister Virgilia is strolling through the cathedral. Enter Sister Grace. Sees Virgilia. Watches her a moment. Approaches.

GRACE: Hi.

(Virgilia kneels before a statue of St. Jude. Grace kneels beside her.)

GRACE: Mind if I join you?

VIRGILIA: If you're here to intimidate me before I testify...

GRACE: No, not at all. I just thought maybe we could...

VIRGILIA: No, we couldn't. Pardon me while I make my devotions to St. Jude.

GRACE: Saint Jude. Saint of hopeless causes. How apropos.

VIRGILIA: Your sarcastic humor is wasted here, Sister Grace. Save it for Phil Donahue. He apparently thinks you're a riot.

GRACE: Virgilia! You watched the show!

VIRGILIA: It was revolting! You had him laughing so hard, he almost swallowed his tongue!

GRACE: Because Phil's a Catholic! Even you must admit, there are some things about us that are just plain funny!

VIRGILIA: No, there aren't.

GRACE: Oh.

VIRGILIA: You'll have to excuse me. I wouldn't want to stand in the way of you and St. Jude yucking it up. (*She crosses to a statue of St. Theresa of Lisieux. Kneels.*)

GRACE: Dear St. Jude...Don't forget...Tomorrow, three o'clock. (*Crosses to Virgilia. Kneels beside her.*) Virgilia...

VIRGILIA: Why are you harassing me!

GRACE: I'm not. Virgilia, please...can't we go somewhere and talk?

VIRGILIA: No. I'd like to be left in peace now.

GRACE: I never see you anymore.

VIRGILIA: How could you see me! You haven't been at choir practice in months! You're too busy sopping up the spotlight instead of the floors! When was the last time you had laundry duty or led Bible study? You shoved all your obligations on Sister Prudence while you chain yourself to the doors of St. Patrick's Cathedral! Just when I'm beginning to enjoy my golden years, I've got *Entertainment Tonight* sticking a microphone in my face outside the convent, asking me if I saw Madonna at your candlelight vigil. And I doubt very much they were referring to the Blessed Mother! They think our convent is a hotbed of revolution and I'm guilty by association!

GRACE: You really don't like me, do you?

VIRGILIA: I think you're dangerous. I think you should be stopped.

GRACE: And you're the one to stop me.

VIRGILIA: God willing.

GRACE: And how are you going to do that, Virgilia? By telling the Spanish Inquisition tomorrow how many times I missed choir practice?

VIRGILIA: I will not allow you to anger me in the House of the Lord.

GRACE: But isn't your very own soul the House of the Lord?

VIRGILIA: *Oh stop it! Just stop it! I am sick and tired of your New Age blasphemy! Your horoscopes and your judo!*

GRACE: It's T'ai Chi, Virgilia

VIRGILIA: You abandon your religion and then scoff at your sisters who remain loyal to the faith! How dare you call us medieval relics!

GRACE: That was a misquote!

VIRGILIA: I am not a medieval relic!

GRACE: Please stay! Just for a minute!

VIRGILIA: I do not cast pearls before swine.

GRACE: Hold it right there!

VIRGILIA: Why? What are you going to do? Lecture me? Attack me? We're in the church. This is *my* territory.

GRACE: God, you can tick me off!

VIRGILIA: Grace is angry. What else is new?

GRACE: All right, Virgilia. It's your turn. What are you angry about? First thing that pops into your head.

VIRGILIA: Your appearance. Most of the time you look more like a suburban mall walker than a Bride of Christ.

GRACE: Next.

VIRGILIA: You've dropped the devotions. We used to pray together till our knees bled.

GRACE: But bleeding knees are not the only way to salvation.

VIRGILIA: Christ said, "Take up thy cross." He didn't say do it as long as it's comfortable! Do it! That's how you gain entrance to paradise, Sister Grace. Not comfort. Have you been saying your rosary?

GRACE: Not as much.

VIRGILIA: What kind of nun are you?

GRACE: A damn good one!

VIRGILIA: No. You're one of the false prophets Christ warned us about.

GRACE: Dear God, how can you say that!

VIRGILIA: You go around telling people that homosexuals, prostitutes, drug addicts and even murderers are all equal in the eyes of God. They are not.

GRACE: I disagree.

VIRGILIA: No wonder they like you so much.

GRACE: Tell me something, Virgilia. Did you never once, just for a fleeting moment, wonder what it would be like to be a priest?

VIRGILIA: No, Sister Grace. I'm quite content with my quiet little life of serving God.

GRACE: And I've been such a disruption to it, haven't I. I'm sorry.

VIRGILIA: But you won't stop?

GRACE: No.

VIRGILIA: Then neither will I. I know who you are. God does not like power mongers, nor do I. And I consider it God's greatest gift to engage you in soul-to-soul combat. And I intend to win.

GRACE: You really believe all that, don't you?

VIRGILIA: With all my heart.

GRACE: You consider me the enemy.

VIRGILIA: Yes, I do.

GRACE: You believe the Church is perfect.

VIRGILIA: Yes.

GRACE: Without question.

VIRGILIA: Without question.

GRACE: I'd give anything to feel that way again. Anything.

(Virgilia exits.)

(Transition.)

ACT II
Scene V

The night before the proceedings. Stage is dark but for four spotlights. In one spotlight kneels Sister Grace. In one spotlight kneels Father Ramon. In one spotlight kneels Cardinal King. In one spotlight kneels Sister Joseph. They are in different locations and therefore are unaware of each other. Grace, King and Ramon pray simultaneously. Sister Joseph's prayer is silent.

GRACE: Archangels Michael, Gabriel, Raphael, surround me with light in my darkest hour. Carry me across the fears and doubts threatening my good resolve. Make me a conqueror only of my own self. Render me an open vessel of healing and deliverance. I pray that this trial be a stepping stone to the paradise of brotherly and sisterly love. Preside over us, and instill in our hearts a profound and abiding respect for each other. May the light of truth illuminate the whole world and bring us all to everlasting peace. I ask these things in Jesus' name, and so they are done. Amen.

KING: My God...most Holy Advocate...help me. Do I betray Your chosen servant, the Pope, for my beloved friend? Or my friend for the Pope? Grant me wisdom in the face of this adversity and the courage to act upon it. Lead me back to our first encounter...among the poor and downhearted, that I may begin again. You know the countless sins that afflict me. I have only to stand in Your shadow, and I am healed. I place all my trust in you. And so it is done. Amen.

RAMON: Hail Mary, full of grace, the Lord is with thee. Blessed art thou among women and blessed is the fruit of thy womb, Jesus. Holy Mary, Mother of God, pray for us sinners, now and at the hour of our death. Amen. Sweet Jesus, help me! I no sooner give my life to God than You test me like this. Why? What have I done to displease You? I don't understand. How can I testify against her? You've taught me through her example. Please don't take her away from us. Stand up with me tomorrow. Put the right words in my mouth. Good Shepherd, my faith is in Your Sacred Heart. And so it is, and so it shall be. Amen.

SISTER JOSEPH: Amen.

(Transition.)

ACT II
Scene VI

The "Community Room" of the Vatican Embassy. Seated are Cardinal King, Father Jerome, Bishop Foley and Monsignor Frigerio. Witness chair is center stage. Enter Sister Joseph.

SISTER JOSEPH: Excuse me, Cardinal King. Shall I ask Sister Virgilia to come in?

KING: Please.

(Sister Joseph exits. Sister Virgilia enters.)

FATHER: Good morning, Sister Virgilia! Thank you for joining us today!

VIRGILIA: It's an honor and privilege.

FATHER: I'm Father Jerome, this is Bishop Foley, Monsignor Frigerio and Cardinal King.

VIRGILIA: I'm overwhelmed…

BISHOP: Yes…well…these things can be quite overwhelming.

MONSIGNOR: They certainly can.

FATHER: We'll try and make this as brief as possible. *(He turns on tape recorder.)*

BISHOP: How long have you known Sister Grace?

VIRGILIA: About thirty years. I remember the first day she came to live at the convent. She made a commotion even then.

BISHOP: And of late? Have Sister Grace's activities had a negative effect on convent life?

VIRGILIA: Most definitely! We are in desperate need of new catechism books. But every penny in our treasury is going for a security system because Sister Grace is getting death threats!

KING: I had no idea the situation was that serious.

VIRGILIA: It is! The children can't possibly use those old books!

KING: I meant Sister Grace's safety.

VIRGILIA: She doesn't care! She's off lunching with Mario Cuomo while men with great beastly dogs come sniffing around for bombs.

MONSIGNOR: I always liked Mario Cuomo.

BISHOP: Sister, did you ever witness Sister Grace administer the sacraments?

VIRGILIA: I think she makes up her own! She's got all these crystals and rocks! Sometimes, late at night, you can hear this weird tinkling music coming from her room! I heard that she…

KING: Sister, we're not interested in rumor or conjecture. Just tell us what you personally witnessed.

VIRGILIA: Then I would have to say nothing. I personally never witnessed her giving a sacrament.

MONSIGNOR: Earlier this morning, your Mother Superior stated that you told her Sister Grace and Father Ramon were developing a particular friendship. Would you tell us about this?

VIRGILIA: Ever since the first day…the first *night*…she brought Ramon to the Center, they were inseparable. They shopped for the groceries, went on clothing drives…anything that would get them out of the Center alone together. Even when Ramon was in seminary I saw them duck into an empty classroom and close the door! It was an hour before they came out! Then at Father Ramon's ordination party, I saw him follow her into that same classroom again! Now what do you think they were doing in there? *(Clergy overlap their responses: "I couldn't tell you," "Bishop, what do you think?" etc.)*

VIRGILIA: Common logic would lead you to believe that the classroom was their secret rendezvous!

KING: Did you ever see Sister Grace break her vow of chastity?

VIRGILIA: They were always touching each other!

KING: Christians openly and joyously proclaim their love for one another. They touch. Sometimes often. Even in empty classrooms. Even shopping for the groceries.

MONSIGNOR: Wait. I'm confused. Did you or did you not see her break her vow of chastity.

VIRGILIA: Well, not the actual…not…no.

KING: Anymore questions for Sister Virgilia? *(Clergy overlap responses: "No," "That about covers it," "No more questions.")*

KING: Thank you, Sister. You're excused.

VIRGILIA: That's all?

KING: Unless there's something relevant we should know.

VIRGILIA: Yes. When the Apocalypse comes, it won't be because of angels raging in the sky. It will come because blasphemers like Sister Grace are paving the way for the Anti-Christ. I urge you to denounce her as vociferously as Christ denounced the money changers in the temple.

KING: We will consider your recommendation.

VIRGILIA: I am at your beck and call.

FATHER: Thank you.

VIRGILIA: *"Stat crux dum volvitur orbis."* The cross remains constant while the world turns.

FATHER: So true. God bless you. *(Virgilia exits. Father Jerome turns off tape recorder.)*

BISHOP: It's always so uplifting to meet such a…a…

MONSIGNOR: Extraordinary…

FATHER: Nun.

BISHOP: Exactly.

KING: Sometimes I think the Church gets a little carried away with this chastity issue.

(Clergy murmur in agreement: "Oh, yes," etc.)

MONSIGNOR: Shall we have Sister Joseph bring us coffee?

(Clergy overlap responses: "None for me, thank you," etc. Enter Sister Joseph with Father Ramon.)

SISTER JOSEPH: Father Ramon is here.

FATHER: Ramon, welcome to the Embassy. How are you today?

RAMON: Nervous.

MONSIGNOR: Don't be nervous, Father Ramon. We'll try and make this as brief and comfortable as possible. Would you like some coffee?

RAMON: No, thank you.

FATHER: I'm Father Jerome, this is Bishop Foley, Monsignor Frigerio and his Eminence Cardinal King.

RAMON: Hey! How ya doin'?

KING: We're sorry to involve you in something like this so soon after your ordination.

BISHOP: We appreciate your cooperation.

FATHER: Sit, sit.

(Father Jerome struggles with tape recorder. It's jammed.)

BISHOP: How long have you known Sister Grace?

FATHER: Hold it. I hate this.

(Bishop fiddles with recorder.)

FATHER: Sister Joseph, I need you. *(Releases button.)* Just hold that thought. This thing is…I can't…

SISTER JOSEPH: If I may…

(Indicating Father's pen. He gives it to her. She puts pen through hole in tape and winds it. Gives pen back. Puts tape in machine.)

FATHER: Thank you.

SISTER JOSEPH: You're welcome.

KING: You may proceed.

RAMON: Yeah…I've known Sister Grace…must be six or seven years.

BISHOP: And what is your relationship?

RAMON: She's like a mother to me.

MONSIGNOR: While you were living at the Houston Street Crisis Center…

RAMON: Excuse me. I was also working there. Sister Grace gave me a job.

MONSIGNOR: Living and working there…fine. During that time, you and Sister
   Grace are accused of developing a particular friendship.

RAMON: I guess all friendships are "particular," aren't they?

BISHOP: The Monsignor is referring to a romantic relationship.

RAMON: I told you. she's like my mother.

MONSIGNOR: Several witnesses have testified that you two were inseparable.
   One of the Sisters said your relationship was very physical.

BISHOP: She didn't say "very physical," she said they were always touching each other.

MONSIGNOR: Yes. Always touching each other. "Very physical."

KING: Ramon, did you ever have a romantic relationship with Sister Grace?

MONSIGNOR: Sexual.

BISHOP: Just trying to keep the record straight.

KING: Father Ramon?

RAMON: See, I had this terrible experience with the Church.

BISHOP: Really!

RAMON: Oh yeah.

BISHOP: I've been hearing that a lot lately.

RAMON: You got to understand something. I'm like the original prodigal son. I
   cut out. I squandered every gift I was ever given until I met Grace. I cut
   out on her, too. But she kept draggin' me home till it stuck. I'm resurrect-
   ed and it's because of her. So, the answer to your question is *no*. Our relationship is based on the highest degree of love and respect.

KING: Any further questions regarding Father Ramon's relationship with Sister Grace?
   (Clergy overlap response: "No, I don't believe so." "No further questions," etc.)

BISHOP: As you know, the Church does not recognize the teaching or belief in
   reincarnation. Does Sister Grace?

KING: I think we're really reaching with this one.

BISHOP: Cardinal King, it's on the list.

MONSIGNOR: It's right here.

KING: Please answer the question, Father Ramon.

RAMON: She has a very open mind.

BISHOP: Does she believe in reincarnation?

RAMON: She believes it's a rare soul who can comprehend the majesty and miracle of God in a single lifetime.

BISHOP: Am I not speaking clearly?

MONSIGNOR: She believes in reincarnation.

BISHOP: Thank you for clearing that up for me, Monsignor Frigerio.

MONSIGNOR: You're welcome, Bishop Foley.

BISHOP: What were her past lives?

KING: I think it's safe to move on. Father Ramon, one more question. Have you ever witnessed Sister Grace perform any of the sacraments? Penance? Marriage?

RAMON: Have any of you been to the Crisis Center? Do you know what this woman does in a day?

KING: We are well aware of her selfless service to others.

FATHER: But that's not the issue.

RAMON: It *is* the issue! Sister Grace lives the Gospels!

BISHOP: That doesn't excuse her attacks on the church.

RAMON: We can't lose her!

KING: The sacraments? A simple yes or no is sufficient.

RAMON: But it wasn't simple! It was an emergency! A couple of years ago, a friend of mine was dying of an overdose. I begged Grace to give him Last Rites.

KING: Did she absolve him of his sins?

RAMON: She didn't want to! She was afraid but I begged her!

BISHOP: Did she hear your friend's confession?

RAMON: It was an act of mercy!

KING: I understand, son.

BISHOP: You're obligated to answer the question.

RAMON: This is all my fault. She would never have done it if I hadn't...

MONSIGNOR: Yes or no.

RAMON: Yes. She did. But let me tell you something. She was as legitimate a priest in that moment in that park as any of us could ever hope to be.

FATHER: I believe we've finished with Father Ramon?

KING: Yes. I hear you're wonderful with the young people of your parish. You've got a bright future with us and we feel very fortunate to have you.

RAMON: Sure.

KING: And try not to worry. It's best you put this behind you.

RAMON: How do I do that?

MONSIGNOR: Pray.

BISHOP: Pray a lot.

KING: God bless you. You're excused.

RAMON: God bless Sister Grace.

FATHER: Good afternoon, Father.

  (Ramon exits.)

KING: Gentlemen, the gravity of the situation requires the utmost care and sensitivity. I suggest you spend the next few hours finding some. Questions?
  (Clergy overlap responses: "No," "No questions, Cardinal." etc.)

KING: We'll be hearing from Sister Grace this afternoon.

(Transition.)

ACT II
Scene VII

That same day. 6:00 in the "Community Room" of the Vatican Embassy. Clergy are present. Sister Grace is before them.

KING: Anymore questions?

(Clergy overlap responses: "No." "No, I believe we've covered everything." etc.)

KING: Is there anything you'd like to say before we adjourn?

GRACE: Why?

KING: Why what?

GRACE: All of it. Why? Please make me understand why I can't be a priest. Why do I qualify for baptism, confirmation, eternal life itself, but not the ministry? I really want to understand.

FATHER: She's digressing again.

MONSIGNOR: You're not here to berate us about the priesthood. You're here to defend yourself against some very serious charges.

GRACE: All these allegations are just smoke screens for the real charge: I'm a woman. And I've become unmanageable.

BISHOP: It's been a very long day.

KING: Bishop Foley, it's not that late.

(Sister Joseph sneaks in the back.)

GRACE: I'm not a threat to you. I want to work with you, not for you. There is one priest for every 1,200 Catholics in this country. What will the ratio be in five years? Ten years? Even now, priests bless massive amounts of communion wafers and distribute them to parishes without any priests at all. The people, both men and women, then give each other communion. Now why am I good enough to give communion, but not good enough to bless the wafer? You'd sooner deny people the keystone of our faith, witnessing the miracle of bread and wine turning into the body and blood of Christ, than have a woman priest. That is sexism. Sexism is a sin. It is ethically, morally and spiritually wrong. It is a sacrilege.

FATHER: Cardinal King, really…

KING: Just listen, Father.

GRACE: The word "Catholic" means "universal," "involving all." Yet every day, you send an implicit message to the world: "God has sanctified the inequality of women." That is a lie. And if you knew, deep in the marrow of your bones, the consequences, you could not bear it. It's like the poisoning of a water supply. The contamination filters down through every aspect of our lives. It's the strongest link in the chain of terminal patriarchy that's choking this planet to death. And I will howl to the heavens and the Vatican and anyone else who'll listen, until that lie is vanquished.

FATHER: You have a gift for self-dramatization.

GRACE: Our seminaries are empty! Do you care? The convents can no longer support themselves! Young people are not attracted to religious vocations! The facts do not need dramatizing!

FATHER: I didn't say you were dramatizing the facts.

GRACE: Father Jerome, women make up three quarters of the world's religious vocations. We are your greatest resource! Look at us! God has our face, too!

FATHER: Sit down, Sister Grace.

GRACE: I will not sit down! And I will not be silenced until you abolish sexual apartheid.

MONSIGNOR: Sister Grace, fortunate as you are...

BISHOP: Sister Grace, you underestimate...

MONSIGNOR: Excuse me, Bishop Foley.

BISHOP: But she can't just...

MONSIGNOR: Excuse me!

BISHOP: This is completely inappropriate!

MONSIGNOR: I was talking!

KING: Gentlemen, please.

MONSIGNOR: Fortunate as you are to have glimpsed the face of God, may I remind you that Christ's chosen disciples were men.

GRACE: But Mary Magdalene was his constant companion! Christ first appeared to her after the resurrection. It was she who brought the good word to the disciples. Doesn't that make her the first missionary?

BISHOP: There were twelve disciples. Twelve. Peter. Matthew. James.

MONSIGNOR: Mark, Thomas, John...

GRACE: Women stayed at the foot of the cross when all the male disciples had fled in fear. We prepared His body for burial. Christ used Mary's body to gain entrance to this world. Through the free will of a woman the course of humanity was forever changed.

FATHER: Look it up in that Bible you know so well. Twelve male disciples.

GRACE: That Bible was written by men, translated by men, and until recently, interpreted by men. You've written us out of history because it was politically expedient. What have we done to warrant such contempt?

BISHOP: I've never heard a more self-serving distortion of scripture in all my...

GRACE: There were no Polish disciples. Is John Paul II distorting scripture? There were no black disciples. Are black priests distorting scripture? Most of the disciples were married. Doesn't that mean...

MONSIGNOR: Oh, we're not going to get into that, are we?

KING: No, we're not.

GRACE: I challenge you because my Creator demands it of me.

FATHER: Sister Grace, you refused to answer all the accusations. Doesn't your Creator demand that you answer us?

GRACE: Definitely not.

BISHOP: We share the same Creator.

GRACE: Let's find a new way to articulate God that includes the feminine. Because as long as we equate God with maleness, we will equate maleness with power. Let's restore original Christianity: to be Christ-like. I'm a priest. This is what a priest looks like. *(Indicating King.)* This is what a priest looks like. *(Crossing to Sister Joseph.)* This is what a priest looks like. It looks like love. Would you bow your heads, please?

(King and Sister Joseph bow their heads. With no recourse, the Clergy reluctantly comply.)

GRACE: Oh Great Redeemer, we converge here to midwife a sacred circle of believers; where no one is first or last, higher or lower, but welcome simply by their kinship to God. We look to You, and all the angels and saints, to light our path. Amen.

SISTER JOSEPH AND KING: Amen.

GRACE: My future and our spiritual integrity lie in your hands. I pray you judge wisely.

(Lights fade.)

KING: We will notify you of our decision as soon as possible.

(Transition.)

ACT II
Scene VIII

One week later. The Church of the Immaculate Conception in New Jersey. Four steps lead up to altar and crucifix, both facing upstage. Father Ramon is alone at prayer. Enter Sister Grace.

GRACE: *Judas!* What did you tell them?

RAMON: I...I told the truth!

GRACE: What did you say!

RAMON: They asked me if I'd ever seen you give the sacraments.

GRACE: Oh God…

RAMON: They must've asked you the same thing!

GRACE: I refused to answer them!

RAMON: And they accepted that?

GRACE: It was the bravest thing I've ever done in my life.

RAMON: Why didn't you just tell them?

GRACE: Why?! Don't you know what you've done?

RAMON: What?

GRACE: They've expelled me from the Sisters of Charity!

RAMON: Oh no. Christ have mercy…

GRACE: This isn't a dismissal, it's an execution. I'm dead. My heart, my love, my family…I am dead.

RAMON: I'll be your family. It's all right. C'mon…sit down. Grace, you've been preparing for this a long time. You've always known.

GRACE: I also know I'm going to die one day. That doesn't mean I won't struggle for the last breath.

RAMON: Easy…

GRACE: Ramon, I'm in such danger…

RAMON: From what?

GRACE: Myself.

RAMON: How?

GRACE: Because…because I think I hate them. Don't let me. Don't let me because if I hate them, I'll never get over this.

RAMON: You have every right to be angry.

GRACE: No. This is not anger. I know anger. This is something so terrifying. Pray for me!

RAMON: We'll pray together.

GRACE: I can't. You do it for me.

RAMON: Holy Mother, we cry out to You in our anguish. Draw us closer as we face this heartbreak together.

GRACE: *Why!*

RAMON: Grant this devoted nun peace of mind and the strength to bear her cross.

GRACE: I'm not a nun. Not anymore. Because…because I hate them.

RAMON: Don't say that.

GRACE: I do! I hate them! And nuns don't feel hate and anger and bitterness. Who can give me penance for this?

RAMON: God can.

GRACE: God. All my life I hammered away at any aspect of my being I thought was displeasing to God. I wanted there to be nothing left of me but love. And now that's the last thing I feel. Is that why God's so angry with me?

RAMON: Don't blame it on God. You're angry with yourself.

GRACE: Who's side are you on?

RAMON: God's.

GRACE: Well, that let's you off the hook, doesn't it? Just float up there in the sky with God while the rest of us spill our guts down here on the battlefield.

RAMON: Hey, if anybody's fought on the battlefield, it's me. You know that. But I've used those experiences to build my church.

GRACE: Your church? *Your church! Who the hell do you think you're talking to!*

RAMON: Right now, I honestly don't know.

GRACE: You wouldn't even have a church if it wasn't for me!

RAMON: I'm a good priest! What do you want me to do? Not be one so you'll feel better?

GRACE: I'm getting out of here before I say something I'll regret the rest of my life.

RAMON: Grace, get a hold of yourself!

GRACE: Get a hold of myself! Go to hell! My Church has just rewarded my lifetime of service by slamming the door in my face! I feel like I could tear this place apart with my bare hands and all you can say is "Get a hold of yourself!" Christ Almighty! I'm being choked to death but I'm supposed to get a hold of myself! I'm telling you I'm losing my faith. Help me, Father.

RAMON: Forgive them.

GRACE: I can't.

RAMON: Offer it up, Grace. Lay your suffering on His altar.

GRACE: What if there's nothing more on that altar than what we imagine? (*A chill runs through Grace. From now till end of scene, She gets progressively colder.*)

RAMON: Don't let them take your faith, Grace. They can take everything, but they can't take your faith.

GRACE: My faith would've never let this happen.

RAMON: Don't you see? It's a blessing. God's kicked everything out from under you so you'll soar to Him. Leave all these distractions and go. Trust me, it's a blessing.

GRACE: Ramon, if I'm not a nun, who am I?

RAMON: You're a priest. And I told them. They should be honored to have you.

GRACE: Look at me. This is not a priest. I don't have the slightest idea who I am.

RAMON: Go find out. That's the real trial.

GRACE: Listen, I'm very upset right now. So if I said anything that hurt you, I'm sorry.

RAMON: You called me Judas.

GRACE: No. You're not Judas. I built my own tomb, stone by stone.

RAMON: I am not one of them.

GRACE: I need to be alone. *(Grace doesn't acknowledge him. By now, she's shivering with cold.)*

(Ramon takes off blazer. Puts it around Grace's shoulders. Rubs her arms while she shivers.)

RAMON: You all right?

(Grace doesn't acknowledge him.)

RAMON: I'll be in the rectory. Stop and see me before you leave.

(Grace nods affirmatively. Ramon exits. Grace kneels before crucifix.)

GRACE: You called my name and I answered "yes." You laid Your hand so heavy on my shoulder, I stumbled beneath the weight of it, Still I answered "yes." But I have nothing left to give You. Release me. For the love of God, let me give up.

(Transition.)

ACT II
Scene IX

Six months later. Washington Square Park. Early morning. Sister Joseph, in full nun regalia, stands timidly clutching a petition and clipboard.

SISTER JOSEPH: Hello sir. We're petitioning for…Oh, excuse me, madam. We're… *(Grace enters.)*

GRACE: How's it going over here?

SISTER JOSEPH: Maybe this was a mistake.

GRACE: You can do it, Sister!

SISTER JOSEPH: I don't think I can.

GRACE: Listen to me. If it wasn't for all your messages and little notes and prayers, I wouldn't be here. O.K., so it took six months, but you still did it. And if you can do that, you can do this.

SISTER JOSEPH: Maybe we should pray first.

GRACE: There's a time for prayer and a time for action!

SISTER JOSEPH: Yes! To everything, there's a season, and this is my springtime! Excuse me, sir? Sir?

GRACE: No, that's One-Eyed Jo Jo. He's signed five times already. Continue.

SISTER JOSEPH: Good morning, Madam! We're…Hi. How are you? We're petitioning for women…women…

GRACE: *Women in the priesthood! Now!*

SISTER JOSEPH: *Yea!*

GRACE: We envision a Church, a nation, a world based on the inherent goodness of every soul! Please sir, join us in heralding this new partnership of woman and man, man and woman! God bless you! Now you try.

SISTER JOSEPH: Hello…uh…Hi…that's an awfully nice handbag you've got there.

GRACE: Sister Joseph!

SISTER JOSEPH: I know. Oh my Savior, what's he doing here?

GRACE: You've nothing to be afraid of.

SISTER JOSEPH: Except profound humiliation and losing my job!

(Enter King.)

KING: I was told this was a hot spot for T'ai Chi practitioners. I didn't expect to find a mecca for radical nuns.

SISTER JOSEPH: Oh, I'm hardly a radical, Your Eminence.

GRACE: How did you find us?

KING: Father Ramon.

GRACE: Ah. He keeps pretty good track of me.

KING: May I speak with you privately?

GRACE: Of course. *(To Sister Joseph.)* Carry on, Sister.

(Lights go down on a bewildered Sister Joseph. Up on nearby park bench. King and Grace sit.)

KING: For God's sake, Grace, what's she doing out here in the cold! She's got arthritis, diabetes, heart disease!

GRACE: You see a woman wracked with the infirmities of old age. I see the Angel of Youth. She is where I was thirty years ago. She asked me to teach her how to storm the barricades. So don't chastise me for recruiting poor Sister Joseph. She recruited me.

KING: That's not why I came. Did you get my letter?

GRACE: No. What did it say?

KING: That I was very worried about you! The newspapers said you were homeless and living on the street!

GRACE: I was for awhile.

KING: You're going to give me a stroke, you know that?

GRACE: After my expulsion, I was flooded with offers: book contracts, the college lecture circuit, talk shows. The feminists branded me their new Messiah. So I went on retreat. Here in the streets.

KING: Grace, I'm sorry. I wish there were a thousand different ways to say it.

GRACE: You don't need my forgiveness. The hardest thing for me was forgiving myself.

KING: For what?

GRACE: For not starting sooner and yelling louder.

KING: Then, you're not giving up.

GRACE: Hell no. This is my ministry. I'm organizing a huge protest in St. Peter's square in the spring.

KING: I should have stood up for you at the hearing.

GRACE: Why didn't you?

KING: It was my job to keep women like you out!

GRACE: You only brought me closer. The nights were long, Michael. I was reduced to nothing. And in that nothing, I found the very center of God. And you know what I learned? That there is no person or power on this earth that can estrange me from God, except myself. And I'm so grateful. I'm so in love.

KING: After the hearing, I was reminded of the man who asked Christ how to get into heaven. He said to sell all you have, give it to the poor, and follow me. I looked around me at the riches and the glory and realized that I was following the letter of the law; not Christ. So I'm going back to work in an Appalachian parish.

GRACE: Michael!

KING: Grace, I'm never happier than when God's left nothing of me but a heap of exhaustion at the end of the day. I can hardly wait.

GRACE: Welcome back.

KING: I need to ask you something I should've asked you a long time ago.

GRACE: What?

KING: Would you hear my confession?

GRACE: I'd be honored. Have you prepared yourself?

KING: Yes. Bless me, Mother, for I have sinned. My last confession was three days ago. I am guilty of the sins of hypocrisy, betrayal and deceit. I am profoundly sorry. I have begged God's forgiveness and the forgiveness of the one person...the women...of my sisters I have betrayed.

GRACE: *(Makes sign of the cross over him.)* I absolve you of your sins in the name of the Father and the Mother, the Divine Child and the Holy Spirit. For your penance, go love and serve those you have betrayed.

(They get to their feet.)

KING: Amen.

(She and King embrace.)

KING: God be with you, Grace.

GRACE: Back at you, Father.

(*Lights up on Sister Joseph. Grace and King cross to her.*)

SISTER JOSEPH: Excuse me sir, we're petitioning for…What did you call me?

KING: Whatcha got there, Sister Joseph?

SISTER JOSEPH: Nothing.

(*King signs Sister Joseph's petition. Offers her his hand. She goes to kiss his ring, King shakes her hand.*)

SISTER JOSEPH: Thank you, Your Eminence.

KING: Michael.

(*King exits. Sister Joseph is awestruck.*)

SISTER JOSEPH: Did you…did you…

GRACE: Yeah, I saw it.

SISTER JOSEPH: *Praise the holy one!*

GRACE: Tell it like it is, girl!

SISTER JOSEPH: My first signature!

GRACE: All things are possible for those who live in faith!

SISTER JOSEPH: I can say, *"Mountain! Be thou moved!"* And that mountain's going to pull up roots and *move!* Now I want some signatures for women in the priesthood and I'm going to stand my ground till I get them!

GRACE: Amen, Sister. Amen!

(*Curtain.*)

END OF PLAY

Vladivostok Blues

Jocelyn A. Beard

Vladivostok Blues was Produced by Love Creek Productions—Rural New York City at the Howard Clurman Theatre, May 13, 1996. It was directed by Sharon Fallon with the following cast:

Piotr	Mark E. Macken
Sophia de la Cruz	Annemarie Downey
Stu bernstein	Chuck Simone
Lena	Terri Monahan
Tasha	Kirsten Walsh
Miguel Fuentes	Sal Brienza
Mrs. Nobokov	John Jordan

BIOGRAPHY

Playwright/Editor Jocelyn A. Beard has edited numerous books on theatre including: *100 Great Monologues from the Renaissance Theatre, The Best Men's Stage Monologues of 1995* and *The Best Stage Scenes of 1995.* A veteran of NYU's film school and the Yale School of Drama, Jocelyn's award-winning plays include *Freakmakers, I Kissed Elvis* and *Perpetual Care.* Her Screenplay, *Igor and the Lunatics,* was made into a feature film and subsequently listed in Heavy Metal magazine as "One of the 10 Sleaziest Movies Ever Made!" Notwithstanding, Jocelyn lives in an old haunted house in the Hudson River Valley with her husband, Kevin Kitowski, their beautiful daughter, Blythe, and lots of dogs.

AUTHOR'S NOTE

A couple of years ago I read an article in the New York Times about a Mexican soap opera star making a personal appearance tour across Russia. Despite the new economic hardships brought about by the end of the communist era, Russians lined up for days to spend their last rubles on tickets to hear their favorite TV star answer questions via an interpreter. Women brought their babies into the auditoriums in hopes that the actress would kiss them and bring them luck. Men shouted marriage proposals. This seemed to me a brilliant juxtaposition of cultures that needed to be exploited as soon as I could fire up my PC. A zillion drafts, many readings and two productions later, *Vladivostok Blues* was finally a living story. This could not have been accomplished without the help of the Schoolhouse Theatre's Playwrights Program, manned by Doug Michael, a great friend and occasional mentor, who allowed me the unconditional gratitude must go to Sharon Fallon at Love Creek Productions in NYC, who saw something worthwhile in the play and brought it to the attention of Le Wilhelm and Philip Galbraith, who were kind enough to accept it into their Developmental Series, which eventually led to a mainstage production. To these people; to Eric and Marisa, who have always believed in me (for whatever strange reason); to my patient and supportive husband, Kevin; my incredible daughter, Blythe and to my wonderful mom, Marilyn: I dedicate *Vladivostok Blues* and it's appearance in this book.

CHARACTERS

Sophia de la Cruz: A Mexican soap opera star. A passionate diva, 20s–30s.

Piotr: An idealistic Russian. Plays blues guitar. 20–30.

Tasha: Piotr's quick-witted sister, 20s.

Stu Bernstein: Sophia's American manager, 30s.

Lena: A lusty Russian policewoman, 20–30.

Miguel Fuentes: Sophia's fiery husband, also a soap star 30–40.

Mrs. Nobokov: Piotr's upstairs neighbor, an offstage voice.

SCENE

A small and depressed apartment in Vladivostok, Russia, and a small and depressed office in the Vladivostok Police Headquarters.

TIME

The present

VLADIVOSTOK BLUES

In the darkness we hear the sounds of a struggle. Someone dragging something heavy up a flight of stairs. A man's voice whispering desperately in Russian, a woman's muffled cries in Spanish. The sound of a door opening. Lights on to reveal Piotr's apartment. It is small and dismal with minimal furnishings. Piotr carries Sophia into the apartment. She has a burlap bag over her head and her wrists and ankles are tied. He quickly carries her to his threadbare couch and unceremoniously dumps her. Sophia struggles wildly against her restraints and shouts curses in Spanish.

PIOTR: *Tikho, goloubushka, tikho! Za nami moghlei ghnatsiia!* (Please, we must be quiet until I make certain we weren't followed.)

SOPHIA: *Quita me esta mierda asquerosa de mi cabeza, carhao!* (Take this disgusting piece of shit off my head, you asshole!)

PIOTR: *Pozhalusta, Angelina!* (Angelina, please!)

SOPHIA: *Para de llamar me asi tu loco! Socorro!* (Stop calling me that, you lunatic! Help! Help!)

PIOTR: *Rady gogha, Angelina, tikho!* (Please, Angelina, you must be quiet!)

SOPHIA: *Socorro! Policia! Un Asesinato!* (Help! Police! Murder!)

(Piotr wrings his hands and rushes anxiously to the window.)

PIOTR: *Angelina, Ia vas proshiu! Onhi vas ulsishiat!* (Angelina, please! They'll hear you!)

SOPHIA: *(Really screaming.) Ayuda me!!!!!!*

(Piotr hesitates for a moment and then pulls the bag off her head. She is amazingly beautiful and glamorous. A brutal juxtaposition to the surroundings. If looks could kill, Piotr would now be a pile of ashes.)

PIOTR: *(Nervously backing away and peering out window.) Vot takh. Nu, tikho, goloubushka, Angelina, tikho! Banda Morales...*(There. Now please, Angelina, you must be quiet. The Morales Gang...)

SOPHIA: *Socorro! Necisito ayuda auxio!!* (Someone help me!!!!)

PIOTR: *(Finally realizing the problem.)* Shhh...okay, okay. Ummm...*Deutsche?* German?

SOPHIA: *(Understanding.)* No. *Français?*

PIOTR: French? No. Persian?

SOPHIA: *Quien?*

PIOTR: *(English.)* Persian?

SOPHIA: *(English.)* Persian? No.

PIOTR: *(Hopefully.)* Serbo-Croatian?

SOPHIA: Serbo…Jesus Christ, somebody get me a fucking Prozac!

PIOTR: *(Joyfully.)* English!

SOPHIA: Of course I speak English! I'm Mexican for chrissakes!

PIOTR: I, too, speak English! Oh, my Angelina, at last we may speak!

SOPHIA: Okay, Boris, let's get one thing straight: My name isn't Angelina. It's Sophia. Sophia Luisa Magdalena de la Cruz, *entiende? (As if to a child.)* Angelina is the character I play on TV. She isn't real. She doesn't exist…

PIOTR: But…

SOPHIA: …and if you dare to call me that name one more time, I swear to you that I will…

PIOTR: Shhhhh! Angelina, please! The Morales Gang may have followed us!

SOPHIA: *(Staring incredulously.)* Morales Gang! That storyline is two years old, for chrissakes! *(Scornfully.)* Morales Gang. What kind of borscht-eating psycho are you, anyway? I told Stu that coming here was a big mistake. I mean, after all, it is Russia. But did he listen? Oh, no. *(Imitating Stu, her manager.)* "Do Russia, babe. It's your biggest market." Market my ass. I've been from one end of this shithole to another and all I've seen are lousy hotels with no toilet paper, undrinkable water, inedible food, bad booze— have you ever tasted Bulgarian Port Wine? And the people! My plastic surgeon could retire here! Oh, and the pollution! Before you say it, it's worse than Mexico City! Have you ever been to Cheliabinsk? The water in my hotel was black, I tell you, black! And this is *my* market? *(Imitating Stu again.)* "They'll treat you like royalty, babe. We'll live like the Czars!" Well, my *gringo* manager forgot one tiny little detail: You idiots had a revolution that wiped out any remnants of civilization! You executed all the good-looking people, for chrissakes! And just look at what it's done to your gene pool! You put the potato farmer and the factory worker at the top of your social ladder where the good-looking civilized people are supposed to be! It's no wonder that what few normal people are left are just dying to get out! Well, when I get out of here I never want to see anyone or anything Russian ever again! I am going to demand that *Forever Angelina* be pulled from this market! Why a Mexican soap opera is the number one show in this mixed-up wasteland is beyond me. It took my management two years—*two years*—to get us a spot on American cable. Two years, and there are people in America who speak Spanish, let me tell you. But here…here in this…this *vat* that you call a country you all speak this Russian! Do you know that the *puta* who dubs my voice in Moscow weighs over three hundred pounds! And she has a disgusting wart *(Thrusting out her chin.)* right here! I tell you I will never make a personal appearance tour again! I shouldn't have to see three-hundred pound women with warts dubbing over my love scenes! I'm a star, for chrissakes! I should be spared things like that!

PIOTR: *(Shocked.)* Angelina!

SOPHIA: *(At the top of her lungs.)* My name is Sophia Luisa Magdalena de la Cruz! Help! Help!!!!!!! *(Sophia thrashes wildly on the couch.)*

PIOTR: Oh dear.

(There is a sudden banging on the ceiling.)

VOICE: Quiet down there!

PIOTR: Sorry, Mrs. Nobokov!

SOPHIA: Help me! Help Me!

(We now hear the sound of Mrs. Nobokov stomping out of her apartment and coming down the stairs. Piotr races to the kitchen area and finds a large roll of duct tape. He tears off a big piece and presses it over Sophia's mouth. She howls with fury.)

MRS. NOBOKOV: *(Pounding on door.)* What going on in there?!?!?

PIOTR: *(Thinking fast.)* Nothing, Mrs. Nobokov! I'm just watching *Forever Angelina.*

MRS. NOBOKOV: It's Sunday night!

PIOTR: Right! It's Sunday night… *(Looking at the roll of tape in his hands.)* it's a tape!

MRS. NOBOKOV: You don't have a tape machine!

PIOTR: No…I don't….it's my sister's, it's Tasha's! She…loaned it to me because… I'm sick! It's a tape, I'm watching a tape.

MRS. NOBOKOV: Well, turn it down!

PIOTR: Sorry.

MRS. NOBOKOV: I have to be at the cannery early in morning!

PIOTR: Sorry, Mrs. Nobokov. I'll turn it down.

MRS. NOBOKOV: It's bad enough that I have to listen to your guitar, day and night!

PIOTR: I'm sorry, Mrs. Nobokov.

MRS. NOBOKOV: Good.

PIOTR: Sorry.

(Piotr listens for a moment. When he doesn't hear anything, he presses his ear to the door. We hear the sounds of Mrs. Nobokov stomping back upstairs and slamming her door. Piotr breathes a sigh of relief and slumps against the door. He then remembers Sophia, who glowers at him from the floor.)

PIOTR: Angelina, please understand, I'm doing this for your own good! That evil Chico Morales has paid half a million American dollars to those wicked thugs, Bernardo and Manuel, to bring you back to Cancun. If he gets you back, he'll never let you escape again! Carlos's death has made him insane. But you'll be safe here, you will. Much safer than at home with your mother drinking so much all the time. Oh! Forgive me, I know how much you love your mother. Tasha—that's my little sister—Tasha is bringing over some clothes for you. I told her they were for Yvonne's wife who just lost job. I cannot wait for her to meet you! What a surprise it will be! So, you see, I have thought of everything. You will have clothes... *(He runs to kitchen area and produces a sorry looking loaf of bread.)* ...you will have food, and most important of all you will be safe from that despicable Chico Morales. You'll be safe if only you'll stay quiet... like when you and Lucia were hiding from the drug cartel in the abandoned fireworks factory, remember? *(Suddenly inspired.)* Tomorrow is Monday, so we can watch the show to see where Chico sent Bernardo and Manuel. We'll know what they're up to. We can stay one step ahead of that dastardly Chico Morales and his crime ring! *(Suddenly inspired.)* Maybe we could even call Ramon and warn him about the baby switch at the hospital in Mexico City! Now that Lucia has the fatal brain tumor, he'll need to know that Maria was carrying his baby! Don't you agree? Then he'd finally be able to confront his grandfather and claim the family hacienda in Tabasco!

(During the above speech, Sophia has begun to make a noise that builds until it sounds like uncontrollable sobbing. Her shoulders and chest shake and heave.)

PIOTR: Oh, dear! Angelina, what is it? Is it Ramon?

(Sophia shakes her head no.)

PIOTR: Lucia's brain tumor?

(No.)

PIOTR: Your mother's drinking? Oh, forgive me! I know you're very sensitive about that...

(But she is shaking her head No, no, no!)

PIOTR: *(Frowning.)* Well, then...

(He gently removes the tape to reveal that Sophia is laughing hysterically.)

PIOTR: Angelina!

SOPHIA: *(Catching her breath.)* In the first place, Boris, Lucia is dead! That's right: *esta muerda!* That old brain tumor did her in for November sweeps two years ago. I cried like a baby at the funeral, but the dress was great.

(Piotr protests, but she plows relentlessly on.)

SOPHIA: And Maria! As it turns out, she didn't die in the explosion. That sleazy lawyer of hers was finally able to negotiate a new contract with the network, so up from the ashes she rose: a Phoenix in red polyester.

PIOTR: I beg you...

SOPHIA: She and I have been competing for the affections of Antonio Paz, new character, multimillionaire and all-around good guy who, of course, is desperately in love with me—that is to say, Angelina, but as you know, I'll never be able to forget that weekend in Cancun with Chico Morales...

(In desperation, Piotr replaces the tape. Sophia has stopped struggling. She stares malevolently at her captor, knowing that the upper hand, at last, is hers.

Lights down on apartment.

Change to: An office in a police station.

A small office that was once a KGB interrogation room. There is a small holding cell in the corner.

Stu Bernstein paces nervously across the floor. Stu is dressed stylishly and with great expense. Armani, Armani, Armani.

Lena enters. She is an attractive young woman dressed in a police uniform. She carries an enormous stack of papers which she deposits on her desk.)

STU: Jesus Christ! It took you long enough! Did you find it?

LENA: I am certain the missing person forms must be in here somewhere, Mr. Bernstein.

STU: Oh for... listen, shouldn't the Inspector be putting some men on this? You know, sending them out *(Gestures dramatically.)* there... to find her?

LENA: I'm afraid we have to go by the book, Mr. Bernstein. First, we fill out the forms.

STU: *(Exasperated.)* Then fill them out for chrissakes!

(As Lena looks through the papers.)

STU: Sophia isn't in that pile of paper! She's out *(Gestures again.)* there!!

LENA: So, you know where she is!

STU: What? No! I don't know where Sophia is! I only know where she isn't, which is right here in this room where nothing is being done to find her! Did you at least make those calls?

LENA: Yes, Mr. Bernstein.

STU: *(After a minute.)* And...?

LENA: And?

STU: The calls...?

LENA: The calls...?

STU: Did you get through? Did you talk to anyone at the embassy?

LENA: *(Smiling.)* Oh, yes!

STU: And...?

LENA: And...? Oh, yes! I spoke with the most delightful man! Some kind of secretary I believe he said he was... Octavio, yes I believe that he said his name was Octavio. Very charming. Said to look him up the next time I am in Moscow.

STU: *(Barely containing his exasperation, through clenched teeth.)* What else did he say?

LENA: *(Thinking.)* Nothing.

STU: Nothing????

LENA: *(Thinking harder.)* No, that was it.

STU: Okay, let me get this straight. You phoned the Mexican Embassy in Moscow and informed a secretary named Octavio—a charming and delightful man—that the most famous citizen of his country has just been kidnapped at gunpoint right here in Vladivostok, and all he had to say was "Look me up the next time you're in town"?!?!

LENA: Oh my!

STU: What? What does that mean, oh my?

LENA: Well, you see, I never told him.

STU: Never told him what?

LENA: About Angelina... I mean, Sophia.

STU: *(Thundering.) You never told him?????*

LENA: Well, you see, I called and asked to speak with the Ambassador who, as it turns out, is at the symphony, so when I wasn't able to speak with the Ambassador, I asked Octavio if I could leave a message for him to call here as soon as he can... and then we just started chatting...

STU: *(Nearly hysterical.)* Chatting? You were chatting?

LENA: Yes, Mr. Bernstein. Chatting.

STU: And it never once occurred to you to tell this Octavio about Sophia?

LENA: Well, I thought it might be a secret.

STU: A secret!?!?

LENA: *(Defensively.)* Yes, Mr. Bernstein, a secret. You Americans are always keeping secrets! Every American I've ever met was keeping some big secret or another.

STU: Okay, okay. Calm down. *(Fumbling in his pockets and finding a bottle of pills. He struggles with the cap and then swallows a handful.)* Okay... okay. *(Taking a deep breath and letting it out.)* Ohmm... ohmmmm... ohmmm mane padne ohmmmmm. (Another deep breath.)* Okay. *(Turns his attention back to Lena.)* Here we go. Miss...?

LENA: Sergeant.

STU: Right. Sergeant?

LENA: Oh, please, call me Lena.

STU: Why, thank you, Lena. Lena?

LENA: Yes?

STU: I want you to go back to your desk and get Octavio back on the line.

LENA: Yes?

STU: I want you to get him back on the line and I want you to tell him that Sophia La Cruz, the star of *Forever Angelina,* the number-one-rated soap opera worldwide, has been kidnapped.

LENA: *(Making a note on a notepad.)* Kidnapped.

STU: That's right, Lena. Tell your friend Octavio that Sophia de la Cruz, the most loved and admired woman in Mexico and personal favorite of the president—who never misses an episode—has been kidnapped.

LENA: *(Still writing.)* Kidnapped.

STU: Yes, kidnapped. You tell that charming Octavio that Sophia de la Cruz, a woman with more international clout than... than... Jimmy Carter, whose face appears every day on television sets from here to kingdomfucking-come, who is adored by miserable people—just like you—everywhere, has been kidnapped right here in your little shithole.

LENA: *(Scribbling frantically.)* ...kidnapped... shithole...

STU: And then you tell this Octavio that in the *(Checks watch.)* five hours that have passed since Sophia was carried kicking and screaming from that wretched excuse of a dressing room by some lunatic waving a gun, that in those five long hours you—the police—have done nothing, *nada,* zilch, to find her.

LENA: *(Writing.)* ...zilch to find her.

STU: Good. Then you tell Octavio to get in his car and drive to the Goddamn symphony and get the Ambassador up off his fat ass and bring him back to the Embassy, because in about (Checks watch again.) oh, five more hours, when I have to inform Sophia's lunatic husband that she's been kid-napped, poor Mr. Ambassador is going to have an international incident on his hands.

LENA: *(Writing.)* International incident...

STU: That's right, an international incident. So you tell Octavio that we've got about five hours before I have to make the call that will end his career. Five hours to find Sophia. Five hours before the end of the world as we know it.

LENA: *(Writing.)* Five hours... end of world.

STU: Any questions?

LENA: *(Looking up with a smile.)* No, I've got it!

STU: So...?

LENA: Yes?

STU: So, go! Make the call.

LENA: I'm on it, Mr. Bernstein!

(Lena exits crisply.)

(Stu seems to collapse in on himself.)

STU: You warned me, Brom. You warned me that taking Sophia the Drama Queen to Russia would be a big mistake. Oh, Brom! Why didn't I listen to you? *(Swallowing more pills.)* Ohmmmm! Ohmmmmm. Ohmmmm mane padne ohmmmm...

(Blackout. Change to: Apartment. Sophia is lying on the couch and appears to be asleep. Her hands and ankles are still bound and she now has a cloth gag in her mouth. The sound of a running shower indicates that Piotr is in the bathroom. We hear the sound of someone walking up several flights of stairs and then a key being inserted into the lock of the door. This wakes Sophia, who starts off the couch and begins inching frantically toward the door. The door finally bursts open and Tasha enters. She is Piotr's younger sister, very pretty and very modern. She carries a large box which is filled with clothes and is wearing a walkman.)

TASHA: *(Calling.)* Piotr! It's me! I have clothes for Yvonne's wife!

(Sophia tries desperately to be noticed while Tasha deposits the box on the couch.)

TASHA: Piotr! *(Hearing shower.)* I have to be back at kiosk in hour! I'll make some tea!

(Tasha goes to the kitchen area and puts on a kettle of water for tea. Sophia slithers awkwardly behind her.)

TASHA: *(Singing as she begins to prepare some tea.)* "At the Copa... Copacabana... the hottest spot north of Havana... at the Copa... Copacabaaaaaana... Music and passion were always the fashion...

(Sophia finally manages to nudge Tasha, who gasps and whirls around.)

TASHA: Oh my... *(Recognizing her immediately.)* Angelina?!?!?

(Sophia makes desperate sounds.)

TASHA: *(Removing the gag.)* What in world...

SOPHIA: *(Hoarsely.)* You've got to help me! He's a lunatic!

(There is a pounding on the upstairs floor.)

TASHA: Oh dear, that's Mrs. Nobokov. Here, let me get this.

(Tasha turns Sophia around and begins to fuss with the knot that ties her wrists.)

SOPHIA: *Esta loco!*

(More pounding.)

TASHA: Shhh…

SOPHIA: *(With great passion.)* I will kill him!!!!

(We now hear the sound of Mrs. Nobokov opening the door to her apartment and pounding down the stairs.)

TASHA: Oh dear…

SOPHIA: *I will rip off his dick…*

(Pounding on the door.)

MRS. NOBOKOV: Hey! You in there!

TASHA: *(Really panicking.)* Oh dear!

SOPHIA: *…And feed it to my Chihuahua!!!!!!!*

(In desperation, Tasha quickly replaces the gag and rushes to the door.)

TASHA: Yes, Mrs. Nobokov?

MRS. NOBOKOV: Is that you, Tasha?

TASHA: Yes, it's me, Mrs. Nobokov.

MRS. NOBOKOV: I demand that you open this door!

TASHA: *(Thinking desperately.)* I can't do that, Mrs. Nobokov.

MRS. NOBOKOV: What?!?!?

TASHA: *(Hearing shower.)* I… uh… just got out of the shower, and I don't have anything on!

MRS. NOBOKOV: *(After a pause.)* Young lady, are you lying to me?

TASHA: Oh, no! Never!

MRS. NOBOKOV: I saw you at kiosk not ten minutes ago!

TASHA: *(Under her breath.) Ucht ti chiort!* (Oh, you Devil!) Yes, yes, I was at kiosk… but a customer spilled coffee all over my smock so I ran over here to take shower! Now I am out of shower.

MRS. NOBOKOV: Then why is it I still hear shower running?

TASHA: Well, I had to run out of the shower, didn't I? To answer the door!

MRS. NOBOKOV: What's all the yelling I heard, then?

TASHA: Yelling?

MRS. NOBOKOV: Yes, yelling!!!! From this apartment! Why is there all this yelling going on. It's the middle of the morning! People do not yell in the middle of the morning!

TASHA: *(To herself.)* Yelling… yelling…

MRS. NOBOKOV: What's that?? What are you saying?

(Tasha looks at Sophia who is pointing to the TV with her hands.)

TASHA: *(To Sophia.)* Oh, thank you! The yelling was on the television! I left the television on, Mrs. Nobokov, while I was in the shower.

MRS. NOBOKOV: What a sinful waste of electricity!

TASHA: But it's off now, isn't it. See *(Pauses for effect.)* there's no more yelling!

(We now hear the very distinct sound of the shower being turned off. Much rattling of pipes, and so forth.)

TASHA: *(Before Mrs. Nobokov can say anything.)* Oh, thank you, Piotr! Piotr's just turned off the shower for me, Mrs. Nobokov.

PIOTR: *(Offstage.)* Tasha?

MRS. NOBOKOV: What's that? What's going on in there?

TASHA: Nothing, Mrs. Nobokov.

(Piotr rushes into the room with a towel wrapped around him. Tasha quickly motions for him to be quiet.)

TASHA: *(Indicating door to Piotr.)* I'm sorry about the television, Mrs. Nobokov, why don't you go back upstairs and get some rest?

MRS. NOBOKOV: *(As she stomps off.)* Well, I'm up now, aren't I?

(Mrs. Nobokov mutters all the way back to her apartment. We hear the sound of her door slamming shut.)

PIOTR: *(Struggling to get Sophia back on the couch.)* Thank you, Tasha! She's been…

TASHA: *(Whirling to face him.)* Piotr, what have you done?

PIOTR: Well, I was going to tell you…

TASHA: Tell me what? That you have Sophia de la Cruz bound and gagged in your apartment? What have you done???!!!?

PIOTR: *(After a moment.)* I'm saving Angelina.

TASHA: What?!?

PIOTR: I'm saving her, Tasha.

TASHA: What do you mean? You are saving her? Saving her from what???

(Sophia watches this exchange with keen interest.)

PIOTR: Someone has to! That evil Chico Morales has goons looking everywhere for her!

TASHA: Who?

PIOTR: She's safe here, don't you see? Even the abominable Chico Morales would never think to look for Angelina here in Vladivostok!

TASHA: *(The emotional wind knocked out of her, sinking into a chair.)* I knew this would be terrible day. As soon as I woke up, I knew. First, kiosk lock was… how do you say it… jammed? Yes, lock on kiosk was jammed. *(Explaining to Sophia.)* I work at corner kiosk where I am selling newspapers, magazines, candy… you know… things that nobody is wanting but everyone is needing. It was only job I could find after university. So first thing this morning I am being shouted at by people who want newspaper but I can't sell because kiosk lock is jammed. When I finally unlock everyone has gone to work, no one wants newspapers anymore, so it only makes sense that my employer makes his first visit since last month. "What are all these newspapers doing here?" What am I to say to that? The news today is boring? Now I have been shouted at by half the people in Vladivostok, my employer and old Nobby from upstairs. My brother has international celebrity tied with rope in his apartment and I haven't eaten anything but boiled egg since yesterday lunch. Oy!

PIOTR: I better get dressed. I'll be right back.

(Piotr exits. Tasha stares at Sophia.)

TASHA: He's flipped, hasn't he?

(Sophia vigorously shakes her head up and down.)

TASHA: He has kidnapped you?

(Yes.)

TASHA: After your appearance at the civic theatre?

(Yes.)

TASHA: Oh my God, poor Piotr!

(Angry sounds from Sophia.)

TASHA: Oh, yes yes, I know, but he really thinks you're Angelina, doesn't he?

(An exasperated yes.)

TASHA: He hasn't hurt you, has he?

(A reluctant no.)

TASHA: Well, that's one good thing then, isn't it? Yes, well, we need a plan, I suppose.

(Angry sounds.)

TASHA: To get you back, of course!

(Yes! Yes! Yes!)

TASHA: But you see, Piotr's my brother, and I don't want him to go to jail.

(An innocent shrug.)

TASHA: I heard what you said about feeding his... well, you know... to your Chihuahua, Miss La Cruz.

(A guilty shrug.)

TASHA: So although you and I both want the same thing, which is to get you back to your people

(Excited yes.)

TASHA: I can't really trust you, can I?

(Oh, please, yes you can!)

TASHA: I mean, look at the way you behaved when I took the gag out of your mouth!

(Oh, that? I'm sorry.)

TASHA: You yelled loud enough to bring old Nobby downstairs and she's deaf like... what is it? A stick of post!

(Can we get to the point?)

TASHA: Well, I'd like to be able to talk with you, but can I trust you not to yell?

(Yes!)

TASHA: Really?

(YES!)

TASHA: All right, then. I'm going to take out gag, but if you make one noise louder than a peeping, it's going right back in. Understand?

(Yes!)

(Tasha gently removes the gag.)

SOPHIA: Oh, thank God! Thank you—*gracias.*

TASHA: It really is you, isn't it?

SOPHIA: Of course it is me, who else would I be?

PIOTR: *(Entering.)* Tasha, what have you done?

TASHA: *(Standing and confronting her brother.)* You've really done it this time, Piotr. Do you have any idea what's going to happen to you if anyone finds out that you've kidnapped international celebrity?

PIOTR: You don't understand…

TASHA: Oh I understand, all right. I understand that you've lost your mind. This isn't "Angelina!" *There is no Angelina!* This is the woman who plays Angelina on television!

SOPHIA: Thank God *someone* got brains in this family.

TASHA: This is really horrible, Piotr. I told you that you've been watching too much television. Ever since you lost your job you've hardly left the apartment, and now look what's become of all that idle time!

SOPHIA: *(Pouting.)* My hands are all tingly.

TASHA: Her hands are tingly, Piotr. *(Indicating box of clothes.)* I suppose that you wanted these for Miss de la Cruz? Oh, Piotr. Can you imagine what a woman who makes, what—forty grand US a week?

SOPHIA: Thirty-nine nine.

TASHA: Can you imagine what a woman who makes thirty-nine thousand dollars US a *week* wears? Can you? *(Pulling a dress out of the box.)* Do you think for a moment that she would wear polyester blend?

PIOTR: Well, I didn't think…

TASHA: No, you didn't think. You didn't think about anything, did you?

PIOTR: You don't understand!

TASHA: Explain to me then.

SOPHIA: Yeah. Explain it to her.

PIOTR: *(After a moment.)* Angelina is… well, last good thing.

TASHA: What do you mean, last good thing?

PIOTR: Look at the world we live in, Tash! Our country is falling apart; drugs, gangsters, democracy... in Chechnya soldiers kill women in the morning and blow up the hospitals where their children lie dying in the afternoon. In Africa, it's tribe against tribe—same thing in the US. We've ruined our air and water. Our children live in despair. These things are real, Tasha. They're not just stories on television. Bad things are happening everywhere. To everyone.

SOPHIA: *(Disgusted.)* Cry me a river.

TASHA: Miss de la Cruz, please.

PIOTR: I've thought about these things, Tasha. All these bad things. And for a time I could see no hope for us. But then, a wonderful thing happened! I lost my job and met Angelina! I'll never forget the first time we met. I'd had to stand on line all day for something—I don't remember what. I was exhausted. My feet hurt.

SOPHIA: My hands hurt!

TASHA: Just a minute more, Miss de la Cruz! He's my only brother and I must know what has driven him to commit such a desperate crime.

SOPHIA: *(To Piotr.)* Then tell the damn story! Concentrate on plot and forget motivation!

PIOTR: When I worked at the docks I never had much time for television, but when I lost my job I suddenly had all the time in the world. So that day, the day my feet hurt, I came home and decided to lie down—on this couch—and watch TV. *(To Sophia.)* You were wearing jungle fatigues.

SOPHIA: Jungle...? Oh, yes. The freedom fighters storyline.

PIOTR: There you were, bravely fighting your way through the streets of that village, risking your life just to make sure that the world press got your video of the leader of the People's Freedom Front giving that young girl CPR. I remember thinking: That was a good thing that woman did for that village.

SOPHIA: *(Agreeing.)* Our ratings went through the roof with that one.

PIOTR: And then, back in Mexico City, you joined forces with Miguel Ramierez to fight corruption in the city government.

SOPHIA: Oh, that was terrible. Three writers lost their jobs over that fiasco.

PIOTR: It was another good thing! Look! *(Piotr rushes to a desk and pulls out a battered notebook.)* I started writing down every good thing you did, Angelina. *(He flips through the pages, showing her.)*

SOPHIA: *Dios Mio!* How long have you been out of work?

PIOTR: You *always* do what you can to help make the world a better place for the rest of us. And I refuse to let that evil man, that... that despicable

Chico Morales get you in his clutches, ever again! *(To Tasha.)* Do you see? Do you see that I am doing a good thing?

TASHA: Piotr, listen to me: *Forever Angelina* is a soap opera—a television show. It's made in a television studio in Mexico.

SOPHIA: *(Defensively.)* We do location work. The freedom fighters story was shot in Hawaii!

TASHA: Miss de la Cruz is an *actress,* Piotr. She isn't Angelina!

SOPHIA: Certainly not in this context.

TASHA: Miss de la Cruz is a married woman, Piotr. She has family and friends. We have to send her back. Vladivostok must be full with police by now— looking for her. Do you understand, Piotr? We have to send her back!

SOPHIA: I demand that you call the police immediately!

TASHA: Please, Miss de la Cruz, just give me a moment to sort this out.

SOPHIA: Maybe Bigfoot upstairs would help me.

TASHA: *(Holding up the gag.)* Only if she can hear you.

SOPHIA: Point taken.

TASHA: Good. Now let me think. *(She paces for a moment.)* Wait a minute! Didn't I read somewhere that you just signed some kind of... what is this being called...? Oh, yes! A "Big Deal"! You have signed "Big Deal" in Hollywood, yes?

SOPHIA: *(Proudly.)* Three pictures.

TASHA: But, no one in America—besides the Spanish-speaking people—knows who you are, do they?

SOPHIA: *(Defensively.)* The studio is planning to...

TASHA: Oh, I'm sure the studio is planning something, all right. They will be paying many rubles to make your name a household word. I read about these things in kiosk every day. But, think of the cost, Miss de la Cruz!

SOPHIA: Everything costs.

TASHA: It doesn't have to! Has it occurred to you that you're now sitting on a... a golden mine of free publicity?

SOPHIA: *(Doubtful.)* Oh, I don't think...

TASHA: The point is, Miss de la Cruz, that no one in America knows you!

SOPHIA: *(Snapping.)* So??

TASHA: *(With a smile.)* So, they will now.

SOPHIA: *(Understanding.)* Ahhhh, I see.

TASHA: If we play this thing right, your new career as a film star will skyrocket before you set foot on the back lot.

SOPHIA: Very interesting. You know, Tasha, I like the way you think. I mean, you were absolutely right about the clothes.

TASHA: By this time tomorrow, your face will be on every American television set!

SOPHIA: *(Excited.)* Oprah will say my name!

TASHA: Forget Oprah! You'll be the lead story on *Hard Copy!*

SOPHIA: *Chiquita,* you are my kind of woman!

TASHA: We better get started!

SOPHIA: Doing what?

TASHA: Writing your ransom note and arranging for your rescue! Here, let's get you untied.

SOPHIA: *(As Tasha unties her.)* You know, I could use a drink. *(With a hateful look at Piotr, who is sitting on the couch, clutching his guitar and looking quite shell-shocked.)* It's been a long night, and I definitely need to visit *el baño.*

TASHA: *(Taking box of clothes.)* Right this way. And don't worry. I will find you some nice things to wear. I don't know about you, but if I have to wear same thing for more than a couple of hours, I start to feel very... *(She makes a little grimace that indicates "grungy.")*

SOPHIA: *(Laughing.)* Then, my dear, you should never become an actress!

(They exit happily. Piotr stares after them and then sinks deeper into the couch.)

PIOTR: *(Somewhat bemused.)* Oh my poor Angelina, what have they done to you?

(Blackout. Change to: Miguel's area. Miguel Fuentes is a handsome and dangerous-looking man in his 30s. He is dialing a number on a cellular phone with one hand and holding a chihuahua in the other.)

MIGUEL: *(To dog.)* Don't worry, Chi Chi, we'll find your mommy. *(Irritated, into phone.)* Sophia, my love, I am leaving this message on your service because the idiotic woman who answers the phone at your hotel in Vladivostok doesn't speak any language in which I am capable of communicating! My darling, you haven't phoned home in over twenty-four hours. What is happening to you in that faraway land that you cannot find five minutes in a day to call your husband?!? *(Pause and change of tone.)* Everyone here is miserable without you, especially little Chi Chi, who shivers beside me in bed at night, wishing that you were there to keep him warm. *(Change of tone.)* The show is a disaster without you. This new director hasn't a clue about storyline. Keeps babbling on about how we should "surrender to our urges" and "feel the moment"—whatever the devil that is supposed to mean. I tell you that woman is as dense as your idiot manager, who, by the way, tried to sneak one of his limo bills onto our account. My love, how you can put up with that donkey boy is beyond me.

OFFSTAGE VOICE: They need you on the set, Miguel!

MIGUEL: In a minute! *(Into phone.)* They need me on the set, my love. Today, Chico is going to set fire to the family hacienda in Tabasco. I wish you could be there to see the flames, *mi amore.* Chi Chi isn't the only one who needs you in the darkest heart of night. *Ciao, my Sophia. Te amo. (Miguel hangs up and closes the phone.)* All right, my little Chi Chi, daddy has to go to work now. I will give you to the nice lady who fantasizes that she is a director of actors to hold during my scenes and should you feel the urge to bite her, I beg you, my little darling, surrender to your urge and by all means feel the moment. *(He then takes a moment to "become" Chico Morales, and exits.)*

(Blackout. Change to: Police Station. Stu is sitting in a chair with his head in his hands. He looks terrible. His suit is rumpled as is his hair. Lena enters. Stu looks up hopefully.)

STU: Anything?

LENA: I'm afraid not, Mr. Bernstein.

STU: This is it, my career is finished. When the studio finds out that I lost one of their new properties in Russia… I'll never work again.

LENA: *(Concerned.)* I am so sorry, Mr. Bernstein!

STU: Do you have any idea what it took to negotiate three pictures? Three pictures!

LENA: So many!

STU: Okay, so it's only three and she's only playing minor roles, but just think of the exposure! The opportunity for career development!

LENA: *(Not understanding.)* It's terrible!

STU: Not to mention the fact that I had to run everything by her Neanderthal husband! God, I hate that man!

LENA: *(Crossing behind him and starting to massage his neck.)* Poor Mr. Bernstein!

STU: Do you know that he once threatened to feed my… well, my member to his dog?!? Dog, now that's a laugh. A little lower… there, that's it. *(Scornfully.)* Dog. I mean how can they get away with calling a Chihuahua a dog? Lassie was a dog. Rin Tin Tin was a dog… Cujo was a *dog.* Oohh, that's good, don't stop.

LENA: *(As she massages.)* I have a dog.

STU: Well, he's going to do more than threaten me with a Chihuahua if he gets wind of this disaster. My life won't be worth a plugged peso… oh why did I ever go into the Mexican market?!?

LENA: His name is Bruce.

STU: What... who?

LENA: My dog! I named him Bruce. After *Die Hard*.

STU: *Die Hard?* You mean you named your dog after Bruce Willis?

LENA: *Da! Da!* Bruce Willis! You know: "Yippie-kay-yay Mutherfucker!"

STU: *(Staring incredulously.)* Oh my God, I'm in a Fellini movie!

LENA: You are? Don't worry, I fix you right up! *(She runs off.)*

STU: Take a good look at this room, Bernstein. This is where it all comes to an end. Bring on the Cossacks!

(Lena enters with a big bottle of vodka and two glasses.)

STU: On the other hand I suppose that you and I could just sit here and get completely shit-faced.

LENA: *(Handing him a glass.)* Da!

STU: Da-da!

LENA: *(Toasting.)* Nostrovya!

STU: Down the hatch, you Slavic she-wolf!

(They gulp down their vodka. Blackout. Change to: Apartment. Tasha and Sophia are sitting on the couch surrounded by crumpled-up pieces of paper. Each has a pad and a pen. Sophia has changed her clothes.)

TASHA: Oh! Okay, how's this: We, the people of the Azarbajinian People's Front have kidnapped Sophia de la Cruz...

SOPHIA: Hold it. Who the hell are the Azarbajinian whatever it was that you said?

TASHA: No one... at least, I don't think they are. You never know these days.

SOPHIA: I don't know, Tasha... I think we should stick to something simple... like a crazed fan kidnapping the object of his psychotic obsession.

TASHA: You think?

SOPHIA: Absolutely. I've been in this business for ten years, and if there's one thing I know, it's storyline.

TASHA: Ten years? But how can that be? You're so young.

SOPHIA: *(Pleased.)* Thank you, but it's true.

TASHA: That's amazing, Miss de la Cruz...

SOPHIA: Please, call me Sophia.

TASHA: Oh, no. I couldn't. It wouldn't be right.

SOPHIA: Why not?

TASHA: *(Embarrassed.)* Well, you know, because of, well, because of my stupid brother kidnapping you.

SOPHIA: *(Dismissively.)* Oh, that. Don't give it another thought, really. Do you realize, Tasha, that this is the first time in three weeks that I've had a moment's rest? On the plane, off the plane. Get in the car, get out of the car. In the hotel, shower, change clothes, leave the hotel. Get in the car, drive to the theatre, get out of the car, wait backstage, get on stage, smile at the audience, sit there like a fool and answer questions for an hour and a half. Smile again, leave the stage, get in the car... *Dios Mio!* It's been hell!

TASHA: *(Concerned.)* I'm so sorry, Miss de la Cruz!

SOPHIA: Sophia.

TASHA: I wish your visit to my country had been more enjoyable!

SOPHIA: In some ways it has been. For one, it's made me appreciate my own country in ways I've never dreamed of, and for another I simply adore listening to Russian.

TASHA: Really?

SOPHIA: Oh, yes. Russian is the most... virile language I've ever heard. Doestoevsky finally makes sense to me now! And the energy! There is an energy here that is both exhilarating and frightening. I see it in your eyes. You are a people who are on the verge of becoming something new—for better or worse, and the energy you generate is very exciting.

TASHA: My!

(At that point, Piotr enters the apartment. He is carrying several shopping bags.)

SOPHIA: Speak of *el diablo.*

TASHA: There you are. *(She rises and takes a bag and looks inside.)* Wonderful, you found Sophia's tea! And black bread! Oh, Sophia, you're going to love this bread! *(Tasha carries the bag to the counter.)*

SOPHIA: *(Holding out her hand to Piotr.)* Cigarettes.

PIOTR: You don't smoke.

TASHA: Give her the cigarettes, Piotr.

(He reluctantly hands them over.)

SOPHIA: Receipt.

(A dejected Piotr fishes a piece of paper out of his pocket and hands it to Sophia.)

SOPHIA: *Gracias. (To Tasha.)* When I get home, I'm going to make that weasel Stu reimburse us for every ruble!

PIOTR: But you don't care about money!

TASHA: *(Warningly.)* Piotr...

PIOTR: Well, she doesn't! Angelina sold her grandmother's priceless diamond brooch so that little Esteban could be flown to Switzerland for his brain transplant, and you know what?

TASHA: Piotr, that's enough!

PIOTR: She didn't ask for a receipt!

(Piotr exits angrily into the bathroom. Sophia stares thoughtfully at the receipt. We hear Piotr's halting blues chords over the rest of the scene.)

TASHA: I'm so sorry.

SOPHIA: *(Shaking it off.)* Don't apologize. I'm starving! What's for lunch?

TASHA: *(Excitedly.)* I'm so happy to have a chance to cook a real Russian meal for you! We'll start with some of my grandmother's *kulibiaka,* that's a cabbage pie—it's delicious—then we'll have some real stroganov, not the stuff they give you in the hotels. And for desert, we'll have a nice fresh cherry pie with *varenya.*

SOPHIA: *(Dubiously.)* It sounds… wonderful.

TASHA: Oh, and look! *(She holds up a bottle of wine.)* I've been saving this for a special occasion!

SOPHIA: What is it?

TASHA: Dry Georgian wine. It's absolutely wonderful!

SOPHIA: *(Taking the bottle and reading the label.)* Esta bueno, *chiquita!* Do you have a corkscrew?

PIOTR: *(Bursting in from the bathroom.)* You don't drink wine! Not after the night your mother had to be flown to the Bunny Ford Clinic in America!

SOPHIA: It was the *Betty* Ford Clinic, and she's *not* my mother! She's the old drunk who used to play my mother until her liver exploded last spring! *(To Tasha.)* The writers made her character an alcoholic when we got sick of having to shoot around her benders.

(Piotr exits into bathroom.)

TASHA: Oh, my! *(Tasha takes several oranges out of the bag and places them in a small bowl.)*

SOPHIA: It was a bad move. One day she passed out on the set and knocked a gaffer right off his ladder. He needed sixteen stitches in his *cabeza.*

TASHA: How terrible! *(She picks up an orange and smells it. This is an unconscious gesture.)* Tell me, I've always wanted to know, what is a gaffer?

SOPHIA: A gaffer? A gaffer… oh, how do you say this… a gaffer uses that thick silver tape to secure all the electrical wires.

TASHA: How fascinating! And a best boy! What is a best boy?

SOPHIA: *(Laughing.)* The kid with the worst job! The best boy plays with electricity.

TASHA: *(Growing more excited.)* And a steadicam operator?

SOPHIA: He operates the steadicam!

TASHA: But, what is it?

SOPHIA: It's a shock-mounted camera… you really have a thing for all this technical stuff, don't you?

TASHA: *(Quickly.)* Oh, not really… it's just that, well, I took cinema course at university, but we only watched Russian films—oh, and great American classic, *Ishtar.*

SOPHIA: *Ishtar!*

TASHA: *Da!* Brilliant! When you read the credits at the end of a movie, it all sounds so fascinating... I've just always wondered what all those people really do.

SOPHIA: *(Studying Tasha.)* It's all pretty boring, believe me.

TASHA: Oh, no! It couldn't be!

SOPHIA: Why do you say that?

TASHA: Well, I mean, it's all so... glamourous! Take you, for example.

SOPHIA: What about me?

TASHA: The life you must live!

SOPHIA: *(Shrugging.)* It's a good life.

TASHA: You get to travel all over the world, meet all kinds of people...

SOPHIA: *Chiquita,* please. All this travel, all these people; it's work, hard work. It's all about the bottom line, which is making money for my network. I am what the Americans call a "cash cow."

PIOTR: *(Entering.)* But Edwardo, your evil brother, just gambled away your family's fortune when he invested everything in the villainous Chico Morales's emerald smuggling scheme! You have no more money!

TASHA: Piotr!

(Piotr exits to bathroom.)

SOPHIA: Ignore him.

TASHA: You're sure you don't mind? He's being quite difficult.

SOPHIA: *(Laughing.)* Tasha, difficult men are my specialty. After spending the last seven years with Miguel Fuentes, I think that it is safe to say that I can handle any difficult man.

TASHA: Miguel is your husband?

SOPHIA: *Si.*

TASHA: He is also an actor on your show?

SOPHIA: *Si. (In a whisper.)* Miguel is the dreaded Chico Morales!

TASHA: *(Timidly.)* And he's difficult... like Piotr?

SOPHIA: Oh, he's difficult, but not like your *loco* brother.

TASHA: Is he... mean to you?

SOPHIA: *(With a smile.)* Constantly!

TASHA: Forgive me, please, but why don't you leave such a man?

SOPHIA: *(With great passion.)* Because I absolutely adore him! Miguel is the sun and the moon and the stars... he is *la vida...* life!

TASHA: But, if he's mean to you...

SOPHIA: You are very young and pretty, Tasha. There must be a difficult young man in your life.

TASHA: *(Shyly.)* No… well, once there was, a long time ago. But he was not difficult. I do not think I would enjoy life with a man who was constantly mean to me.

SOPHIA: Tasha, Miguel and I are mean to each other, like all married couples, but we'd be lost without one another… which is why you and I have got to get this ransom note to the police as soon as possible! When that idiot Stu tells Miguel that I have been kidnapped you can bet your last peso that the big lug will be on the first plane to Vladivostok.

TASHA: And that would be bad?

SOPHIA: My dear, that would be horrible! Miguel would tear this town apart to find me. He is like *el gato montes*—a mountain lion—when he is angry!

TASHA: *(Alarmed, clutching an orange.)* Oh, dear!

SOPHIA: So you cook and I'll write!

(They both turn back to their assigned tasks. Sophia starts humming "Copacabana" as she writes. Tasha smiles and softly joins in. Before long the two women are wailing: "Music and passion were always the fashion at the Copa…" The guitar playing stops.)

PIOTR: *(From bathroom.)* Angelina, you hate Barry Manilow! Ever since that time the odious Chico Morales tried to…

SOPHIA AND TASHA: *(Singing forcefully.)* "They fell in love!"

(Mrs. Nobokov begins to pound on the ceiling.)

MRS. NOBOKOV: Stop singing that "Copabanana" song!

(The two women automatically start whispering: "At the Copa, Copacabana…" Slow fade to black. Change to: Miguel's space. Miguel stands with phone, He looks terrible. We hear the sounds of an international airport terminal.)

MIGUEL: *(Into phone.)* Sophie, my love, what have you done to me? I've been in this airport for *(Checks watch and counts fingers.) Jesus Christo!* I've been in this airport for nine hours trying to get a connecting flight to Vladivostok. I don't even know what country I am in! *(Looking around.)* I mean, this could be anyplace! *(He calls to an unseen passerby.)* Excuse me, senor, what country is this, please?

OFFSTAGE VOICE: *(Angrily.)* Chekistonbula!

MIGUEL: *(Angrily.)* The same to you, senor! Ay! These Eastern Europeans are worse than New Yorkers! *(Shouting to any who will listen.)* You cannot treat me this way! I am an actor, for the love of God! I am the star of one of the world's highest rated television shows! Is this how you would treat Mr. Robert Urich? Is this how you would treat Mr. *William Shatner?!?* Who do you miserable little people think you are???? *(To phone.)* I tell you Bill Shatner has never been forced to suffer such indignity! Sophie, my love, what has become of you? Why does no one in Vladivostok know where you are? I am insane with not knowing! And I burn, my love. I burn! *(Change of tone.)* Uh, Sophie, about poor little Chi Chi. I know that we vowed to never... well... damn it, Sophie, I had to put Chi Chi into a kennel! Please forgive me! I had no choice, I swear this to you! Esteban is in Fiji for two weeks and cannot Chi Chi-sit. My love, how is it that our secretary can afford two weeks in the South Pacific? What are we paying him, for the love of God? Forgive me, my treasure, I know that by now you must be frantic, but I assure you that our little darling is in the very finest kennel in all Mexico City! He has his favorite toys and all his sweaters... oh, and I had his Elavil prescription refilled, just in case he has one of his episodes... but he won't, my darling. *(He listens for a brief moment.)* Sophie, my love, I'm not sure, but I think they just called my flight. *Ciao, mi amore. Ciao.*

(Miguel pockets the phone and strides off. Blackout. Change to: Police Station. At lights up, Stu is discovered in a state of general dishevelment, passed out upon Lena's desk. We hear the sound of a record skipping. Lena enters. She has discarded her uniform and now wears a black slip, stockings and gun holster. She is carrying a new bottle of vodka.)

LENA: Oh, Stu-uuu! Look what I found in the evidence room!
(Stu groans.)
LENA: *(Pouting.)* Oh, Mister Stu! You have passed out! *(A lightbulb going on in her mind.)* Music! We need more music! *(Lena scampers to an old record player and flips the record over.)*
STU: *(Rousing.)* No... no more music...
LENA: *(Reading the label.)* Ahhh, here we go, Mister Stu! *(She puts the record on and the tinny speaker begins to play Miami Sound Machine's "Shake Your Body" or similar). She then turns to the supine Stu and holds her arms out.)* Come and dance with me, Mister Stu!
STU: *(Struggling to curl up in a ball on the desk.)* No... no... no more dancing...
LENA: *(Starting to dance in a nearly provocative manner.)* Oooh, come on, baby... shake your body!!!!
(Stu groans and struggles to cover his ears with his hands.)

LENA: *(Pulling Stu roughly to his feet.)* Come on and dance, you big American Cowman!

STU: Cowboy…

LENA: *(Swinging him around.)* Yippie!!!!

STU: *(Weakly.)* Oh, help.

LENA: I do the rumba with you, Stewie! *(She pulls Stu's head down upon her ample bosom.)*

STU: Mommy, help me!

LENA: *(As she whips him away.)* You do it good, baby! Just like Johnny Travolta!

STU: Help!!!

LENA: *(Pulling him close.)* Go ahead and scream, lover boy, no one will hear you.

STU: What are you talking about, this place is full of people! Help! Help!

LENA: *(Giggling, in a singsong.)* Interrogation room!

STU: What?

LENA: Interrogation room. KGB design. Soundproof.

STU: Ohmygod, help! *(He runs to the door.)* Help! I'm trapped in here with a woman with a gun!

LENA: *(Leaning back on desk as she takes another mighty swallow of the vodka.)* They can't hear you.

STU: *(Trying to overcome his state of inebriety to adopt an authoritarian demeanor.)* Officer… whatever your name is…

LENA: *(Drawing it out, sexily.)* Leeeenaaaah.

STU: Officer Lena, I demand that you unlock this door immediately!

LENA: *(Dangling keys in front of him.)* With one of these?
(Stu reaches for the keys, but she snatches them away. He is very drunk and falls down. Lena laughs and jingles the keys again.)

STU: *(As he struggles to his feet.)* It's not funny! Don't you realize that you're creating an… international incident? Give me those keys!

LENA: *(Wagging her finger at him.)* Ah ah ah! Be nice to Lena. Then maybe I'll unlock door for you.

STU: Listen, you… you… cat woman, you! You can't hold me against my will! I'm a citizen of the United States of America!
(Lena smiles and drips the keys into her cleavage.)

STU: No! No, not in there! Take them out!

LENA: Come and get them, big American cowguy.

STU: This… this is sexual harassment! At home there are laws…
(Lena slowly shakes her bodice.)

STU: …there are laws… awwww, shit. *(Stu resignedly takes a few steps toward Lena.)*

LENA: *(Encouragingly.)* That's a good boy, Bruce.

STU: I thought your dog was Bruce.

LENA: *(Grabbing him.)* Not tonight, baby! Tonight we *Die Hard* together! Say it!

STU: *(Glumly.)* Say what?

LENA: Be Bruce Willis for Lena.

STU: *(Heaving a sigh.)* Yippie-kay-a.

(Lena grabs him roughly.)

STU: Be gentle.

LENA: Not a chance, stud-boy!

STU: Brom! Brom! Wherever you are, forgive me! History will note that I had no choice!

LENA: Baby, history is what you are in the dark.

(Stu whimpers plaintively as the lights Blackout. Change to: Apartment. Sophia and Tasha are watching television. Piotr is in the bathroom, playing his chords. There is a small bowl of oranges on the table.)

SOPHIA: *Dios mio!* This is terrible! What do you call it?

TASHA: *(Holding an orange that she will never eat but smells constantly.)* Forever Means Forever. It is very popular Russian show.

SOPHIA: Forever means *mierda.* Turn it off.

TASHA: But...

SOPHIA: Turn it off, turn it off. I can't bear to watch another frame. It's no wonder your country is so... wacked. *(She takes an orange and begins to peel it.)*

TASHA: Wacked?

SOPHIA: *Si,* wacked. Tell me, when you were a small girl, what was your favorite TV show?

TASHA: We didn't have a television.

SOPHIA: Ah ha! You see? The worst deprivation that can be inflicted upon a child!

TASHA: Oh, but we didn't mind.

SOPHIA: *Ay Chihuahua!* Have you people no shame?

TASHA: Is it so terrible to grow up without a television in the house?

SOPHIA: Girlfriend, it is beyond terrible. It is criminal! Okay, tell me, when you were ten, who did you want to be?

TASHA: When I was ten? I don't know... a nurse or a gymnast, I suppose.

SOPHIA: No, no. Not what, *who.* Who did you want to be?

TASHA: I don't understand.

SOPHIA: *(Dreamily, enjoying the memory.)* I wanted to be Alexis Carrington.

TASHA: Who?

SOPHIA: Alexis Carrington... Blake's first wife. The most powerful, glamorous and wonderfully evil woman in the entire world.

TASHA: At ten you wanted to be the most evil woman in the world?

SOPHIA: I said *wonderfully* evil, darling. Oh, I spent hours and hours watching Alexis do her thing.

TASHA: Ahhh, this was someone you knew!

SOPHIA: *(Regarding her sadly.)* Tasha, darling: Alexis was a character on *Dynasty.*

TASHA: The TV show?

SOPHIA: Bite your tongue, *muchacha!* *Dynasty* wasn't a "TV show"! *Dynasty* was… it was a lifestyle!

TASHA: Lifestyle?

(The guitar stops, as if Piotr is listening to her story.)

SOPHIA: When I was a little girl growing up in Mexico City, *Dynasty* was my world! *(She starts to hum the* Dynasty *theme song.)* Every Wednesday night my mother and sister and I would make a bed on the floor in front of the TV set. First we'd spread out this old cotton blanket, then we'd get all our pillows from our beds and prop them up against the bottom of the couch. Then the three of us would sit and snuggle all through the Wednesday night lineup.

TASHA: *(Wistfully.)* It sounds nice.

SOPHIA: *(Eating a wedge of orange.)* Say, this is a good orange!

TASHA: My mother insisted that we all eat an orange every day.

SOPHIA: Smart woman.

TASHA: *Da.* She was. "Eat an orange every day just like Rudolph Valentino."

SOPHIA: Rudolph Valentino!

TASHA: He was Mama's favorite. He loved oranges.

SOPHIA: *Ay, Chihuahua.* You do need to catch up!

TASHA: So please tell me more about this… Wednesday night lineup.

SOPHIA: *Sin falta, muchacha.* First came *Wheel of Fortune.* Now don't even try to tell me you've never heard of The Wheel.

TASHA: Is that letter-guessing game?

SOPHIA: *Si!* Poor Francesca—that's my little sister—she never solved the puzzles. She was much better at *The Price is Right.* Ay! that girl can shop!

(Tasha giggles.)

SOPHIA: *(Resetting the mood.)* Anyway, after the Wheel it was time for Ricardo Montalban to welcome us to *Fantasy Island.*

TASHA: My, that sounds exotic!

SOPHIA: Mama's favorite show—except for *Star Trek.* She just loved Ricardo Montalban. Hey, that's something we have in common, *muchacha!*

TASHA: What?

SOPHIA: Both of our mothers had a thing for macho latinos who can't act!

TASHA: Ahh. Please, tell me more about this *Fantasy Island.*

SOPHIA: *(As Ricardo Montalban.) Fanstasy Island!* Well, a wealthy and mysterious man owned this island that was kind of like a supernatural Club Med.

TASHA: Club Med?

SOPHIA: *Ay, Dios mio!* You went to the island, for a vacation, and for a price, this man could make your favorite fantasy come true.

TASHA: *(Impressed.)* Any fantasy?

SOPHIA: Any fantasy. But you had to pay the price.

TASHA: So it was a morality play.

SOPHIA: Will you stop thinking like a Russian? Listen: Imagine a beautiful tropical paradise. The sun is shining, the sea is blue, the air is scented with frangipani and coconut... a light warm breeze is blowing off the ocean making the palm fronds rustle. Do you hear them?

TASHA: *(Dubiously.)* I... guess so.

(Piotr quietly opens the bathroom door and leans against the frame, listening. Tasha holds the orange to her nose and closes her eyes as she breathes in its scent.)

SOPHIA: Try harder. A light warm breeze is blowing off the ocean... but wait! Do you hear that?

TASHA: The rustling fronds?

SOPHIA: No! No, that other noise! It sounds like a plane! *(Without warning, Sophia drops to her knees ad becomes "Tattoo.")* Boss! Boss! The plane! The Plane! *(She then leaps to her feet and becomes Ricardo Montalban.)* Ah, Tattoo! Are you ready to greet our new guests? Yes? Good. Today, Tattoo, we will meet Tasha...

TASHA: Me?

SOPHIA: Silence, Tattoo! You know you must never interrupt me during my opening monologue. Today we will meet Tasha, a young woman with a most unusual fantasy. *(As Tattoo.)* Really, Boss? What would that be? *(As Ricardo.)* Well, my little friend, this young woman's fantasy is to have a fantasy, for this poor young woman has none of her own. *(As Tattoo.)* No fantasies? *(As Ricardo.)* Yes, Tattoo, I'm afraid it's true: This lovely young woman was raised without a television!

TASHA: You are so lucky, Sophia. We've had some American television shows, but it's never *ever* been enough. Well, not for me. I mean...

SOPHIA: *Muchacha,* you really *do* have a thing for show biz.

TASHA: Oh, no! It is only that... well, sitting in kiosk day after day with nothing to do except read magazines filled with pictures of faraway lands like California with everyone looking so happy and so... how do you say it... tan! I have always wondered about the lives these tan and happy people must live.

SOPHIA: *(Studying her.)* Looking happy is easy, *muchacha.* The people in your magazines may look happy, but in here *(Pointing to heart.)* they are miserable, believe me.

TASHA: *(Wishing to keep the mood up.)* Please, tell me more about this Alexis.

SOPHIA: Okay. After *Fantasy Island* it would finally be time for *Dynasty. (She hums the theme song.)* We'd all sit up straight and get ready for Alexis. *(Sophia becomes Alexis/JoanCollins.)* Blake, darling! I see that you and Crystal have decided to throw a little barbecue. I hope you don't mind that I've decided to stop by. *(As Blake/John Forsythe.)* Damn it, Alexis! I've told you that you're no longer welcome here! The children hate you, the servants hate you, the dog hates you and damn it, I hate you, too! *(As Alexis.)* That's a shame, darling. Well, I suppose I must be going then. Oh, Blake, by the way, my twenty-year-old stud lover and I have just purchased Denver-Carrington for a billion dollars so you're out of a job. Oh, yes, and your lawyers threw in this house as an incentive for paying cash, so I'll expect you and Crystal to be moved out by, say, this time tomorrow? And, Blake, don't forget to take the dog.

TASHA: Oh, Sophia! That's marvelous! It's no wonder you grew up to be a star!

SOPHIA: I'm no Joan Collins, believe me.

PIOTR: You're no Angelina, either.

TASHA: Piotr!

SOPHIA: Wrong, Boris! I am Angelina! *Solamente mio, comprende?*

PIOTR: Oh, I understand, Miss Fancy Pants! I understand that you've taken over the life of a brave and noble woman. I see now that you're not the real Angelina. You know what I hope? I hope that Chico Morales does find you. You deserve each other! *(Piotr begins to storm off into the bathroom and then pauses at the door.)* You want to know why my country is so wacked? It's because there is an Angelina but everyone thinks its *you! (Piotr exits.)*

SOPHIA: *(After a moment.)* Your brother is off the deep end, *muchacha.*
(Piotr resumes practicing his blues chords.)

TASHA: Oh, forget about Piotr. Tell me more about this *Star Trek.*

SOPHIA: *(Hums the theme song as lights begin to dim. As Shatner.)* Stardate, 2134. Captain James T. Kirk… *(An aside to Tasha.)* Did you know that the "T" is for Tiberius? Not many people know that. Of course, my Miguel knows everything about William Shatner. You know, he played a recurring role on *T.J.Hooker.* Colombian drug lord. I know, typecasting. We hate it, believe me. But Bill was always so nice to Miguel, and we always have so much fun going shopping in LA…

TASHA: Does this William Shatner work for Captain James T. Kirk?

SOPHIA: *(Exasperated.)* No, darling! Bill Shatner *is* Captain Kirk!! Now, pay attention. *(As Shatner.)* Stardate 2134. Captain James Kirk...

TASHA: T! You forgot T!

SOPHIA: What?!?

TASHA: *(Proudly.)* T for Tiberius!

SOPHIA: *(With a sigh.)* James T. Kirk reporting. We've just entered the Alpha Quadrant, and Dr. McCoy has brought it to my attention that Mr. Spock is behaving very strangely...

(Blackout. Change to: Police Station. We hear the sound of the interrogation room being unlocked from the outside. The door opens and Miguel Fuentes enters.)

MIGUEL: Bernstein! Stu! *Donde esta?*

STU: *(A loud groan from behind the desk.)* Oh, no!

LENA: *(Also from behind the desk.)* What is it, my cowpoke?

MIGUEL: Bernstein, what the devil is going on here?

STU: Will you look and tell me if you see a big handsome brute of a man standing on the other side of this desk?

(Lena peeks up over the desk. She looks terrible.)

STU: Well?

LENA: *Da!* It's him!

MIGUEL: Bernstein! Come out from behind that desk.

STU: *(Peeking up from behind desk.)* Umm, I'm afraid I have a small problem with that, Miguel.

MIGUEL: You're going to have more than a small problem if you don't come out from behind that desk!

STU: *(Pointing across the room to a pile of clothes.)* Would you be so kind?

MIGUEL: What?!?

STU: *(Sounding amazingly embarrassed.)* My clothes. Could you please throw me my clothes?

MIGUEL: *(Incredulously.)* You have no clothes under there?

STU: *(Miserably.)* No.

MIGUEL: *(Suddenly noticing the room's state of disarray.)* There is a woman under there with you?

STU: *(A squeak.)* Yes.

MIGUEL: *(Picking up an empty vodka bottle.)* Is she wearing clothes?

STU: Barely... if you'll forgive the pun.

MIGUEL: Were the two of you not wearing clothes... together?

STU: *(Squirming.)* In a manner of speaking.

MIGUEL: *(Astonished.)* Are you no longer gay, Stu?

STU: Miguel, please! My clothes.

MIGUEL: *(Turning to collect the clothes.)* Bernstein, you have exactly one minute to get dressed, and then I want answers about Sophia. If I thought for one minute that you were… what is it you call it? Schtuping? If I thought for one minute that you were schtuping some Russian *caliente* while my Sophia is out there at the mercy of a madman I'd hang your ass on my wall! *Comprende, muchacho?*

(Miguel turns back around just as Lena leaps up from behind the desk. She is magnificent in black lace bra and panties. She is aiming her revolver at Miguel.)

LENA: Freeze!

(Stu slowly stands holding a wastepaper basket in front of himself.)

STU: Oh, wait a second, Lena. You don't want to do this.

LENA: Not now, Stewy.

MIGUEL: What the hell is this? Cagney and Lacey?

LENA: Put your hands up, Morales!

MIGUEL: Oh, for the love of God!

LENA: *(Indicating interrogation cell.)* In there, Morales. Don't make me have to use force.

STU: Lena, darling, there's seems to be a little confusion…

LENA: *(As Miguel moves slowly toward the cell.)* Quite an interesting coincidence, wouldn't you say, senor? First Angelina disappears without a trace and now you show up out of the blue?

MIGUEL: Without a trace? Out of the blue? Who writes your dialogue? *(To Stu.)* Where's Sophia?

LENA: Good question, Chico! Perhaps *you'd* like to tell us where she is!

STU: Uh, Lena…

(Lena shoves a protesting Miguel into the cell and slams the door.)

MIGUEL: Bernstein! Tell this woman who I am or you're dead!

STU: *(Sinking wearily into a chair with the wastepaper basket still on his lap.)* The way I figure it, *Chico,* I'm dead no matter what happens.

MIGUEL: You sonofabitch!

(Lena throws open the office door.)

LENA: Everyone come and see! I, Sgt. Lena Klyachko, have single-handedly apprehended the notorious Chico Morales *and* cured homosexuality! All in the same day!

MIGUEL: *Bernstein!!!!!!*

STU: *(Very weakly.)* Yippie kay-a.

END OF ACT ONE

ACT TWO

The Apartment
Sophia and Tasha are sitting cross-legged on the floor doing meditation exercises.

SOPHIA: That's it, just let the energy flow through. Let it flow... you're a reed in the wind... you're a...

(At that moment, Piotr storms in. He throws several newspapers on the floor in front of Tasha and Sophia and then stomps angrily into the bathroom. We hear the sound of blues chords.)

SOPHIA: *Dio mio!* Girlfriend, your brother could bring down Carnival. *(Meaning the newspapers.)* How're we doing today?

TASHA: *(Holding up paper with a smile.)* Front page!

SOPHIA: Let me see!

(Tasha hands her the paper.)

SOPHIA: *Mierda!*

TASHA: What's wrong?

SOPHIA: I hate this picture! Oh, it figures that my idiot manager would give this photogenic catastrophe to the press!

(Piotr re-enters from bathroom and busies himself in making tea.)

TASHA: *(Studying photo.)* I must disagree, Sophia. The photographer has captured you in a very sophisticated light.

SOPHIA: *(Studying photo.)* Sophisticated?

TASHA: Oh, yes. You see how the light fills in there? That makes you look... what is the word...? Glamorous? Like the stars of the 30s, yes?

SOPHIA: You think?

TASHA: Absolutely.

(Piotr slams the kettle meaningfully on the stove. The women ignore him.)

TASHA: With your hair like that you look something like a young Rita Hayworth.

SOPHIA: It's funny you should say that.

TASHA: Funny? Why?

SOPHIA: Miguel has said the same... you know that I look like Rita Hayworth. Oh, my poor Miguel. He must be frantic by now.

TASHA: Do you think he knows?

SOPHIA: I haven't phoned home in days. Believe me, he knows.

TASHA: Then he is on his way here, yes?

SOPHIA: We better hope that he isn't.

TASHA: But, Sophia! That would be perfect! The brave husband flies halfway round the world to rescue his beloved wife, succeeding where the authorities have failed! Think of the copy that would make for the evening news!

(The kettle begins to whistle.)

SOPHIA: You don't understand. My Miguel is a lunatic. The first place he would go to here is straight to jail, for killing Stu.

(The phone rings. They all jump and stare at it fearfully.)

SOPHIA: Is someone going to answer that?

(Tasha picks up the phone.)

TASHA: Hello? Yes…? Oh, Selina! *(To Piotr.)* It's cousin Selina calling from San Diego!

SOPHIA: California?

TASHA: *(To Sophia.)* Yes! How are you Selina? Yes? Yes? And how is Fa Fa? What? In a *(Pronouncing each syllable.)* gar-bage com-pac-tor? How did such a thing happen? Really? Oh, that's too bad. What? He lost it?? Well, how often did he change the dressing? Oh. Well, he has nine good ones left… oh, only eight? Oh, Selina, I am so sorry. What's that? Sophia de la Cruz? yes, that's right, she has been kidnapped right here in Vladivostok! What's that? It was? *(Looks excitedly at Sophia.)* The story was on CNN?

SOPHIA: CNN!

TASHA: Wait a minute, Selina, I can't hear you. What's that? They interviewed our mayor on *Entertainment Tonight?*

(Sophia drops to her knees and crosses herself.)

TASHA: It was on *Hard Copy and A Current Affair?*

(Sophia picks up a pillow from the sofa and screams into it.)

TASHA: It was on David Letterman's Ten Best List?

(Sophia screams into the pillow.)

TASHA: *(Putting her hand over the receiver.)* They've been playing clips from *Forever Angelina* on the American news for two days!

(Sophia screams into the pillow again.)

TASHA: Yes, Selina. We're all excited. Well… yes, yes I will. I promise to call you as soon as she's found. I will. Give our love to Fa Fa, and tell him we hope he's better soon. Good-bye, Selina. Good-bye!

(As soon as the phone is hung up, Tasha and Sophia hug and squeal like teenagers.)

SOPHIA: I can't believe it!

TASHA: I knew this would work! I knew it!

SOPHIA: You're a genius, *muchacha!* Awoo! *(She starts chanting.)* *Hard Copy* and *David Letterman*… *Hard Copy* and *David Letterman*…

(Tasha joins in and they make a little conga line. They proceed around the apartment until they are suddenly confronted by Piotr, who regards them crossly. He makes a curious hand motion.)

SOPHIA: Oh, look. Boris wants to play charades. Okay, shoot.

(Piotr holds up five fingers.)

SOPHIA: Five?

(Piotr holds up four fingers.)

SOPHIA: Four.

(Piotr holds up three fingers.)

SOPHIA AND TASHA: Three!

(Piotr holds up two fingers.)

SOPHIA AND TASHA: Two!

(Piotr holds up one finger, which he points at the ceiling.)

SOPHIA AND TASHA: One!

(Mrs. Nobokov begins to pound furiously.)

MRS. NOBOKOV: What's going on down there?

TASHA: Nothing, Mrs. Nobokov! *(To Piotr.)* You think you're so clever.

(Piotr shrugs and exits through the the bathroom door. Guitar.)

TASHA: Oh, anyway, it's just a few more days, Sophia. A few more days and we will be free at home.

SOPHIA: Why wait? I've been on *David Letterman!*

TASHA: Is that good?

SOPHIA: It's to die for. So why should I wait?

TASHA: For the news to spread. In another couple of days, *the whole world* will be wondering what happened to Sophia de la Cruz!

SOPHIA: *(Appraisingly.)* You know, you think pretty big for someone who grew up without fantasies.

TASHA: Sophia, I said I grew up without television, not without fantasies.

(Sophia regards her speculatively for a moment and then turns back to the newspaper.)

SOPHIA: You really think I look sophisticated here?

TASHA: Absolutely. It's the light and your hair. You know, I studied photography at university.

SOPHIA: Really? You studied photography?

TASHA: Yes. Three years.

SOPHIA: As well as cinema?

TASHA: Oh, that was only one course…

SOPHIA: Then why do you sit on your behind in kiosk day after day?

TASHA: Times are hard in Vladivostok. No one is needing photographer. But I am good enough one to know that this is good shot.

SOPHIA: Do you think I should do all my shots like this?

TASHA: Oh, no. You need a whole array.

SOPHIA: Array?

    (As the lights begin to dim.)

TASHA: You need sophisticated poses, girlish poses, perky poses...

SOPHIA: Perky?

TASHA: Yes, perky...

    (Blackout. Change to: Police Station. Miguel paces like an animal in the cell Stu enters and Miguel lunges through the bars at him. Stu neatly sidesteps Miguel's reach.)

STU: Now, now. Strangling me isn't going to help.

MIGUEL: *(Darkly.)* Oh, yes it will.

STU: Since I'm the only one in town who can actually prove that you're Miguel Fuentes and not the evil Chico Morales, my well-being should be your primary concern.

MIGUEL: *Sophia* is my primary concern you Donkey Boy!

STU: Donkey Boy? Oooh, that's a real zinger, Miguel.

MIGUEL: I'm warning you, Bernstein...

STU: No, I'm warning you! For the last five years I've had to sit and take your inane threats and insults. You've threatened to feed every part of my anatomy to that horrid little rabid beast you call a dog; you've referred to me in public as "the Gay Blade," "Stu the Gazoo"—whatever that means— "Sophie's Bad Choice," "the Bag Man" and now we've finally arrived at "Donkey Boy." You've pushed me, pulled me, knocked me down, made me drink bad tequila...

MIGUEL: Is this where you start singing?

STU: That's right. This is where I start singing the song about the cruel Chico Morales.

MIGUEL: It's ridiculous. No one besides your butch girlfriend will believe that I'm the character I play on TV!

STU: I wouldn't be too sure about that, *Chico.* You don't know these people like I do.

MIGUEL: Yes, you do seem to have acquainted yourself with the locals in ways I never would have guessed.

STU: I was drunk! She made me drink that awful vodka, and then she took advantage of me!

MIGUEL: Well, I hope that... what is that name you call him? Ah, yes. I hope that *Brom* will be understanding of this.

STU: You leave Brom out of this!

MIGUEL: I certainly would hate to have to describe what I saw when I walked in here today.

STU: Oh, no! You're not going to blackmail *me*, you… you… overgrown *mariachi!* Brom would *never* believe anything that you would have to say!

MIGUEL: Probably not. Hmmm… I wonder how your buxom friend would like an all expenses paid trip to LA?

STU: That's enough! You better start being nice to me! These crazy Russians think that you're Chico Morales, remember? And let me tell you something, they *hate* Chico Morales. So as long as Sophia is missing, you just better be nice to me! I'm your only ticket out of here, baby.

MIGUEL: *(Darkly.)* Donkey Boy, you better hope that I rot in this cage.

STU: You know what? I don't have to listen to this! *(He heads for the door.) Das Vidanya, Chico. (Stu exits.)*

(Miguel sinks down onto his stool.)

MIGUEL: *(With great despair.)* Sophie, my love, what has become of you?

(Suddenly, the cell phone in his pocket rings. Miguel starts and then joyfully remembers the phone, which he quickly opens.)

MIGUEL: Hello? Sophie? My love, is that you? What…? No, this isn't Courtney at Fox publicity. No, this isn't Fox publicity at all. Don't be ridiculous, senor, do I sound like a "Courtney"? This isn't Courtney's phone, this is my phone. This is my phone… I have a phone! *Adios, senor!* I have a phone! I will dial 911! *(Dials and waits.)* My God are there no 911 operators in this wretched city? *(A Russian operator answers.)* Hello? Hello? Is this a 911 operator? What? Not in Russian, I beg you! Do you speak Spanish or English? English? *Bueno!* Is this 911? What? Oh, Just an operator? Oh, no, I do value operators, *senora!* To a wretched soul like me you are the angels of the fiber optic heavens! I was just hoping for a 911 operator. That's right! Like on American television! Do I have an emergency? Indeed I do, Madame! My name is Miguel Fuentes and I am being held against my will in the Vladivostok police station… wait! Hello! Do not put this call through to the police! I repeat! Do not…

(Lena enters.)

LENA: *(Holding out her hand.)* Phone.

(Miguel reluctantly hands it over.)

LENA: You are pathetic, Morales. *(She exits.)*

(Miguel slumps back down on his chair.)

MIGUEL: Sophie, my love, you've really done it this time.

(Blackout. Change to: The Apartment. At lights up, we discover Sophia alone

in the apartment. She is cantering around the small area much in the same manner as a child pretending to ride a horse, complete with hoof noises.)

SOPHIA: *(Pulling back on invisible reins.)* Whoa, boy! Whoa! *(She pats the horse's neck.)* Good boy! Let's try that again.

(Piotr has entered and watches as Sophia spurs her mount forward. She canters in a small circle and then stops when she sees Piotr. She then makes a show of pulling the horse to a stop and dismounting.)

SOPHIA: Is there something I can do for you, Boris?

PIOTR: It's Piotr. What are you doing, Angelina?

SOPHIA: It's Sophia. As any fool can see, I am practicing.

PIOTR: Practicing?

SOPHIA: *Si.*

PIOTR: Practicing what?

SOPHIA: *(As if to a moron.)* Horseback riding. I have to ride a horse in my first American film, so I am practicing.

PIOTR: Oh, no, Angelina! You cannot do such a thing!

SOPHIA: Why not?

PIOTR: Don't you remember? You've been terrified of horses ever since you fell off that wild mustang when you were a child on your family's hacienda! Edwardo, your evil brother, put the chili peppers under the saddle pad and...

SOPHIA: *(Too tired to argue with a lunatic.)* Exactly why I must practice now!

PIOTR: Without the horse?

SOPHIA: You have a problem with this, *gringo?*

PIOTR: Well, no. But... I really think you should practice on a horse.

SOPHIA: *(Making a dismissive gesture.)* Don't be ridiculous. *(She touches the side of her head.)* It's all up here.

PIOTR: Horseback riding is in your head?

SOPHIA: *Si!*

PIOTR: And you're not afraid that when you finally climb onto a real horse that you'll fall off?

SOPHIA: Of course not! Listen, Boris...

PIOTR: Piotr.

SOPHIA: Whatever. Listen to me: Everything in life is already up here *(Touches head.)* and in here. *(Touches heart.)* Do you know what will happen when I climb on that horse?

PIOTR: I shudder to think.

SOPHIA: *(Ignoring him.)* I will gather up the reins, like so. *(She gathers the reins with professional flourish.)* I will urge him forward, like this. *(She makes a soft clicking sound and begins to move forward.)* And I will trot around that set like a *gaucho*. Any why? Because I've already done it thousands of times, up here in my *cabeza*.

PIOTR: You better hope the horse has done it thousands of times in his *cabeza*.

SOPHIA: What a tiresome man you are! Listen, have you ever kissed a girl?

PIOTR: I beg your… that's not really any of your…

SOPHIA: *Si o no?*

PIOTR: *(Giving in.) Si.*

SOPHIA: Aha! And how was this kiss?

PIOTR: What do you mean?

SOPHIA: I mean, how was it? Did you know what to do, or did you fumble? Was it mush or was it magic?

PIOTR: *(Remembering, with a half-smile.)* It wasn't half bad, actually.

SOPHIA: You see!? That's what I'm talking about. That kiss wasn't half bad because you'd probably been thinking about doing it for a long time.

PIOTR: *(Agreeing absently.)* At least a year.

SOPHIA: All day every day?

PIOTR: Of course not!

SOPHIA: Ahh, but think of how wonderful that kiss would have been if you'd practiced it whenever you could!

PIOTR: But, that's obscene! One doesn't spend an entire day thinking about kissing!
(Without warning, Sophia suddenly grabs Piotr and kisses him. The kiss turns quite passionate in short order. After a steamy moment, Sophia pushes him away. Piotr is dazed and gasps for air.)

SOPHIA: There. Just imagine what that would have been like if you'd ever bothered to *practice. (Sophia walks triumphantly to the bathroom door. She pauses and turns back to Piotr.)* I'm going to take a bath. Next month, Angelina gets lost at sea. *(She exits into the bathroom.)*
(Piotr sinks onto the sofa. He leans back and closes his eyes. Tasha enters through the the apartment door carrying a bag.)

TASHA: I found a great outfit for Sophia's rescue! *(She pulls a tattered garment out of the bag.)* She'll look great in this, don't you think? Piotr? Piotr?
(Piotr sits silently on the sofa, a vacant expression on his face.)

TASHA: Piotr, are you all right?

PIOTR: *(As if from a great distance.)* I'm fine, Tasha.

TASHA: What are you doing?

PIOTR: *(A smile spreading across his face.)* Practicing.

(Blackout. Change to: The Police Station. Stu sits at the desk, his feet propped

up. He is happily eating an apple. Miguel looks worse than before. He is obviously at the end of his endurance.)

STU: You know, this has got to be one of the tastiest apples I've ever had!

MIGUEL: Be quiet, you banty cock! I'm trying to think.

STU: Don't hurt yourself. *(He takes a big bite.)* Mmmm-mmm!

MIGUEL: Stop that!

STU: You know, I find myself wondering how such a tasty apple found it's way to such a miserable spot. Do you suppose they hand these out in the prison, to the *criminals?*

MIGUEL: All right, all right! That's enough! Read me the paper!

STU: *(Sitting up straight and getting a piece of paper off the desk.)* "I, Miguel Fuentes, that's you, do hereby swear to hold Stuart Aaron Bernstein, that's me, harmless in all matters regarding the disappearance of my wife, Sophia de la Cruz. I do hereby further agree to refrain from any physical contact with Stuart Aaron Bernstein and to remain at least ten feet away from his person at all times. I further agree to keep my Chihuahua, a canine entity know as "Chi Chi" at least fifty feet away from the person of Stuart Aaron Bernstein. And finally—this is my favorite—I do hereby promise to never again refer to Stuart Aaron Bernstein as anything other than Stuart, Stu or Mr. Bernstein. This agreement is legal and binding and will expire on the day of my death, whenever that may be. Etcetera, etcetera.

MIGUEL: And in return, you'll have me released?

STU: Absolutely!

MIGUEL: Give me the paper.

STU: Somehow I just knew you'd come around.

   (Stu rises and cautiously approaches the cage. He gingerly passes the paper and a pen to Miguel, who takes a moment to scan over the text of the agreement. Miguel sighs and is about to sign, but a thought occurs to him and he pauses.)

MIGUEL: Wait a minute, *Mr.* Bernstein. What kind of guarantee do I have that you're going to keep your word and get me out of here?

STU: Miguel, Miguel. That woman is crazy about me. She'll do whatever I say.

MIGUEL: I agree that she's crazy, but as for the rest…

STU: Oh, come on, Miguel! I promise you that I can get you out of this.

MIGUEL: First give me some proof, then I'll sign.

STU: *(Making a huge show of heaving a big sigh.)* Very well, very well. If it's proof you want… *(He marches to the door and yanks it open.)* Oh, Lena, darling! Could you come in here, please?

   (Lena enters the office.)

LENA: You wanted to see me, Mr. Bernstein?

(She closes the door behind her and immediately drags Stu into a passionate embrace.)

STU: *(Trying to disengage.)* Not now, my little dumpling. We have an important matter to discuss…

LENA: *(Whispering.)* I'm not wearing any underwear!

STU: That's… that's quite a concept. Really, it is, but we have to talk about…

LENA: Let's do the wild thing, baby!

(Miguel clears his throat.)

LENA: *(Crossing to the cage.)* Oh, yes. I had almost forgotten about you, Mister Big Shot Drug Lord.

MIGUEL: I'm not…

LENA: Silence! You may be interested to know that your government has no record at all of anyone named Chico Morales leaving the country and that my government has no record of a Chico Morales entering the country.

MIGUEL: That's because I'm not…

LENA: Curious, don't you think?

STU: Lena, you really should…

LENA: Who else could sneak out of Mexico and into Russia besides a master criminal such as yourself!

MIGUEL: *(Pointing to the desk.)* Read my passport and visa, for God's sake!

LENA: *(Picking up the papers without looking at them.)* Ha! Cheap forgeries! *(She tosses them into the wastepaper basket.)* Did you think you could fool us with such chicanery?

MIGUEL: Bernstein!

(Stu dives after the passport.)

LENA: Well, Senor, it may interest you to know that I have just received word that we are to be visited by Senior Investigator Borodin. In the days of the Soviet Union, Senior Investigator Borodin was a master interrogator for KGB. His techniques are… legendary. It should take him no time to find out what you have done with Angelina!

MIGUEL: *(Roaring.)* Bernstein!!!!

STU: Lena, there really has been a dreadful mistake made here…

LENA: I have to go back to work now. *(She grabs him in another embrace.)* Maybe we do quickie for lunch?

(Lena kisses Stu again and then releases him. She exits as he collapses to the floor.
After a moment, we hear the slow and deliberate sounds of Miguel tearing the agreement into strips.)

MIGUEL: *(Quietly, as he rips the paper.)* Do you know what a Donkey Boy is, Bernstein?

STU: *(Putting his hands over his ears.)* I don't want to hear this!

MIGUEL: In Tijuana, the Donkey Boy is something of a folk hero.

STU: *(Marching as far as he can from the cage.)* I'm not listening!
(As the lights begin to dim…)

MIGUEL: First they find a nice big donkey.

STU: *(Loudly, with his fingers in his ears.)* La la la! I'm not listening! La la la la!

MIGUEL: And then they find a boy like you, Stu. A boy who likes donkeys…

STU: La, la, la, la, *la!!!!!*

(Blackout. Change to: The Apartment. Piotr sits glumly on the sofa, playing his chords. Sophia stands up on a stool. She is wearing the tattered dress that Tasha brought home and indeed looks as though she's on the cover of a Harlequin Romance Novel. Her bodice is ripped, her skirt has suffered a tear that goes all the way up the side of her thigh, and her hair flies wildly around her head. Tasha stands to one side and examines her handiwork.)

TASHA: Perfect! It's just the right look.

SOPHIA: What about shoes?

TASHA: Oh, go barefoot!

SOPHIA: You think?

TASHA: Most assuredly. It will enhance your captivelike appearance. Like cover of romance novel!

PIOTR: *(Scornfully.)* Listen to the two of you! You're behaving as though you are preparing for adolescent dance, not a daring escape.

SOPHIA: Men just don't understand. *(As she steps down from the stool.)* Take my Miguel, for example. If I spend two pesos on a new dress he goes crazy loco. What does he expect me to wear to have dinner with *El Presidente?* The same old rag I wore the last time?

TASHA: You've actually had dinner with the president of Mexico?

SOPHIA: *(What an unbelievable thought.)* The president of Mexico?? Please, *muchacha.*

TASHA: Which president, then? Wait! Oh, Sophia! Surely you cannot mean the president of the…

SOPHIA: *(Dismissing it as unimportant.)* Si, si. Whenever they're in Mexico City or LA. He's too busy to watch the show, and the wife *(With admiration.)* now there's a real ball-buster! The wife can't be bothered to watch, so he likes Miguel and I to catch him up.

TASHA: Oh, my!

SOPHIA: It's so rude of him. Even Aaron Spelling manages to have someone tape the show for him, and he's a busy man!

TASHA: *(Wistfully.)* What a life you must lead.

PIOTR: Not for long.

SOPHIA: What do you mean by that?

PIOTR: *(With a satisfied smile.)* I mean, that I hope you've been *practicing* living a life without your precious Chico Morales.

SOPHIA: What are you talking about?

PIOTR: *(Pointing to a newspaper on the floor.)* Read today's paper.

SOPHIA: I can't read it! I can't read Russian! No one in their right mind can read Russian!

(Tasha grabs the paper and starts paging through it. Suddenly, she stops and gasps.)

TASHA: *Uch ti tchiort! (Oh, you devil.)*

SOPHIA: *Dios mio,* what is it!?

TASHA: It's Chico! I mean, Miguel!

SOPHIA: *(Grabbing the paper.)* What? In here? *(She thrusts the paper back at Tasha.)* What does it say? What does it say?

TASHA: Oh, dear. Be strong, Sophia. *(Reading.)* Well-known Mexican crime lord, Chico Morales, was apprehended at the police station in Vladivostok today when he attempted to gain information concerning the disappearance of Angelina Montoya, beloved television star who has been missing for nearly a week and may soon be presumed dead.

SOPHIA: *Dead?!?*

TASHA: Morales was taken into police custody when he walked into the central police office and physically attacked Miss Montoya's American manager, whose round-the-clock vigil has touched the heart of every Russian. He is being held pending interrogation.

PIOTR: Ha! You know what that means!

SOPHIA: *(To Tasha.)* What does it mean? What does it mean?

PIOTR: It means that Chico Morales is finally going to get what he deserves!

SOPHIA: *There is no Chico Morales!!!!! When will you finally understand that Chico and Angelina don't exist?????*

PIOTR: When the interrogator is finished doing his job, the question of Chico's existence will be moot.

SOPHIA: Moot!? What does this mean: *moot!?*

TASHA: Try to calm down. Sophia…

SOPHIA: I will not calm down! This… this interrogator, this brute of a man has my Chico! I mean Miguel! *Jesu Christo!* You crazy Russians are making me crazy, too!

TASHA: Sophia, please!

SOPHIA: *(Grabbing Tasha by the arms.)* I must go to him! I must save the man I love from this horrible interrogator person! Please, Tasha, you must take me to the police station!

(Mrs. Nobokov begins to pound on the ceiling.)

MRS. NOBOKOV: What's going on down there?!

PIOTR: Quiet, you fool! Do you want the whole world to know?

SOPHIA: *Si! Si!* You worm of a man! I want the whole world to know! I am a woman of Mexico! In these veins courses the very blood of the Aztecas and the Mayas, who ripped the skin and the hearts from their sacrificial victims while they were still alive!!!!

(More pounding.)

MRS. NOBOKOV: Quiet down there!

SOPHIA: *(Shouting up at the ceiling.)* I will not be quiet! Do you hear, you old bat?!? I will not! I am Sophia Magdalena de la Cruz! I live only for passion, and I will not be quiet! *(To Tasha.)* Take me to the police station! *(Sophia marches to the door.)* Are you coming?

TASHA: *(Timidly.)* Only if you promise not to get Piotr in trouble and to follow our plan.

(Sophia throws open the door and stands before it: Barefoot ad wildly dramatic in her ripped dress.)

SOPHIA: Muchacha, you are about to witness the performance of a lifetime.

TASHA: I'll get my bag!

SOPHIA: *(To Piotr.)* And you! If anything has happened to my darling Miguel, I swear to you that I will hunt you down like the dog that you are. I will hunt you down and I will…

TASHA: I'm ready.

(Sophia takes one last look around the little apartment and then sweeps out dramatically.)

TASHA: *(To Piotr as she follows.)* Don't worry, Piotr. It's almost over. *(She exits.)*

(Piotr tries to catch his breath as the lights Fade to Black. Change to: Police Station. Miguel and Stu both pace their respective areas.)

MIGUEL: Any word from the embassy?

STU: Not yet. Apparently the charming and delightful Octavio had to fly to Oslo for a root canal. The only person I can get on the phone is the neither charming nor delightful Annunciada who bursts into tears every time I say Sophia's name.

MIGUEL: What about the Colonel?

STU: Useless. Does nothing but sit around here all day drinking Bulgarian Port Wine. Ugh, revolting swill. I'm afraid Lena is running the show.

MIGUEL: Ahh, yes. Your... enthusiastic girlfriend.

STU: She is *not* my girlfriend...

MIGUEL: No? What then?

STU: She's... she's an acquaintance.

MIGUEL: An *acquaintance?!* Bernstein, I've been forced to watch you and your acquaintance do things that I'd never do with my wife, let alone with an acquaintance!

STU: I would like to point out, Miguel, that at no time was I ever a willing participant in these... activities. that woman... that woman has abused me! When I get home...

MIGUEL: *If* you get home.

STU: Oh, I'll get home, but unless Sophia shows up in the next *(Checks watch.)* five minutes or so, I can't vouch for your return ticket.

MIGUEL: Oh my poor Sophia. What has become of you?

(They are quiet for a moment, then Miguel starts to chuckle.)

STU: I fail to see the humor in this situation.

MIGUEL: I was just thinking of Gogol.

STU: Who?

MIGUEL: Gogol. *The Inspector General.*

STU: She said his name was Borodin.

MIGUEL: *The Inspector General,* my ignorant... acquaintance, is a play by Nikolay Gogol.

STU: *(Unimpressed.)* Oh. *(He begins to fuss with his eye.)*

MIGUEL: It is the story of mistaken identity in a provincial Russian town. *(Sardonically.)* I don't know what made me think of it.

STU: Does it look to you like I'm getting pink eye?

MIGUEL: You see, this is why I detest you, Bernstein. how can anyone represent actors for a living and not know the greatest play ever written in the Russian language?

STU: I don't represent actors, Miguel, I represent movie stars.

(There is a sudden commotion outside the office. Both men recognize Sophia's voice.)

SOPHIA: *(Offstage.)* Unhand me you idiot! I demand to be taken to my husband!

MIGUEL: In here! In here, my beloved! *(To Stu.)* You're a dead man, Donkey Boy.

SOPHIA: *(Offstage.)* Get out of my way!

(Stu panics and races to the door, but it is thrown open by Sophia, still looking wildly dramatic in her ripped dress. She advances on Stu.)

SOPHIA: You! I might have known you'd be behind this...

(Lena rushes in and tries to restrain Sophia.)

SOPHIA: *(Whirling around to face Lena.)* If you touch me one more time, I will kill you, you... you potato-eating bitch!

STU: *(Weakly.)* Sophia, you're alive!

SOPHIA: Don't even try it! As of this moment, you're fired!

STU: You can't do that! We have a contract!

SOPHIA: We have *mierda!* And when I am through with you, you will be lucky if you can book El Mysterioso the Magician at children's birthday parties! Now leave this room, both of you. I refuse to even look at my husband while you pollute the air with your negativity! Go on! Get out! *(To Lena.)* You! Steroid Sally! Keys!

(Lena reluctantly hands Sophia the keys to the cage.)

LENA: *(To Stu as they begin to exit.)* It's okey dokey, Donkey Boy. We can go to my place.

STU: You can't do this to me, Sophia! I got you three pictures! Three!

SOPHIA: I will dance on your grave with a red dress and spike heels, you... you... *cucaracha! Largo de aqui!* Get out, before I unlock this cage!

(Miguel rattles the cage threateningly as Stu cowers against Lena, who puts her arms around him protectively.)

STU: Sophia! Listen to reason! You can't do this to me!

(Lena picks up Stu, either throwing him over her shoulder or carrying him in her arms and exiting as he shouts.)

STU: I mean it! I'll sue! I'll sue! No! I'll sell! I'm calling NBC film development right now and sign off faster than you can chug a fifth of tequilla! Your sorry little life will be a TV movie before your plane lands! A *network* TV movie! That's right, I said network! And they'll need some big old drama queen to play you... Fran Drescher will play you! No, wait! They'll need someone *older!* To be realistic! I've got it! They'll give it to *Susan Lucci!* I can see it now! Erica Cane plays Angelina Montoya! Oh, God that's beautiful! That's just...

(Sophia slams the door.)

SOPHIA: *Dios mio!* I will never be played by Susan Lucci! Do you hear? *Never!*

(Sophia takes a moment to catch her breath and then whirls dramatically to face Miguel.) My love!

MIGUEL: My treasure!

(They kiss through the bars as Sophia unlocks the door. When Miguel is free, he sweeps her up into his arms.)

MIGUEL: My darling, what has happened? Who has done this to you? Who has dressed you so poorly?

SOPHIA: I'm not sure I can talk about it just yet.

MIGUEL: *(With a smile, He knows that she's good and ready.)* Try.

(Tasha has opened the door. She watches anxiously.)

SOPHIA: Oh, look, Miguel! It's Tasha! She saved my life! Tasha, darling, come and meet my husband, Chico Morales… I mean Miguel Fuentes!

TASHA: *(Timidly.)* It's an honor, sir.

MIGUEL: Is this true? Have you saved the life of my Sophia?

TASHA: Well, I…

SOPHIA: Don't be so modest, Tasha! She's very modest, but brilliant! Absolutely brilliant, and you know what?

MIGUEL: What?

SOPHIA: I'm going to give her a job as my new assistant!

TASHA: Oh, no! I mean, I couldn't! I wouldn't know what to do!

SOPHIA: Nonsense! You already know more about the business than Stu.

TASHA: I don't think…

SOPHIA: And besides, what kind of a life do you have here?

TASHA: It's not so…

SOPHIA: No, it's all settled. You're coming back on the plane with Miguel and me.

TASHA: Sophia, it's not that I don't appreciate what you're tying to do, but I wouldn't know what to do! I'd never fit into your world!

SOPHIA: Now you're being silly. Tasha, you always know what to do, and anyone can fit into our world.

MIGUEL: Do you like dogs, Miss…?

TASHA: Oh, call me Tasha, Mr. Fuentes. And yes, I adore dogs, especially little ones.

MIGUEL: There you have it. Let's go.

SOPHIA: *(To Tasha.)* Well, what's it going to be, *chiquita?* Come to Hollywood with us or stay here selling magazines and candy in your little kiosk?

(Tasha takes a look around the tiny office. She looks down at her clothes and her shoes and then back at Sophia with a smile.)

TASHA: With you. I'll go with you!

(The two women impulsively hug.)

MIGUEL: Now wait a minute! You haven't said one word about your kidnapper! Do you know that you've got the entire world, including me, in an uproar? Have the police taken him into custody?

(There is a tense moment of silence.)

SOPHIA: The most terrible thing was, my darling, that I never even saw the brute! *(Tasha visibly relaxes.)*

MIGUEL: Never saw him?

SOPHIA: Never! He wore a black ski mask the entire time! It was dreadful, I tell you, dreadful!

MIGUEL: *(To Tasha.)* And just how, exactly, do you fit into this scenario, Tasha?

SOPHIA: *(Steering them both towards the door.)* That, my darling husband is the most remarkable story!

MIGUEL: I'd love to hear it.

SOPHIA: You will… you will… You know, I'd kill for a shot of tequila, you didn't happen to bring any with you, did you, darling?

MIGUEL: In my bag at the hotel.

SOPHIA: *(As they exit.)* Ahhh, *es muy bueno.*

(Blackout. Change to: The Apartment. Piotr waits anxiously for any word from Tasha. Suddenly we hear the sound of feet running up stairs.)

TASHA: *(Offstage.)* Piotr! Piotr!

PIOTR: Tasha!

(Tasha races in through the door. The two meet in a fierce hug.)

PIOTR: I was so worried!

TASHA: You needn't have been.

PIOTR: *(Holding her at arm's length.)* It worked?

TASHA: *(Joyously.)* Yes! Yes, my brilliant brother! Your plan is a complete success!

PIOTR: She's taking you back with her?

TASHA: We leave in fifteen minutes.

PIOTR: *(Hugging her again.)* So soon?

TASHA: Yes, so I have to hurry, Piotr. They'll be here any minute to pick me up… *(Tasha pauses and sinks onto the sofa.)*

PIOTR: Tasha, what's the matter?

TASHA: *(Tearfully.)* Well, it's just that when we planned all this, I always thought that I'd have plenty of time to say good-bye!

PIOTR: Oh, Tasha!

(There is a sudden pounding on the door.)

PIOTR: Who is it?

MRS. NOBOKOV: It's me, Piotr! So, did your plan work? Is Tasha going to Hollywood with that Mexican?

PIOTR: Yes, Mrs. Nobokov! It worked. Thanks for all your help!

MRS. NOBOKOV: *(As she stomps back to her apartment.)* Well, whatever. I do what I can.

(Mrs. Nobokov stomps back upstairs, muttering about Trotsky going to Mexico and getting shot.)

TASHA: Oh, Piotr! I'm going to miss you so!

PIOTR: Now, now. Don't cry.

(She cries harder.)

PIOTR: When you're a big film director I'll… I'll come for a visit.

TASHA: *(Collecting herself.)* We both know that isn't true. You'll never leave Vladivostok.

(Lena suddenly bursts through the door.)

LENA: Well?

PIOTR: My God, Lena! You nearly scared me to death!

LENA: Well? Well?

TASHA: You can't stay! They'll be here any minute!

LENA: *(Shrugging.)* I'll hide in the bathroom. Well?

PIOTR: She's going.

LENA: *(Hugging Tasha.)* How wonderful! Oh, Piotr, our little sister is going to Hollywood!

TASHA: I have to get ready!

LENA: Thank God *one* of us is going to get out of this toxic dump! Oh, Tasha, make sure you get MCI Friends and Family like cousin Selina.

(Tasha starts gathering things from around the room and throwing them into a small bag.)

PIOTR: You must be glad that your part in this is over.

LENA: *(Shrugging.)* It was fun, little brother, although probably not as much fun as pretending to be a crazed soap opera fan!

TASHA: *(As she packs.)* Piotr was wonderful.

PIOTR: What has happened to our Mr. Bernstein?

LENA: When I left him at his hotel he was still on the phone with King Larry.

PIOTR: King Larry?

LENA: *(Shrugging.)* Another American on television.

PIOTR: Ah.

(Lena picks up a framed photograph and studies it.)

LENA: I wonder what Mama and Papa would say if they could see us now?

PIOTR: They'd say, Brava, Tasha! Go to Hollywood and realize your dream! Make wonderful movies and keep a nice orange grove.

ALL THREE: Like Rudolph Valentino!

TASHA: Mama's favorite.

LENA: *(Holding out the photo to Tasha.)* You better take this.

TASHA: *(Takes the photo and smiles.)* They look so happy. So young. I was just thinking about that time we all went to...

(There is a knock on the door.)

SOPHIA: *(Offstage.)* Tasha? Tasha, it's me! It's time to go!

(Tasha looks up and realizes that she has no time to say good-bye. The three gather in a silent hug. Lena wipes a tear from Tasha's eye and silently slips into the bathroom. Piotr opens the door. Sophia strides in followed by Miguel, who is arguing with someone on the phone.)

MIGUEL: ...and I tell you no! I will not do another publicity shot in this wretched country! You're my agent, for the love of God! You're supposed to be my friend!!! *(Looking up.)* Hello, Tasha. *(Back to phone.)* What??? Didn't you hear me...

(Sophia gently pushes Miguel out the door.)

SOPHIA: Wait right there, my darling. We'll be right out. *(To Piotr.)* Boris!

PIOTR: Angelina.

SOPHIA: *(To Tasha.)* Are you ready?

TASHA: *(Looking around forlornly.)* I guess so.

SOPHIA: Come on then, you'll feel better after a week or two in Acapulco.

TASHA: Oh, I definitely advise against the sun, Sophia!

SOPHIA: Really? Why?

TASHA: *(Suddenly sounding a bit professional—but not overwhelmingly so.)* Well, you're scheduled to start filming in LA in a month and a half. They're not going to want you too dark, it'll screw up everything from costumes to makeup.

SOPHIA: I love this girl! You see, already you're earning your salary! Now, say good-bye.

TASHA: *(Turning back to Piotr.)* Good-bye, Piotr. Take care of yourself.

PIOTR: *(Softly.)* I will. Good-bye, little Tasha.

SOPHIA: Now run down to the car. I'll be along in a minute. There's something I want to say to your *loco* brother.

(Tasha looks fearful, but Piotr indicates that she should leave. Suddenly inspired, he grabs an orange from the bowl.)

PIOTR: Tasha!

(He tosses her the orange. She smiles and exits. Sophia closes the door behind her. She regards Piotr speculatively.)

SOPHIA: I don't want you to worry about Tasha. We'll take good care of her.

PIOTR: Who will? You and the evil Chico Morales?

(Sophia holds up a hand, silencing him.)

SOPHIA: I came to ask you for something.

PIOTR: Haven't you taken enough?

SOPHIA: Perhaps, but I still want more.

PIOTR: What? What could I possibly have that you could want?

SOPHIA: Your book. Isn't that it, over there? *(Sophia walks to the sofa and retrieves the book that Piotr claimed contains every good deed committed by Angelina.)* Yes, this is it. Your "Last Good Thing" book? I'd like to have it.

PIOTR: Why?

SOPHIA: Well, I'm a collector.

PIOTR: Of what?

SOPHIA: Props. I collect properties.

PIOTR: What do you mean?

SOPHIA: Usually what I say. Listen, Piotr, when Tasha is finally settled into her new life, when she has her own home, friends, a good man, a child perhaps; when all these things have come to pass, I'd like to give her this book.

PIOTR: But, why?

SOPHIA: Because it will be good for her soul to be able to laugh with me about this... this... *como se dice?...* this grand charade of yours one day.

PIOTR: *(Realizing.)* Charade? ...You knew.

SOPHIA: Boris, I get paid the big bucks because I'm good... *really* good at making people believe that up is down and down is up.

PIOTR: What is expression... you saw us coming...

SOPHIA: *Si!* A mile away.

PIOTR: But why play along? Why take Tasha with you?

SOPHIA: Because I *like* her, foolish boy. To even attempt a scam like this one is *muy formidable.*

(Miguel bursts back in.)

MIGUEL: Quickly, Sophia! We must leave now if we are ever to escape this black hole! I have been on the phone with Paramount all morning and they are threatening to sign Pamela Anderson to play you!

SOPHIA: *(Exploding.) What!!!!* Pamela Anderson??? *Are they insane????*

MIGUEL: *(Into phone.)* Did you hear that? You better find a good place to hide, my friend. When Sophia gets back to LA she will use bloodhounds to hunt you! *(To Sophia.)* We must hurry, my love. *(Into phone.)* What? You're not listening to me. *(Noticing Piotr for the first time.)* Do you watch *Baywatch,* senior?

PIOTR: *(Alarmed to be noticed by Miguel.)* Well... I suppose that I have seen a few episodes...

MIGUEL: *(Holding out phone.)* Then will you kindly explain to the man on the other end of this phone why Pamela Anderson could never portray my wife.

PIOTR: *(Gingerly taking phone.)* Hello…?

(Miguel draws Sophia aside and pantomimes the need for haste.)

PIOTR: I'm afraid that Pamela Anderson would be a very bad choice to play Angelina. Who would *I* cast? *(Thinks, and then with great definity.)* I would cast Miss Shannen Doroghty of *Beverly Hills 90210!*

(Sophia screams and Miguel snatches back the phone.)

MIGUEL: *(Over Sophia's ranting about how she would never be played by Shannen Doroghty.)* Forget you ever heard that! I will call you as soon as we land in Mexico City. *(He closes phone and turns to Sophia.)* There, there, my love. *(Meaning Piotr.)* Who is this person?

SOPHIA: Oh! This, my darling, is Tasha's brother, Piotr. He's a very big fan of our show.

MIGUEL: A fan? Then I forgive you, *senior*.

(Miguel offers his hand and the two men shake.)

MIGUEL: We are indebted to your charming sister, *senior*, for helping to rescue my Sophia from the vicious criminal who abducted her.

PIOTR: Well…

MIGUEL: Did you know, *senior*, that this brute of a man only wanted to steal my wife's underwear?

SOPHIA: Oh, they have all kinds of lunatics here, my darling. Go on down to the car and I'll be right along.

MIGUEL: Very well, my treasure. *(To Piotr.)* Adios, *senior*. You must come visit sometime! Tasha's brother will always be welcome in our home.

PIOTR: Thank you.

MIGUEL: *(To Sophia.)* One minute, my love, then we must go. *(He exits.)*

SOPHIA: *(Exploding.)* Shannen Doroghty???

PIOTR: Your underwear???

(They both laugh.)

SOPHIA: It seems, Boris, that we are even. And now I must say *adios*. As you know, it's harder to get out of this *loco* country than it is to get in. *(Sophia heads for the door.)* Oh, and Boris?

PIOTR: Yes, Angelina?

SOPHIA: I just thought you should know, I've ridden horses all my life.

PIOTR: *(Smiling.)* Then you should know that I practiced that kiss for five years.

SOPHIA: Really? Keep it up. You're getting… warmer. *(Sophia turns around and shouts into the door.)* Good-bye, Mrs. Nobokov!!!!!

MRS. NOBOKOV: *(From just outside the door.)* What?! Can't a person walk up the stairs without getting shouted at by Mexicans? *(She stomps back upstairs, muttering all the way about Trotsky going to Mexico and getting shot.)*

(Sophia opens the door and looks out in the hall.)

SOPHIA: I guess it's safe. *Ciao,* Boris.

PIOTR: *Das Vidanya, Angelina.*

SOPHIA: *(With a smile.)* Keep practicing your blues. *(And she is gone.)*
   (Piotr sadly closes the door and heads for the sofa and his guitar. He sits and begins to strum his blues chords. Lena comes out of the bathroom, sighs, and proceeds to make tea. Both their movements echo the melancholy tones of the guitar.)

LENA: *(After a moment.)* Your blues are very blue today, little brother.
   (Piotr pauses and smiles sadly to himself. He then plays a single note.)

PIOTR: *(Singing softly.)* Her name was Lola…

LENA: *(Fondly.)* Tasha's song.

PIOTR: Remember when she was a little girl? She'd dance around the kitchen singing that song…

LENA: *(Enjoying the memory.)* She drove us crazy. Especially Papa.

PIOTR: *(Imitating.)* "Stop singing that stupid American song!"

LENA: But Mama didn't mind. "Let the child sing, Misha!" Remember?

PIOTR: "If she can sing, she can also fly." It was Mama who taught Tasha to love the movies. They went every Saturday while we cleaned apartment and Papa napped. Mama would bundle Tasha up in that red wool coat…

LENA: I had forgotten that coat! Tasha wore it for years, even when it was too small because it looked just like the coat Elizabeth Taylor wore in *National Velvet.*

PIOTR: They must have seen hundreds of movies together. *(Strums.)* And now she can finally make her own. All with happy endings.

LENA: Mama knew Tasha would fly one day.

PIOTR: We all knew. Tasha is special.

LENA: So are you, Piotr.
   (He hits the note again.)

PIOTR: *(Singing.)* Her name was Lola…

LENA: *(Joining in.)* She was a showgirl…

PIOTR: With yellow feathers in her hair…

BOTH: And a dress cut down to there! She would meringue and do the cha cha!

PIOTR: *(Shouting.)* Cha cha!
   (Piotr puts down his guitar and swings Lena into a cha cha.)

PIOTR: Here at the Copa…

BOTH: Copacabana! Music and passion were always the fashion at the Copa…
   (Mrs. Nobokov bangs on wall.)

MRS. NOBOKOV: *They fell in love!!!!*
   (They continue to dance and sing while the lights Fade to Black.)

END OF PLAY